SURPRISE ATTACK

*Written under the auspices of
the Jaffee Center for Strategic Studies,
Tel-Aviv University*

SURPRISE ATTACK

The Victim's Perspective

With a New Preface

Ephraim Kam

Harvard University Press
Cambridge, Massachusetts
London, England

First Harvard University Press paperback edition, 2004

Library of Congress Cataloging-in-Publication Data
Kam, Ephraim, 1941–
    Surprise attack : the victim's perspective / Ephraim Kam.
        p.   cm.
    Bibliography: p.
    Includes index.
    ISBN 0-674-85745-3 (alk. paper)
    ISBN 0–674–01354–9 (pbk.)
    1. Surprise.   2. Military art and science.   3. International
relations.   4. Preemptive attack (Military science).   5. Military
history, Modern—20th century.   I. Title.
U163.K27   1988   88–15395
355.4'3—dc19

To Matia

Acknowledgments

I wish to acknowledge my gratitude to Thomas Schelling and Stanley Hoffmann of Harvard University, who followed this study from its inception and never failed to offer their encouragement and advice. Without their help this book could never have been completed.

Robert Jervis commented on an earlier draft; his writings on misperception spurred this study. I also have a special obligation to Richard Betts for his help as well as his elaborate comments.

I owe much to the advice of those colleagues and friends who read the manuscript, in whole or in part, and contributed valuable criticisms and suggestions: Abraham Ben-Zvi, Ruth Beyth-Marom, Zvi Lanir, Amnon Rapoport, Aryeh Shalev, and Amos Tversky. I benefited much from discussions with Michael Handel.

Two institutions kindly offered their assistance. The Jaffee Center for Strategic Studies at Tel-Aviv University generously supported the final stages of the study, and I owe particular thanks to Major-General (Reserves) Aharon Yariv, the head of the Center. I am also grateful to the Leonard Davis Institute for International Relations at the Hebrew University of Jerusalem, and especially to its director, Gabriel Sheffer, for its help in editing this book. Tamar and Joseph Alpher provided valuable editorial assistance.

Finally, I am indebted to Harvard University Press, especially to Michael Aronson and Maria Ascher, for guidance and advice.

Contents

Foreword

by Thomas C. Schelling

Twenty-five years ago Roberta Wohlstetter asked me to write a foreword to her superb study of surprise attack, *Pearl Harbor: Warning and Decision.* When I was asked to write something for Ephraim Kam's book, I couldn't resist. I took the occasion to reread Wohlstetter, and my recollection was confirmed that where the two works overlap they are remarkably in agreement.

Wohlstetter began as an amateur, but by the time she had read through thirty-nine volumes of the *Congressional Hearings* on the Pearl Harbor attack and most of the literature pertinent to it, she was expertly professional. Her book is acknowledged everywhere to be not only the definitive examination of what, to Americans, is the most infamous surprise attack in history, but a perceptive analysis of why there can be no assurance that strategic surprise will not happen again.

Ephraim Kam was already a professional when he began work on this book, more than a dozen years ago, from his career as an analyst in the Israeli Ministry of Defense. Israel achieved surprise in 1956 and 1967 only to be surprised, with devastating though not disastrous results, in 1973. Kam has an expert's knowledge of the most modern techniques of collecting and analyzing data. More than that, he is a trained political scientist who has had extensive opportunity to see how intelligence is not only gathered and analyzed but used (or not used) in plans, policies, and decisions.

Kam studies in detail the German invasion of Norway and Denmark, the North Korean attack on South Korea, the Chinese attack on India, and eight other surprises including Pearl Harbor. But his vantage point is altogether different from Wohlstetter's: small nation, not superpower; enemies adjacent, not on the other side of the globe; multiple adversaries, not just one; and the military and intelligence technologies available in the 1980s, not the technologies of the late thirties and early forties.

His final chapter is entitled "Is Surprise Attack Inevitable?" I regret to inform that his conclusion is pessimistic. Worse, it seems to be solidly based on evidence.

Quite in the spirit of Wohlstetter, he asserts that "lack of information and warning indicators is usually not the reason for failures of estimates." And if you searched Wohlstetter carefully, you would find anticipations of Kam's observations that "the greater the amount of information collected, the more confusing and contradictory the noise received"; "the more information coming in, the more difficult it is to process the data"; and "the more sensitive the information, the stronger the demand to protect sources and limit dissemination."

Let me quote a favorite paragraph from my foreword of 1962: "Surprise, when it happens to a government, is likely to be a complicated, diffuse, bureaucratic thing. It includes neglect of responsibility, but also responsibility so poorly defined or so ambiguously delegated that action gets lost. It includes gaps in intelligence, but also intelligence that, like a string of pearls too precious to wear, is too sensitive to give to those who need it. It includes the alarm that fails to work, but also the alarm that has gone off so often it has been disconnected. It includes the unalert watchman, but also the one who knows he'll be chewed out by his superior if he gets higher authority out of bed. It includes the contingencies that occur to no one, but also those that everyone assumes somebody else is taking care of. It includes straightforward procrastination, but also decisions protracted by internal disagreement. It includes, in addition, the inability of individual human beings to rise to the occasion until they are sure it is the occasion—which is usually too late. (Unlike the movies, real life provides no musical background to tip us off to the climax.) Finally, as at Pearl Harbor, surprise includes some measures of genuine novelty introduced by the enemy, and possibly some sheer bad luck."

That paragraph fits this foreword as well. Does it mean that if you have already read other good books on surprise attack, you needn't read Kam? It does not, for several reasons. First, Kam's analysis of the institutional role of intelligence and the relation of analysts to decision-makers does not duplicate earlier work. It is based on eleven case studies and reflects his own personal experience. Second, fantastic advances in electronic and other techniques of surveillance and intelligence collection make altogether different the questions of how to know what the Egyptians and Syrians were up to on Yom Kippur; and the collation of sources and data over the past quarter century gives us a sharper picture of what the Japanese were up to the week before that Day of Infamy. And third, for countries as disparate as the United States, Israel, the Soviet Union, and even Britain in the Falkland Islands, there are few subjects more vitally important or more intellectually tantalizing than why surprise attack is so often successful and what might be done to avert it.

One lesson that comes through loud and clear is that there are no easy lessons. In her final paragraph Wohlstetter said, "If the study of Pearl Harbor has anything to offer for the future, it is this: we have to accept the fact of uncertainty and learn to live with it." In his final paragraph Kam says, "History does not encourage potential victims of surprise attacks."

But reading this book can help.

Preface, 2004: Old Patterns, New Lessons

Since *Surprise Attack: The Victim's Perspective* was published fifteen years ago, several new members have joined the unenviable club of victims surprised by an enemy's offensive. The background to these new surprise attacks has been generally similar to those of previous attacks: a combination of faulty security concepts; misjudgment of the enemy's motivation, intentions, and capabilities, and hence misperception of the imminent threat; lack of critical hard evidence of the coming attack; and organizational obstacles. Both Kuwait and the United States were surprised by the Iraqi invasion of Kuwait in August 1990. For several reasons they assumed that Saddam Hussein had intended to threaten and blackmail Kuwait, but not to occupy it: for generations no Arab state had occupied another; Kuwait had been a close ally of Iraq and had actively supported it during its war against Iran just a few years earlier; and it was expected that American support would deter Hussein from attacking the oil-rich emirate.

It is not evident to what extent Saddam Hussein was strategically surprised by the American attacks in 1991 and 2003. When Hussein's army invaded Kuwait, he clearly had not expected to be attacked by the U.S.-led coalition. Less certain is whether he modified this assessment in the months leading up to the Gulf War. Even if he anticipated an American military move, however, he most likely did not expect such a massive operation or such a devastating defeat. For his part, Hussein surprised many Israeli decision makers and analysts by launching thirty-nine Scud missiles into Israeli territory. In 2003, Hussein perhaps envisioned a large-scale American offensive in Iraq, the likes of which he encountered in 1991. This time, however, he misunderstood the meaning and implications of the modern battlefield. He apparently did not expect that within a month his entire country, including Baghdad, would be occupied and his army completely dismantled.

Yet the most illuminating recent case for studying surprise attack is certainly the September 11, 2001, terror attack in the United States. This attack differs from traditional cases of surprise attack, since it did not involve fighting between regular armed forces or an invasion of a country. Nevertheless it has many similarities with conventional surprise attacks, and because of its strategic importance, it can shed new light on the nature of future strategic surprises. Its similarities to other cases of strategic surprise include its many instances of intelligence failure: with so many contributing factors, it is difficult to locate the weak links in the chain of assumptions and operations and prevent a surprise before it occurs.

As the U.S. Congressional Joint Inquiry reported, since 1998 the American intelligence community has acquired and disseminated intelligence reports advising in general terms that Osama bin Laden's Al Qaeda organization intended to carry out terrorist attacks inside the United States in the very near future. One of the attack scenarios indicated by that information involved using aircraft as weapons by crashing into buildings, yet as in other cases of surprise attack, the intelligence that accrued was not specific as to time and place. Yet in the view of the Joint Inquiry, the information should have been sufficient to foster a heightened sense of alert and to prompt implementation of additional defensive measures. As it happened, the U.S. government failed to undertake any comprehensive effort to carry out such measures.

There were various reasons for this failure. Despite information on the immediacy of the Al Qaeda threat in the spring and summer of 2001, the assumption prevailed in the U.S. government that attacks of the magnitude of what was to occur on September 11 could not happen in the United States. The general view of the intelligence community was that Al Qaeda attacks would most likely occur against U.S. targets overseas. Moreover, the intelligence community's understanding of Al Qaeda was hampered by inadequate quality of evidence and lack of analytical focus. Intelligence was more oriented toward tactical analysis in support of operations than on the strategic analysis needed to develop a broader understanding of Al Qaeda and the threat it posed. Hence, prior to September 11, 2001, the community failed to tap available information and analyze its collective significance in terms of a probable terrorist attack. As a result, some significant pieces of information were overlooked entirely, while others were not identified as potentially important and therefore not disseminated.

The intelligence failure testified to organizational obstacles as well. Intelligence agencies did not adequately share relevant information. This communication malfunction resulted from the agencies' respective missions, legal mandates, and organizational cultures. Various FBI agents who investigated critical activities of Al Qaeda in the United States knew nothing about other aspects of that investigation and therefore could not possibly understand the significance of these activities; no one at FBI headquarters processed isolated activities into a comprehensive, meaningful picture. Some of the shortcomings in analytical capabilities also emanated from the fact that analysts were often inexperienced, undertrained, or underqualified for their responsibilities.

Predicting Conventional Attacks: New Difficulties

The two recent wars in the Gulf as well as the terror attack in the United States reflect new difficulties in coping with future enemy attacks. The traditional surprise attack involves an offensive launched by the conventional armed forces of one country against the territory and/or armed forces of another one. This book, which examines all major conventional surprise attacks between 1939 and 1982, argues that in most of them the victim of the attack failed to foresee its imminence, or at least failed to understand its critical aspects.

The two wars in the Gulf have made it clear that the problem of correctly perceiving a strategic threat and predicting the weight of an impending attack has become even more complicated. The 1991 Gulf War demonstrated for the first time the devastating power of the so-called Revolution in Military Affairs. This revolution, which started in the 1980s, relies on thorough use of modern sophisticated military technology by highly trained soldiers and is based on several pillars: precision-guided munitions, capable of striking targets accurately; control of space, which provides an accurate intelligence picture of enemy targets, as well as other advantages such as communications of unlimited ranges; dominant maneuvering on the battlefield; and information warfare, which includes several features, among them cyber-warfare and electronic warfare.

This revolution augurs poorly for potential victims of conventional attacks. It provides an attacker whose military resources have modernized according to the Revolution in Military Affairs with new means of surprise, from technology to weapon systems to military doctrine. It enables the attacker to overcome difficulties—for example, geographical obstacles or fortifications—in ways that previously seemed beyond its capabilities and therefore were not taken into account by the victim. Even if the victim might not ignore the possibility of attack, it may find itself surprised, more than in the past, by the attack's timing, location, or the enemy's use of doctrine and weaponry. Thus even if Saddam Hussein eventually grasped, both in 1991 and in 2003, that he was about to be attacked, he probably failed to foresee the nature and impact of the wars.

The growing superiority of modern conventional armed forces over non-sophisticated ones has led to further complexities. The inability to compete against high-technology conventional warfare is one of the reasons why weaker opponents might either resort to terrorism or try to acquire chemical, biological, or nuclear weapons of mass destruction, as well as long-range ballistic missiles, in order to neutralize their enemy's conventional superiority. The greatest concern refers to a combination of both measures: that terror organizations, or terror-sponsoring states, will acquire non-conventional weapons. The increasing recourse to terrorism and weapons of mass destruction, which is particularly notable in the Middle East, leads to further difficulties in predicting imminent attacks.

Predicting Terror Attacks

Terrorism, of course, is a very old mode of warfare. Terrorist organizations usually pose a difficult challenge for their victims in part because they have a greater capability to surprise. Terrorist organizations are relatively small and flexible and often innovative—and therefore less predictable. Their leadership is a small, closed circle, and some of the leaders are unknown to the victims' intelligence. They can easily choose the target, time, and location of their attack, often with little notice, and successfully conceal their intentions and plans. Since in most cases they are ideologically motivated and highly compartmentalized, it is difficult to infiltrate their cells in order to gather intelligence about their planning and activities. They do not use major weapon systems, nor do they have large units and military bases; furthermore, they do not need lengthy, intensive, or visible preparations for their attack. Hence they do not create many early warning indicators that could provide their victim's intelligence community with some indication of the impending attack or with visible and qualitative military targets for preemptive attacks.

From the viewpoint of the victim's intelligence, the most impenetrable kind of terrorist operation is the suicide bombing. The preparations for such an operation are simple and quick, the materials needed to prepare the bomb can be easily obtained, and the number of individuals involved in the operation is small. It takes no more than a few days to prepare and send a suicide bomber, who acts like a human precision bomb. Moreover, once bombers are on their way to the target, they are difficult to stop: the victim's intelligence community has to be very lucky, or needs very accurate and specific information, in order to prevent the operation at this advanced stage.

Al Qaeda represents a new type of terrorism. It comprises violent, radical Islamic cells that are not linked to any specific country but are united in their Islamic fundamentalism and their anti-American/anti-Western zeal. While many terrorist organizations pose a rather limited threat, Al Qaeda poses a formidable strategic threat to its opponents: it aims at deposing moderate Islamic regimes around the world and undermining American and Western influence by inflicting mass casualties. Details of potential major terrorist operations are not widely shared within Al Qaeda, which makes it difficult to collect and process the intelligence needed to preempt or disrupt attacks. September 11 demonstrated the organization's capability to surprise through the choice of unexpected targets and accurate planning. It also reflected highly innovative thinking, which turned Boeing aircraft into precise bombs with the help of simple box cutters.

Although the September 11 attack highlighted plainly the severity of the threat posed by organizations like Al Qaeda, the potential for future strategic surprise caused by such organizations is still high. The American military operation in Afghanistan that began in late 2001 eliminated this country as a safe haven for Al Qaeda, and the capture of hundreds of Al Qaeda operatives provided the American intelligence community with valuable information about the organization's structure, activities, and plans. The countermeasures taken by the American security agencies limit the capabilities of terrorist organizations to carry out future operations, and the willingness of many governments, including Muslim governments, to cooperate with the American administration in the war against terrorism has yielded significant assistance. Nonetheless, Al Qaeda activists are now scattered in many Muslim countries around the world, planning surprise terrorist attacks, and—as the attacks in Indonesia, Morocco, Kenya, Turkey, and Iraq have demonstrated—it is still difficult to locate and obstruct them. As the U.S. Congressional Joint Inquiry emphasized, the emergence of a threat posed by international terrorists who operate across national borders demands huge changes in focus and approach from intelligence agencies organized and trained primarily to deal with more traditional types of terrorist organizations. Such changes take time, training, experience, imagination, and openness to become fully effective.

Non-Conventional Attacks

The possible use of weapons of mass destruction enhances the potential severity of a surprise attack. Today, the club of nuclear powers already includes eight countries, and it may well grow in coming years. Moreover, a relatively large number of countries possess chemical warfare capabilities as well as long-range ballistic missiles, and some of them have also acquired biological weapons.

Owners of non-conventional weapons pose more complicated challenges for their victims' intelligence communities. Awareness of the danger of a non-conventional attack is now relatively great, and potential victims of such an attack usually take into consideration that their enemies, given the possibility, might use weapons of mass destruction. However, there is little experience regarding the practical use of such weapons: atomic bombs were dropped only twice, six decades ago, and biological weapons have never been used on a large-scale basis. Hence it is more difficult to analyze and assess the likelihood of such an attack, because the enemy's considerations and constraints pertaining to non-conventional attack are not sufficiently familiar, and therefore its intentions are not well understood. The acquisition of weapons of mass destruction by many countries creates a new conundrum for the potential victim: will the enemy use these weapons in the next attack, or will it reserve them as a last resort?

Moreover, the difficulties encountered by Western intelligence communities regarding the availability of Iraqi chemical, biological, and missile capabilities in advance of the 2003 war reflect the great challenges involved in assessing non-conventional capabilities. The number of operatives who participate in the launching of a non-conventional attack is rather small, and the preparations for the operation are well hidden, often in underground facilities. In order to assess conventional capabilities, intelligence communities must, among other requirements, check the quantities and analyze the qualities of the enemy's weapon systems, follow its behavior in the battlefield and in military training, and estimate the quality of its military leadership and the functioning of its maintenance system. As this book intends to show, this is a difficult mission by itself. It is even more complicated to assess chemical and biological warfare capabilities, since intelligence communities are required to know and analyze what happens inside relatively small laboratories and other facilities, often disguised as civilian plants.

The limited visible enemy activity linked to the development, acquisition, and use of weapons of mass destruction affects both the quantity and the quality of early warning indicators of a non-conventional attack. Early warning indicators, which must appear before an attack, are usually activated by the enemy's preparations for its offensive, and serve as the main body of information that can be obtained by intelligence communities prior to an attack. In the case of conventional attacks the quantity of such indicators is rather great, since such an attack requires massive visible preparations. In the case of a non-conventional attack the quantity of early indicators is likely to be small, since the preparations for such an attack are fewer and much less visible. Furthermore, many of the warning indicators prior to a non-conventional attack may resemble those appearing before a conventional attack, and cannot be specifically identified: the launching of a ballistic missile armed with a chemical warhead might look identical to that of a conventional missile. And since there is little experience with non-conventional attacks, it will be difficult to define and identify warning indicators and use them as alerts against the impending attack.

Improvements in Intelligence Collection

While the Revolution in Military Affairs, the increasing use of weapons of mass destruction, and the growing sophistication of terrorist operations are providing the attacker with additional capabilities to surprise the victim, new developments in intelligence collection could improve the technical capabilities of intelligence communities to predict future attacks. Indeed, new technologies have brought about impressive advances in intelligence collection during recent decades, progress that has enabled intelligence communities to draw a more detailed and accurate picture of the enemy's activities. The problem is that these advances are much less helpful in improving assessment and prediction capabilities to prevent surprise attacks. What is needed in order to assess the enemy's strategic intentions, especially to identify its possible decision to go to war, is new intelligence capabilities to penetrate the top level of the enemy's decision makers. So far, the progress in intelligence collection has not improved the capabilities of such penetration.

The improvement in intelligence collection in recent decades has been especially remarkable in three relevant fields. The first field relates to various aspects of signal intelligence, communications intelligence, and electronic intelligence. The information collected through these channels is very helpful regarding enemy activities at the tactical and operational levels, and may shed some light on strategic decisions. Yet hard evidence pertaining to the enemy's decisions on highly sensitive issues such as initiating war is not likely to be available in this kind of information: leaders are usually careful not to use these channels of communication to exchange messages regarding secret strategic decisions, because of the vulnerability to monitoring.

Impressive progress in collecting information has also been achieved in visual intelligence, especially through the use of satellites and unmanned aerial vehicles, as well as high-resolution cameras. However, while overhead reconnaissance can provide high-quality, accurate information about the enemy's activities in real time, it too does not provide the crucial element: explaining the intentions behind these activities. And since usually these activities can be interpreted in several different ways, such information is not sufficiently helpful in assessing the likelihood of a coming attack.

A third area of enhanced intelligence collection is the acquisition and dissemination of nonclassified information, especially through rolling news networks and the Internet. Twenty-four-hour news networks and Internet databases provide valuable information that had not been available before, part of it in real time. Yet again, while this revolution contributes to clarifying the picture of the enemy's activities, one cannot expect to find hard evidence pertaining to the enemy's secret strategic decisions in nonclassified material.

One of the best ways to penetrate the enemy's upper echelons of intelligence is through reliable and knowledgeable human sources. The most important information in advance of the Egyptian–Syrian attack against Israel in 1973 came from a Mossad agent. The crucial information concerning the Iraqi biological warfare program was provided by Saddam Hussein's son-in-law, who defected to the West in 1995. Indeed, the Congressional Joint Inquiry emphasized that the American intelligence community failed to develop and use human sources effectively in order to penetrate the Al Qaeda inner circle; the lack of such sources significantly limited the community's ability to acquire intelligence that could have been acted upon before the September 11 attack. The problem is, of course, that it is very difficult to develop such high-quality human sources, and their recruitment is often a matter of luck, not necessarily intensive efforts.

Looking to the Future

Surprise Attack: The Victim's Perspective presents a rather pessimistic conclusion, namely, that it is at best very difficult to prevent surprise attacks. The lessons of the last fifteen years seem to support this conclusion. These lessons are also reflected in the words of FBI director Robert Mueller to the Joint Inquiry committee. Referring to the question of whether anything could have been done to stop the hijackers from carrying out the September 11 attack, Mueller said: "Looking at each of the areas that we could have done better, I'm not certain you get to the point where we stop these individuals." In the competition between the growing capabilities of the attacker to surprise its victim and the improving intelligence capabilities that can help to prevent the surprise, the attacker's capabilities apparently have the upper hand. If this lesson proves to be true, then the vulnerability of our grandchildren to surprise attack will be greater than the vulnerability of our grandparents.

At the same time, this book posits a complementary observation: although surprise attacks occur often, they are not inevitable, like natural disasters. Encouraging a spirit of openness, caution, skepticism, and imagination within intelligence communities and among decision makers can reduce the severity of surprise attacks. The lessons of the past fifteen years pose an additional challenge for intelligence communities: to reorganize themselves, conceptually and practically, to cope with the new missions on all three levels—conventional, non-conventional, and terrorist. This requires the heads of intelligence communities to look at threats beyond the horizon, to define a new order of priorities for allocating resources, to learn how to deal with new sets of early warning indicators, to try reducing organizational obstacles within the intelligence community, and to cultivate effective human resources to undertake the new missions.

SURPRISE
ATTACK

Introduction

Throughout the long history of warfare, the strategy of surprise attack has frequently been used. That it succeeded in ancient times is understandable, since armies then had at their disposal few means to prevent it; but it has also occurred in the wars of our own century. During the Second World War, for example, each of the great powers was taken unaware: the British by the German invasion of Norway and the Japanese attack on Singapore; the French by the German invasion of their country; the Russians by "Barbarossa," the German invasion of 1941; the Americans by the Japanese attack on Pearl Harbor; and the Germans by the Allied landing in Normandy. The best intelligence services have failed to predict war: Russian intelligence, the largest in the world, and Israeli intelligence, considered to be one of the best, were surprised in 1941 and 1973 respectively. And in five separate instances between 1941 and 1973 American intelligence failed to anticipate an attack that significantly affected U.S. armed forces or interests.[1]

Nor has history been a good teacher. The United States, surprised in June 1950 by the North Korean invasion of South Korea, was surprised again five months later by China's intervention in the same war; Egypt, surprised by Israel in 1956, failed to apply that lesson in 1967; and Israel, having managed to surprise the Egyptians twice, was in turn surprised by them in the ensuing round of hostilities in 1973. And the failure to anticipate attack does not discriminate among types of states and regimes: superpowers and small states have both been victims, and totalitarian regimes have fared no better than democratic ones.

Although employed in ancient warfare, surprise attack did not become a common strategy until recent times, especially the past century. By the beginning of the twentieth century a combination of developments—improvements in communications, transportation, and weapon systems, including the use of tanks and air power; new bureaucratic structures and advanced procedures for systematic problem solving—had altered the nature of war. The resulting increase in opportunities for strategic surprise overshadowed a parallel significant improvement in the collection of information (Knorr and Morgan, 1983, pp. 2–3).

The striking thing about a surprise attack is that in retrospect one can never quite understand how it could have happened. In international affairs violent measures are usually taken only after a period of protracted friction, and military action requires lengthy preparations that cannot be concealed. In fact, in almost all the cases of surprise attack that we shall be looking at, the victim possessed subtle evidence that war was imminent. Yet this was not enough to prevent the surprise.

This study deals with the problem of strategic rather than tactical surprise. More concretely, it deals with the outbreak of war by surprise attack as a specific—indeed the most complex—instance of strategic surprise. We shall observe the issue from the vantage point of the victims, in order to comprehend the causes of their failure to anticipate the initiation of hostilities.

Most explanations for the success of surprise attack focus either on biases in perception and information processing or on the impact of organizational processes and breakdowns in communication. I take a much broader approach. My basic assumption is that anticipating the coming of war is more complicated than any other problem of strategic estimation. It involves many interdependent analytical difficulties and judgmental biases, organizational obstacles, and political as well as military constraints. Falling victim to surprise attack—the most costly case of all estimate failures—signals more than a failure of intelligence. Indeed it is the very complexity of the surprise attack that renders it so difficult to predict and prevent.

This study does not present one central explanation, because no one explanation can take into account the complexity of the issue. Rather I attempt to follow the behavior of the victim at various functional levels and from several viewpoints, in order to examine the difficulties, mistakes, and biases that permit a nation to be surprised by an attack. The study tackles the problem on four levels. The first is that of the individual analyst—how he builds his hypotheses and treats information, and how misperceptions and biases of judgment occur. My central assumption is that mistakes made at this level determine the failure to anticipate war. Hence a major part of this study is devoted to an examination of the difficulties and biases inherent in the intelligence process at the level of the individual analyst. I use the term *analyst* to refer to both the intelligence analyst and the political or military decision maker; in cases where the term refers to only one of these two functions, this is indicated explicitly or contextually. Second, I look at the small group of analysts—the way the group works and influences the perceptions of its members and their willingness to offer risky assessments. Third, I examine the larger structure of the intelligence community and the military organization, its reaction to the imminence of war, the role of organizational inefficiency, and the pertinent characteristics of these organizations. Last, I return for a closer look at the decision makers and their relationship with the intelligence community.

My analysis is based on an examination of eleven major surprise attacks that have occurred since the outbreak of the Second World War:

German invasion of Denmark and Norway, April 9, 1940
German invasion of France, the Netherlands, and Belgium, May 10, 1940
"Barbarossa"—the German invasion of Russia, June 22, 1941
Japanese attack on Pearl Harbor, December 7, 1941
Japanese invasion of Malaya and Singapore, December 7, 1941– February 15, 1942
North Korean attack on South Korea, June 25, 1950
Chinese invasion of Korea, October 25, 1950
Israeli conquest of Egypt's Sinai Peninsula, October 29, 1956
Chinese attack on India, October 20, 1962
Israeli attack on Egypt, June 5, 1967
Egyptian-Syrian attack on Israel, October 6, 1973

This list does not include all cases of surprise attack since 1939. Additional instances are the Soviet invasion of Czechoslovakia on August 21, 1968; the Chinese invasion of Vietnam in February 1979 (Pao-min Chang, 1982); the Iraqi attack on Iran on September 23, 1980; and the Argentine invasion of the Falkland Islands on April 2, 1982 (Hopple, 1984). My study does not refer to these cases inasmuch as available material dealing with the victims of these surprise attacks adds little to what we can learn from the other cases.

Furthermore, the quantity of case material available for study is not uniform. In some instances (especially those of Pearl Harbor and the Yom Kippur War) there exists a great deal of information; in others (such as the Egyptian instances of 1956 and 1967) data on the behavior of the victim are relatively sparse. Occasionally too I shall refer to additional cases of strategic surprise that did not involve war, such as the Cuban missile crisis or the fall of the Shah of Iran.

There is more than one kind of surprise attack. Hence this study commences with a distinction between various aspects and degrees of surprise attack. By and large I attempt to pinpoint and analyze those elements that seem to be common to surprise attacks in general. Basing the study mainly on cases of estimate failure seems justified insofar as most relevant material has come to light as a result of such failures, not of successes. Yet in order to complement the analysis I make passing reference to two additional kinds of strategic estimate: erroneous predictions of attack (the "worst-case analysis" and the "cry wolf" syndrome) and, in the conclusion, estimates that did anticipate a coming attack.

PART ONE

The Components of Surprise Attack

1

The Essence of Surprise Attack

To understand the essence of surprise attack, it is necessary to examine the nature of surprise itself. Surprise is a basic and recurring event in human life. Still, neither the repeated occurrence of surprises nor our assumption that life has surprises in store for us makes us any less vulnerable to its impact.

In most cases of surprise we do not ignore the probability of a potential occurrence but rather tend to reject it as unlikely. Therefore, when it actually does happen, it takes us "by surprise" since we had expected it to occur later or in a different place or manner. Sometimes our imagination is too limited even to entertain the possibility of surprise, preventing us from envisaging the event in any way.

Surprise is complex. For one thing it means that an act or development has taken place contrary to our expectations, thus proving our assumptions to be ill founded. Then too a surprise comes without warning, catching us unprepared; hence our inadequate response. Finally, the sudden happening provokes our emotions, which, when strong enough, may throw us off balance, at least for a while.

Surprise is a matter of degree, and its strength and nature may vary from one situation to another. On a theoretical scale, we might identify at one end a complete *absence* of surprise, where the actual development precisely matches our expectations; a complete absence of surprise finds us well prepared. At the other end of the scale is *total* surprise, in which the event, having never been envisaged, takes us completely unprepared. Between these two extremes we might pinpoint varying degrees of surprise, using as criteria the extent to which our expectations and beliefs prove wrong, the level of preparedness, and the outcome of the sudden event.

From these general characteristics, one may turn more specifically to surprise attack. Several attempts have been made to distinguish among the various kinds (see, for example, Knorr 1964a; Ben-Zvi, 1979). Lanir (1983) distinguishes between *situational surprise* and *fundamental surprise*. Situational surprise exposes errors in assumptions and predictions but does not undermine basic conceptions. Fundamental surprise is essentially a national problem, abruptly exposing very basic conceptual flaws.

More detailed attempts to break down the concept of surprise attack are presented by George (1979) and Brodin (1978). George looks at surprise attack from the standpoint of the victim's assessment, and finds that the victim can be surprised by various aspects of an attack. These include the basic question of *whether* an attack will occur as well as additional questions such as *what kind* of attack, *where*, *when*, and *why*. In some cases an attack comes as a complete surprise because the victim has failed to answer several of these questions. In other cases the surprise is only partial, as when the attack itself was foreseen but the victim is surprised by its nature, location, or timing.

Brodin deals with the degree of surprise from a different angle. According to her, a surprise attack is "an attack launched against an opponent who is insufficiently prepared in relation to his potential (mobilization) resources" (1978, p. 99). The defender's level of preparedness is thus the measure of the surprise. A total surprise implies a fundamental miscalculation on the part of the victim. Partial surprise occurs when an attack is thought to be a real possibility yet reaction proves insufficient.

Both George and Brodin distinguish between various degrees of surprise attack, yet each deals with just a part of the process. George addresses the expectations that lead to surprise, while Brodin concentrates on their outcome—that is, on the victim's state of preparedness. Proceeding from where their analyses leave off, I shall attempt to deal with the whole process of surprise attack.

Each case of surprise attack is unique. No two instances are identical or even similar. The concept of surprise attack nonetheless appears to contain three main elements. First, surprise attack is a military act that is not consistent with the victim's *expectations* and assumptions. From this viewpoint the strength of the surprise depends on the nature and depth of these assumptions. Second, surprise attack implies a failure of advance *warning*. In this sense the strength of the surprise is in reverse proportion to the timing and clarity of the early warning, if any. Last, a surprise attack exposes the victim's failure to meet the danger adequately. In this sense the degree of surprise can be deduced from the victim's level of *preparedness* at the moment of attack. The degree of surprise cannot be measured by the outcome of the war, however, since the outcome is determined by many other factors, and it is impossible to isolate the effect of the initial surprise.

Obviously there is a clear connection among these three elements. Assumptions and expectations regarding a possible attack determine the clarity and timing of any advance warning; and the preciseness of the warning determines both the speed of response and the extent of preparedness for war. The wider the range of the victim's erroneous assumptions, the more belated and vague the advance warning; and the less accurate the warning, the more inadequate the level of preparedness.

Reaction to Disasters and Warnings

Before we look more closely at these elements of surprise attack, let us briefly examine the more general topic of reaction to disasters and warnings of impending danger.

According to Turner (1976, pp. 381, 393–394) disasters—as distinguished from accidents—involve "a basic disruption of the social context and a radical departure from the pattern of normal expectations for a significant portion of the community." Disasters are potentially foreseeable and avoidable because they are not created overnight; rather they are the result of a long, complex chains of errors, inaccuracies, and inadequacies in accepted beliefs about hazards and in practices and norms for avoiding them. Turner asserts that during the critical stage prior to the disaster—the incubation period—a series of events accumulates that is at odds with these norms. These events are unnoticed, misperceived, or ignored because of erroneous assumptions, information-handling difficulties, lack of standards and precautions, and reluctance to fear the worst.

An extensive body of data suggests that the risk of disasters and natural hazards is usually misjudged (Slovic, Kunreuther, and White, 1974). Facing an impending disaster, people tend to assume their invulnerability and deny danger, underestimate the hazard, and overestimate their capability of dealing with it. In a psychological study of disaster Wolfenstein (1957, pp. 17–18, 23–24) describes such a reaction:

> In relation to remote threats the usual reaction is one of being unworried, with the more or less explicit belief that the threat will not materialize, or will not affect oneself. This tendency to deny danger is likely to carry over into situations of more imminent threat.
>
> A threat, particularly of a danger not previously experienced, is simply not believed . . . The pre-disaster conviction seems to be: it can't happen, but if it does I will remain immune.
>
> One does not believe it until one sees it. So, for instance, in Kansas, in the face of a predicted and oncoming flood, people were inclined to say: "We'll wait and see what happens."
>
> Even where the past provides a precedent for disaster . . . there is a tendency to deny that this is any portent for the future. One expects things to be better now than in the bad old days.

To a large extent this reaction reflects a tendency toward optimism. According to Withey (1962, p. 113) people are inclined to estimate the probability of favorable events as somewhat higher than the "objective" probability, and the probability of threatening events as somewhat lower. In the latter case people feel that the disaster will not really happen or will not be as bad as predicted. In part this reaction may also reflect a social constraint. Since many societies and cultures repudiate fearful tendencies, for most people anxiety is not only unnecessary but incompatible with a positive self-image (Wolfenstein, 1957, p. 21). Yet observations indicate that advance warning can sometimes produce a sensitizing effect too, thus increasing rather than decreasing vigilant reactions to danger (Janis, 1962, p. 78).

A variety of factors, then, appears to determine whether people will be alert or insensitive to warnings of imminent disaster. Some of these are relevant to the understanding of surprise attack. To begin with, the perception of threats and the reaction to warnings of impending disaster vary with people's beliefs about their ability to take effective countermeasures. In other words, the feeling of immunity may be strong when people feel that there is nothing they can do to ward off the danger. In this case "denial of the threat continues to recommend itself as a defense against anxiety" (Wolfenstein, 1957, p. 20). Moreover, "people feeling more ineffective should be less sensitive to incoming information. People feeling overconfident should be equally indifferent, but not as a defense—just because they feel they do not need the information" (Withey, 1962, p. 114).

Such a tendency explains in part why weak states may be surprised by stronger ones. When the inferior victim feels that it lacks the capacity to deter or repel an attack, it may develop a degree of indifference toward the possibility of war. The German invasions of Norway and of the Netherlands in April and May 1940 fall into this category. Yet the behavior of people prior to disasters reveals that even when they believe that something can be done, their tendency to deny the danger is further reinforced if taking action involves considerable inconvenience. This is reflected, for example, in people's attitudes toward evacuating their homes when threatened with floods or hurricanes (Wolfenstein, 1957, p. 21). Such behavior provides an additional perspective on the tendency of policy makers to postpone a decision to take countermeasures against a possible attack because of the political and economic price involved, a point I discuss later in this chapter.

Janis suggests that there is a marked difference in responsiveness to warnings concerning disasters that build up slowly (floods) and disasters that have a more rapid onset (tornadoes). Warnings delivered just before the onset of nonprecipitant disasters are frequently ignored, whereas those given before precipitant disasters are not. When warned about a flood, people may assume that their inaction involves no serious risks because they will have ample time to escape later if the flooding reaches their neighborhood (Janis, 1962, p. 81; Janis and Mann, 1977, p. 56). Surprise attack can be regarded as a kind of nonprecipitant disaster, since warning indicators appear gradually. Thus Janis's suggestion provides another explanation for the lack of vigilant response: people may assume that numerous warnings will be issued before the final warning is given.

Then too there is a tendency to interpret new stimuli within a framework of the familiar, for the familiar is seen as more probable than the unfamiliar. Since disasters occur infrequently, the tendency is to interpret indicators "in terms of most probable occurrences, which implies interpreting them in nonstressful terms." This leads to discounting the threat, although "when a set for the 'worst' exists, this tendency may be reversed" (Withey, 1962, pp. 114–116).

In addition, familiarity derives from past experience with disasters. Apprehension about a future disaster is probably greater among people who have been caught unprepared in the past. In such a case people tend to be on the alert in order to avoid being again taken by surprise. Yet experience of past disaster may also have the opposite effect. Having survived one disaster, people may feel over-confident with regard to future dangers. In any case, as time passes apprehensiveness appears to decrease gradually. Thus it has been found that the purchase of earthquake insurance increases sharply immediately after a quake but decreases steadily as memories became less vivid (Wolfenstein, 1957, pp. 154, 158; Slovic, Kunreuther, and White, 1974).

Similarly analysts and policy makers who have had past experience with a surprise attack seem to be more alert—sometimes even oversensitive—to the danger of future attacks and are likely to be impressed by any evidence that another such attack is impending. Yet this sensitivity may decrease with the passage of time, eventually weakened by overconfidence that the lessons of that shocking experience have been learned and that one cannot be caught napping twice. The history of surprise attack teaches us that being surprised once is no guarantee against being surprised again.

Finally, familiarity also arises from repeated warnings of danger. As Janis (1962, pp. 81–82) suggests, vigilance aroused by a warning will be dampened if the recipients have been exposed to previous warnings about the same threat, provided that the new warning does not add information about increased vulnerability to the danger. If former warnings have heightened the awareness of vulnerability to an impending disaster, the recipients will become sensitized to new warnings, especially if the new warning refers to a severe threat; but if the new warning is perceived as referring to a very mild threat that can be safely ignored, the sensitization effect promotes adaptive compromise formations.

From this general discussion let us now return to the three main elements of surprise attack: erroneous assumptions, failure of warning, and inadequate preparedness.

Aspects of Erroneous Estimates

Assumptions pertaining to a possible attack address four questions: (1) whether the attack will actually happen, (2) its timing, (3) its location, and (4) the way in which it will be carried out. If an attack is to take its victim by surprise, it must find him wrong about at least one of these four questions, and usually more.

The basic question, of course, is *whether* an attack is expected at all. To a large extent this is related to how nations perceive other nations as a threat to their national security. One nation's threat perception is derived from another nation's behavior and is a function of both estimated capabilities and intentions (for a definition of theat perception see Singer, 1958, p. 94; Knorr, 1976, pp. 84, 97–98).

In this context one can distinguish between the perception of a potential threat and the perception of war as a concrete possibility. The more that war is perceived as only a long-term possibility, the more it is conceived as a hypothetical event. Even when the chance of war is hypothetically accepted, the tendency might be "to treat it merely as abstract knowledge rather than as a trigger to specific and vigorous action. To make an intelligent prediction of the likelihood of war is one thing, to project oneself imaginatively and seriously into an expected war situation is quite another" (Brodie, 1965, p. 187). Yet the perception of war as a potential threat presents a twofold problem. First, potential threats are not necessarily restricted to long-range plans, since they can become imminent suddenly and unexpectedly. And second, when war is perceived as only a potential threat, the preparations for facing it may in extreme cases lack a clear orientation and detailed concept of the circumstances under which it might occur. Such a perception may even distort the understanding of the concrete conditions under which an alarm should be sounded (Knorr, 1979, p. 70; Harkabi, 1975, p. 121).

Thus a victim who erroneously believes that no attack should be expected at all will be taken completely by surprise, for if war is not expected at all, no warning will have been issued and no preparations will have been made to face it. Such total surprise is very rare, since no state under threat can completely exclude the possibility of war. It would mean that the victim's most basic conceptions about the attacker and himself had proved totally wrong; that no tension was recognized to exist between the two parties prior to the attack; and that the attacker had managed to conceal both his intentions and his military preparations so completely that no significant early warning indicators were available to the victim. In fact, no surprise attack since 1939 falls into this category. Theoretically, if France were to attack Switzerland tomorrow morning, we would have a surprise of this magnitude.

It is conceivable, however, that a nation generally does not expect war, assigns it a low probability, but does not exclude the possiblity altogether. It may foresee other kinds of hostile action short of war.

In this case it may issue a vague warning to its troops or even take some early precautions. In a sense this was the case with the Japanese attack on Pearl Harbor. Most American decision makers had not expected Japan to attack American territories, though they gave some credence to the possibility of an attack on the Philippines or to a submarine attack or raids against U.S. naval forces (Sherwood, 1950, p. 414). Since an attack against non-American territories was expected, and since some hostile acts against American units were considered possible, a vague warning had been issued; but it was insufficient to bring about even minimal military preparedness.

A victim that basically does not believe that an attack will be launched will obviously be surprised by the timing of the attack, and perhaps by other aspects as well. This kind of surprise involves such a fundamental misperception of the enemy's motives, intentions, and relative capabilities that it can be considered a national failure, not merely a result of intelligence misjudgment.

Failure to anticipate *when* an attack will occur is probably the most common reason for successful surprise attack. In a typical case the victim recognizes that a threat exists and takes the possibility of war into account, yet is surprised when the attack is launched earlier, or sometimes later, than expected.

All surprise attacks since 1939 have involved a surprise in timing. For example Stalin regarded war with Germany as quite likely, even inevitable, but he thought that he might have another few months before its actual outbreak (Ainsztein, 1966). Likewise, Secretary of State Dean Acheson claimed that although there was a measure of prior consensus concerning the possibility of a North Korean attack on South Korea, it did not appear imminent in the summer of 1950 (Rees, 1970, p. 18). And in 1973 Israeli intelligence estimated that the Arabs would not be in a position to carry out their threat of war until sometime in 1975 or 1976, while Israeli Defense Minister Moshe Dayan claimed in July 1973 that no general war was expected during the next ten years (Herzog, 1975, p. 41; *Time*, July 30, 1973; Bar-Lev, 1975, p. 261).

There are various reasons for erroneous estimates of the timing of an attack. Typically the victim believes that the military balance is so strong in his favor that his opponent needs more time to get ready for war. This was the basis of the Israeli estimate in 1973: the expected timing of war was predicated on the assumption that by 1975 or 1976 the Arabs would have acquired and absorbed medium-range bombers that could strike at Israel's airfields (Herzog, 1975,

p. 48; Bartov, 1978, p. 287). The victim also commonly tends to believe that the current political circumstances do not enable the enemy to attack. Thus the assessment that Israel was politically isolated and that the United States would not support an Israeli attack probably led to Egypt's mistake concerning the timing of the Six-Day War in 1967. Similarly, a week before the Yom Kippur War, the U.S. State Department's INR (Intelligence and Research) assessed that the political climate in the Arab states argued against a major Syrian attack on Israel at that time (Cline, 1974, pp. 131–134; *Pike Papers*, 1976, p. 7).

Another kind of erroneous estimate of the enemy's timing occurs when the victim believes that his opponent prefers to achieve its goals by other means, such as political pressure, guerrilla warfare, or clandestine activity, and that the enemy might resort to military action only if all other means failed. The best example of such an assumption was Stalin's belief that Hitler would first try political blackmail against the Soviet Union before turning to costly and risky war. Alternatively the victim may believe that the optimal time for its opponent to launch an attack has already passed; the victim assumes that the attacker is waiting for more favorable circumstances before going to war. Thus before the Chinese intervention in Korea U.S. intelligence estimated on October 28, 1950, that "with victorious U.S. Divisions in full deployment, it would appear that the auspicious time for such [Chinese] intervention had long since passed." Having refrained from intervention at a time when an attack might have resulted in an American Dunkirk, the Chinese, it was thought, would not be so foolish as to throw their army into battle at a later stage (Appleman, 1961, p. 761; see also Spanier, 1965, p. 98; Rees, 1970, p. 111). In another common instance the victim finds it difficult to pinpoint the timing of the attack because the enemy's own schedule has changed. Whaley (1969, p. 177; 1976, p. 4) found that of sixty-seven strategic surprises, the attack actually began on schedule in only twenty-six.

Surprise related to the timing of an attack is a matter of degree as well. If the victim thinks of the possibility of war in terms of many months or years, as was the case with Israel in 1973, the surprise may be relatively great, since his military preparedness is at a low level.[1] In fact such a case comes close to misjudging whether war will occur at all. If, however, the victim does not believe that war is imminent but considers it in terms of weeks or a few months, the surprise may be decreased. This was the case in the German invasion of France in 1940. In the least severe cases, when the victim is surprised only in terms of days, the surprise may be defined as merely a tactical one.

The victim may also be surprised by *where* the attack is launched, though war may generally be expected. In this sense strategic surprise may result when an attack is launched in an area considerably distant from the expected theater. A surprise concerning location can occur either when the opponent has the option of attacking several states or when the attacked state is a relatively large one. When the potential area of attack is small, as in the case of Israel, the surprise in location is confined to the operational or tactical level.

Perhaps the best example of strategic surprise in location is the attack on Pearl Harbor. On the eve of the attack, the list of feasible targets as estimated by American analysts included the Burma Road, Thailand, Malaya, the Netherlands East Indies, the Philippines, and the Russian Maritime Provinces. Hawaii and other American territories were not included even as potential targets (U.S. Congress, 1946a, p. 390).

The German invasion of France was also a surprise in location. The Allies believed that the German Army was not capable of launching an all-out attack on France and would therefore direct its land assault against Belgium or Holland. Four main possibilities were considered: an attack limited to the Low Countries, perhaps Holland alone; an offensive through the Low Countries aimed at flanking the Maginot Line in the north; a frontal attack on the Maginot Line; and an attack through Switzerland. The French command's attention focused on the first two and discounted the possibility that the main German thrust would come through the Ardennes (Hinsley, 1979, p. 129; Knorr, 1983, p. 31). Similarly before the Chinese intervention in Korea American analysts assumed that if China were to move offensively, it would most likely push into Southeast Asia or launch its long-anticipated invasion of Formosa (Paige, 1968, p. 172). And in October 1956 Egypt probably believed that Israel might launch an attack against Jordan, as most of the indicators suggested, as a reprisal for terrorist activities directed against Israel from Jordanian territory.

There appear to be two specific explanations for surprise regarding location. First, erroneous or outdated analysis on the part of the victim pertaining to both the terrain or arena and the enemy's capabilities may lead the victim to conclude that the enemy is incapable of overcoming a difficult ground obstacle; in some cases such an operation may even be regarded as a "mission impossible." Consequently the victim neglects a certain direction of possible attack. One of the problems concerning terrain analysis is that sometimes it is possible to prove its feasibility only under actual combat conditions. Another problem is that a terrain analysis that proved correct a few years ago may prove misleading today if the enemy has in the interim developed a means of overcoming the obstacle. Thus, before the attack on Pearl Harbor, American decision makers felt that Hawaii was a near-impregnable fortress, one that Japan would not risk attacking (U.S. Congress, 1946a, p. 234). The same mistake was made by the French, who believed in 1940 that the Ardennes were impassable (Hinsley, 1979, pp. 128–129). And the British command in Singapore believed in 1941 that a Japanese landing on the mainland in Johore with the object of launching an attack on Singapore Island would, owing to the nature of the ground to be crossed and the thick jungle, constitute such a difficult military operation that the Japanese would never attempt it on a large scale (Kirby, 1957, pp. 7–8).

The second explanation is that the victim may misjudge the motives and intentions of the enemy, especially when there is an option of attacking more than one country. This was the dilemma in assessing whether Hitler intended to attack France or Belgium and Holland in 1940; whether Hitler wanted to invade the Soviet Union or Great Britain in 1941; whether Japan planned to attack American territories or Dutch or British or Soviet territories in 1941; and whether Israel was going to attack Egypt or Jordan in 1956. Severe misjudgment of the enemy's basic motives and considerations may put the resulting attack in the category of high-level surprise. This is especially true when the victim's assessment of the target leads him to conclude that no significant precautions are called for on his part. To a large extent this was the case at Pearl Harbor.

At the strategic level surprise regarding *how* the attack is carried out occurs when the means and methods used by the enemy render its military operation more feasible than expected. The victim's perception of the future battlefield may be wrong if he misjudges critical components such as the nature of the anticipated conflict (clandestine activity, guerrilla warfare, conventional fighting, or nuclear war), the size and type of forces employed, the doctrine and tactics used, and the weapon systems and technological capabilities involved.

The main cause for surprise regarding means lies in innovations developed by the enemy, either in technology or in doctrine and tactics, that increase the enemy's capabilities beyond what was known or assumed by the victim.[2] Innovations may surprise in two ways. In the first instance the victim does not know about the developing innovation because of the lack of information or because erroneous interpretation of information, especially when the innovation is a very recent one. For example, the U.S. Navy assumed that warships anchored in the shallow water of Pearl Harbor could not be sunk by torpedo bombs launched from the air. This belief was based on the fact that in 1940 the only air-launched torpedoes the Navy knew about required a minimum depth of about sixty feet, whereas the depth of the water in Pearl Harbor was only thirty to forty feet. The Japanese managed, however, a week before their fleet sailed to develop torpedoes that could function even in the shallow water of Pearl Harbor (Wohlstetter, 1962, pp. 369–370). Similarly Egypt's decision to change tactics, abandon the search for long-range aerial attack capability, and rely on the neutralization of Israeli aerial superiority with a massive antiaircraft system was apparently made shortly before October 1973; this change was unknown to Israeli intelligence.

A second way in which innovations may surprise occurs when the existence of a technical or doctrinal development is known to the victim but the way in which it is used and its full impact under combat conditions come as a surprise. Thus the supply to the Egyptian Army of Sagger antitank missiles and that weapon's main technical characteristics were known to the Israelis. The Israeli Army had already encountered these missiles before 1973 during the War of Attrition; but the impact of their large-scale use on the battlefield by the Egyptians came as a surprise to the Israelis. Again in 1967 the Israeli strike against Egyptian airfields at the opening of the Six-Day War was not really an innovation; the Germans and the Japanese had already used this method during the Second World War. Its full devastating impact when employed with such accuracy against most of their airfields, however, surprised the Egyptians. The fact that this method was an innovation in Middle Eastern wars probably contributed to the surprise.

Surprise in means is a matter of degree as well. Here one can distinguish between surprise generated by the sudden appearance of new weapons and their impact and surprise concerning the very nature of a war. The employment of a new type of weapon or military technology can be considered a low-level surprise. Indeed, as Zeev

Bonen, the former director of the Israel Armament Development Authority, notes, technological surprise is difficult to achieve nowadays. Prior to the Second World War, armies were largely unaware of the possible impact of new technological development on warfare, and scientific intelligence was neglected; hence technological surprises did occur. Today "the long and leaky process of weapon acquisition is full of opportunities for timely detection." Since it takes a long time to produce and deploy new weapons in quantities capable of changing the military balance between nations, information on their characteristics usually becomes available in the interim. It is somewhat easier to achieve surprise when security is tight, as in the case of producing equipment in small quantities or during actual war (Bonen, n.d., pp. 3–5).

The main problem concerning technological surprise lies in the development of countermeasures. In many cases, taking effective countermeasures requires information about internal components of the new equipment, the acquistion of which takes time. Hence the development of countermeasures may lag considerably behind the deployment of the enemy's equipment. If war breaks out during this period, a technological surprise may be achieved in the sense that the countermeasures are not yet available (Bonen, n.d., p. 4). In some cases delayed knowledge of internal characteristics of a weapon may cause technological surprise with regard to the weapon itself if war breaks out in the interim. Thus American intelligence estimated that the range of Japanese fighters based on Formosa was insufficient for an attack on the Philippines. This was true until a month before the attack, when the Japanese succeeded in increasing the range by reducing the engine cruising speed, setting the fuel mixture as lean as possible, and training the pilots to ensure constant flight speed (Wohlstetter, 1962, pp. 357–361).

In any case most technological surprises are minor ones nowadays. Similarly under most circumstances misjudgments with regard to the order-of-battle employed by the enemy (especially a long-time enemy) are generally not greatly erroneous. Moreover, even when surprised in this way, the victim may still have a chance to adapt to the unexpected innovation. Thus, although Israel was surprised in 1973 by the impact of the massive use of Sagger antitank missiles, it managed partly to neutralize their effect before the end of the war.

A higher degree of surprise may occur when the victim misperceives the very nature of the coming war. Such a misperception reflects a long-term misjudgment and may lead the victim to base the central conception of his defense on faulty assumptions. In this case it is much more difficult for the victim to adapt. There are various reasons for such a fundamental surprise: it can be the outcome of prolonged ignorance of revolutionary doctrinal innovations or an accumulation of severe misjudgments with regard to technical developments. Then too it may reflect a basic misperception concerning the enemy's mental capabilities for conducting modern warfare.

This level of surprise is represented by the German blitzkrieg against Poland and, to a lesser extent, against France and the Soviet Union. Before the attack the Allies were aware of the technical capabilities of tanks, but they were surprised by their revolutionary operational potential when deployed independently of infantry and in coordination with air support. Thus the Soviet General Staff believed that the Germans would not view blitzkrieg tactics as feasible on a front so broad and so open to counterattack. The Soviets assumed that the main German forces would be engaged only after several days of probing frontier battles (Betts, 1980b, p. 569; Knorr, 1983, p. 30; Erickson, 1984, p. 418). Similarly the appearance of Japanese tanks in Malaya came as a great surprise to the British, who had insisted that tanks could never operate in a jungle and thus had retained not a single tank in Malaya. As it happened, the Japanese tanks moved easily between the spacious rows of rubber trees. Thus "the Japanese speed of movement, their ability to overcome obstacles and their bold use of tanks, came as a complete surprise" (Kirby, 1957, p. 211; see also Barber, 1968, p. 60).

At this point we may draw a number of conclusions regarding the level of the victim's expectations. As we have seen, four main questions form the basis of the victim's expectations of surprise attack: *whether* an attack will occur, and *when*, *where*, and *how* it will be launched. In each case it is possible to distinguish between high and low degrees of expectation and hence surprise. Let us now look at how these various issues operated in the examples of surprise attack listed earlier.

Table 1 demonstrates, first, that the degree of surprise and the aspects of surprise attack vary from case to case. Second, we see that a high degree of surprise concerning the actual occurrence of war is relatively rare; when it does happen, it is usually because the states involved have no history of hostility. The only cases that come close to this definition are the German invasion of Norway, the Japanese attack on Singapore, and the Chinese intervention in Korea. Low-

Table 1.   Degree of surprise across four aspects of suprise attack

Case	Whether	When	Where	How
Norway, 1940	high	high	high	none
France, 1940	none	low	low	high
Holland, 1940	none	low	low	low
Russia, 1941	none	high	low	low
Pearl Harbor, 1941	low	high	high	high
Singapore, 1941–42	high	high	high	high
North Korea, 1950	low	low	none	low
China-Korea, 1950	high	high	low	low
Egypt, 1956	low	high	high	high
China-India, 1962	low	high	none	low
Egypt, 1967	none	low	low	high
Israel, 1973	none	high	none	low

degree misjudgment as to the occurrence of war is more common. This may happen either when the victim has never been attacked by that enemy or when the enemy has an option of attacking another country.

The table also shows that surprise over timing is the most familiar case: it happened in all the attacks cited here. We may postulate that in modern warfare surprise in timing is the most vital aspect of successful surprise attack and is probably the easiest to achieve.

We see that in most cases the victim was surprised by more than one aspect of the attack. This is not incidental. Erroneous assumptions about whether the attack will occur must lead to erroneous expectations with regard to its timing, and sometimes to its location and the way it is carried out. More important, strategic surprise is caused not by one wrong hypothesis but by a whole set of misconceptions. It is only natural that these misconceptions should lead to surprise on more than one level.

Finally, the degree of expectation may change and hence influence the degree of surprise. Thus during 1971 Israeli intelligence believed that war might break out in the near future. This assumption changed during 1972, as President Anwar Sadat's "Year of Decision" (1971) passed without overt evidence of Egypt's capability or intent to attack. In 1973 Israeli intelligence further reviewed its assessment that war was not expected before 1975 or 1976. Defense Minister Dayan's estimate underwent a striking change during the spring and summer of 1973 from a perception of high threat and high probability of war to the assumption that war would not occur in the near future. He even went beyond the intelligence estimate, predicting, as we have seen, that there would not be a major war within the next ten years. The final days before the 1973 war, however, witnessed a gradual change in the assumptions of Israeli decision makers with regard to the timing of the coming war; and in the last twenty-four hours prior to the attack many believed that war was imminent (Brecher, 1980, pp. 53, 62; Herzog, 1975, p. 41; *Time*, July 30, 1973). A somewhat similar process of reevaluation took place among Soviet leaders on the eve of the German invasion in 1941.

The Strategic Warning

Advance warning is the vital link connecting intelligence assessment with countermeasures designed to enhance readiness. Without adequate advance warning military preparedness can never be sufficient to face the threat. In this sense surprise can be regarded as the result of failure to issue an advance warning to decison makers and troops that would enable them to take appropriate precautions.

Advance warning comprises two elements. *Early warning indicators* are those signals that show that the enemy may be intending or preparing to launch an attack. They are the raw materials for the formation of an intelligence assessment pertaining to the possibility of war. The *strategic warning* is the message sent by the intelligence community to the decision makers, and from the decision makers to the troops, warning that war or hostile military action is a possibility. Strategic warning results from assessing the possibility of war, and it is aimed at bringing the decision makers and troops to the point where they can take appropriate measures to face a threat.

Intelligence analysts distinguish between two kinds of strategic warning. The first is warning with regard to the enemy's *capabilities*—that is, the determination that the enemy has the forces and means sufficient for launching an attack. The second type of warning concerns the enemy's *intentions*; it determines that the enemy has decided, or is about to decide, to launch an attack. Intelligence analysts believe that they can frequently determine whether and at what point the enemy has completed its preparations toward an offensive military option; but they are reluctant to issue warnings regarding the enemy's intentions because they feel that this kind of warning is risky and likely to be erroneous. They emphasize that they cannot guarantee that they will provide an early warning pertaining to the enemy's intentions; hence responsibility for such warnings should be shared by decision makers as well. Yet decision makers often ask their intelligence agencies about the enemy's likely behavior and intentions, and usually they get answers. Thus, despite their reservations, intelligence analysts are pressed to provide assessments and warnings concerning the enemy's intentions—and are blamed whenever they fail to issue such warnings. Consequently, in practice the distinction between the two kinds of strategic warning is blurred.

Here I am interested in the *process* of strategic warning. In most cases the warning communicated to the troops reflects, or is identical with, the warning provided by the intelligence community to the decision makers, although sometimes the decision makers may delay or change the intelligence warning. For our purposes the two stages of strategic warning—the intelligence warning and the warning issued by the decision makers to the troops—will be regarded as one process.

The failure to issue a strategic warning can also vary in degree. As Table 2 demonstrates, in most of our cases of surprise attack an advance warning was issued by the intelligence community and the decision makers but proved insufficient. A satisfactory warning must contain two elements.[3] First, the warning should be phrased in spe-

Table 2.   The strategic warning

Case	Kind of warning	Time between warning and attack
Norway, 1940	no warning	no warning
France, 1940	general, ambiguous	about six weeks
Holland, 1940	general	twenty-four hours
Russia, 1941	partly clear	a few hours
Pearl Harbor, 1941	general, ambiguous	two weeks
Singapore, 1941–42	no warning	no warning
North Korea, 1950	general	a few weeks
China-Korea, 1950	no warning	no warning
Egypt, 1956	no warning[a]	no warning[a]
China-India, 1962	general	six weeks
Egypt, 1967	no warning	no warning
Israel, 1973	mostly clear	eleven to twelve hours

a. Conclusion based on limited data.

cific and unambiguous terms. The ideal warning should be reasonably clear in terms of probability as to whether the enemy is going to attack, as well as to when, where, and how he will attack. Second, the warning should be communicated in a timely way to the decision makers and troops. Unfortunately most strategic warnings are deficient in at least one of these qualities and usually in both.

The Wording of Strategic Warnings

One of the complaints voiced most often by the Pearl Harbor commanders after the attack was that they had not been unambiguously warned by Washington that war was imminent. Admiral Husband Kimmel, then Commander in Chief of the Pacific Fleet, complained in his memoirs (1955, pp. 35–36, 45) that none of the reports from the U.S. ambassador in Tokyo warned of an imminent attack in the area of Hawaii or indicated that an attack there was even probable. The "war warning" dispatch sent by Naval Operations on November 27, 1941, did not warn the Pacific Fleet of such an attack nor did it repeal or modify the advice previously given to the admiral by the Navy Department that no move against Pearl Harbor was being planned by Japan. "The phrase 'war warning' cannot be made a catchall for all the contingencies hindsight may suggest," he claims.

The advance warning issued before the attack on Pearl Harbor deserves close attention, since it provides the best example of a much larger problem—the ambiguous language of intelligence.

Prior to the attack on Pearl Harbor, Washington had issued several general warnings. On November 24, 1941, Admiral Kimmel received the following message from the Chief of Naval Operations: "Chances of favorable outcome of negotiations with Japan very doubtful. This situation coupled with statements of Japanese government and movements their naval and military forces indicate in our opinion that a *surprise aggressive movement in any direction* including attack on Philippines or Guam is a possibility" (Wohlstetter, 1962, p. 44; emphasis added).

The Committee on the Investigation of the Pearl Harbor Attack concluded that this dispatch carried no orders for Kimmel; it appeared to have been designed to acquaint him with the mounting tensions as well as to supply him with an estimation of probable Japanese movements. Kimmel took no action pursuant to this dispatch; indeed he later stated that he felt the message required no action other than that which he had already taken.

The main warning was the November 27 dispatch sent by the Chief of Naval Operations. It opened with the words "This is to be considered a war warning," and went on: "An aggressive move by Japan is expected within the next few days ... The number and equipment of Japanese troops and the organization of naval task forces indicated an amphibious expedition against either the Philippines, Thai or Kra Peninsula, or possibly Borneo." Kimmel was ordered "to execute an appropriate defensive deployment" (U.S. Congress, 1946a, pp. 104–105).

This warning constitutes a more complicated case. It does contain most of the required elements of an advance warning: it includes the concrete term *war warning*; it projects a short time before the attack, offers an outline of the possible attack, and gives an operational order. But it was not specific enough, and, worse, it was misleading. Its main deficiency was that it mentioned specific possible targets for the attack, but not Hawaii. In Kimmel's words: "It did not state expressly or by implication that an attack in the Hawaiian area was imminent or probable." General Walter Short, Commander of the Army's Hawaiian Department, concluded from the same dispatch that "the War Department expected the war to break out, if at all, only in the far Pacific and not at Hawaii" (U.S. Congress, 1946a, pp. 105, 126).

In fact the analysis by the recipients of these warnings reflected the tenor of estimates being made in Washington. The War Council did assume low probabiliity for an attack on Pearl Harbor. It thought that by sending out the warning it was alerting Hawaii to the possibility of danger, but its own estimate affected the wording of the dispatch. The officers in Hawaii, by contrast, gave the message an extreme interpretation. "They believed it meant that the government leaders agreed with their assumption that there was no chance at all of a Japanese attack against Pearl Harbor, that the only threats to be considered were minor ones" (Janis, 1972, p. 96–97).

The next warning was sent by War Department on November 27. It stated that "negotiations with Japan appear to be terminated ... hostile action possible at any moment" (U.S. Congress, 1946a, p. 102). This dispatch provides another example of the caution that characterizes the phrasing of warnings. Secretary of War Henry Stimson and General Leonard Gerow, Head of the Army War Plans Division, had opened the draft of the warning with the words "Negotiations with Japan have been terminated." Stimson, however, after a conversation with Secretary of State Cordell Hull, altered this definite statement to read: "Negotiations with Japan *appear* to be terminated to all practical purposes with only the barest possibilities that the Japanese Government *might* come back to continue." Thus, as the investigation committe stated, he introduced confusion into a sentence of crucial importance (U.S. Congress, 1946b, p. 65).

The last example is the message sent by Naval Operations on December 3. This message was not a full, direct warning. Nevertheless, many officers in Washington regarded it, after the actual event, as the most significant tip-off to the theater commanders and an unambiguous signal for a full alert. It read as follows: "Highly reliable information has been received that categoric and urgent instructions were sent yesterday to Japanese diplomatic and consular posts at Hongkong, Singapore, Batavia, Manila, Washington, and London to destroy most of their codes and ciphers at once and to burn all other important confidential and secret documents" (U.S. Congress, 1946a, p. 100). The wording of this message created two problems. First, it reported that the Japanese consulates had been ordered to destroy *most* of their codes. Kimmel later claimed that since not *all* of the Japanese codes were to be destroyed, he "didn't consider that [message] of vital importance." Rather it indicated to him "that Japan was taking precautionary measures preparatory to going into Thai, and because they thought that the British or the Americans, or both of them, might jump on them and seize their codes and ciphers after they went into Thailand" (Wohlstetter, 1962, p. 52).

Second, the message contained neither conclusions or orders and could be seen as nothing more than a transfer of information for the receiver's passive knowledge. Consequently Kimmel could claim that since such reports had been made to him three or four times during the year, this message did not seem extraordinary (Wohlstetter, 1962, p. 53).

Of course this kind of mutual misunderstanding is not peculiar to intelligence but belongs to the larger problem of communication in general. Jervis suggests that "when messages are sent from a different background of concerns and information than is possessed by the receiver, misunderstanding is likely" (1969, p. 250). That is, two people will read the same message quite differently if one of them lacks relevant information known to the other. The difference will be compounded if each assumes a shared background. The sender will make the unwarranted assumption that his intentions are clear, while the receiver of the message will believe that he has grasped its intended implications.

Thus when Washington advised General Short in Pearl Harbor to expect "hostile actions at any moment," the sender of the message meant him to expect attack on American possessions from without; but Short understood the message to refer to sabotage. Washington did not realize the extent to which Hawaii considered the danger of sabotage to be primary. Also it incorrectly assumed that Short had received the extraordinary information provided by the "Magic" intercepts of the diplomatic communications between Tokyo and the Japanese embassy in Washington, which indicated that surprise attack was a distinct possibility. In fact Short's actions were heavily influenced by the message sent to him by the War Department on July 8 saying that a Japanese attack on Russia was the most probable form of aggression, and that an attack on British and Dutch targets ranked next in probability. Short did not believe that he had received notice of any change with regard to the views stated in that message. Indeed, the officers in Hawaii felt so confident of their interpretation that they thought it unnecessary to check with Washington to make sure that they had grasped exactly what had been intended. Needless to say, Washington maintained a mirror-image misperception. The crucial importance of having the relevant background information is proved by the fact that all other American outpost commanders who received the warning messages of November 27 in substantially the same form took full measures to effect a state of readiness commensurate with imminent warfare. Hawaii was the only outpost that failed to institute a proper alert (Wohlstetter, 1962, pp. 74, 101; Janis, 1972, p. 80; U.S. Congress, 1946a, p. 236).

Similarly, while Kimmel strongly criticized Washington's ambiguous warning, he himself was to be criticized for the same error. Two months before the attack Kimmel, in a confidential letter to his staff, had spoken of a probable Japanese surprise attack and had added a list of instructions in case of submarine action: "It must be remembered, too, that a single submarine attack may indicate the presence of a considerable surface force" (Wohlstetter, 1962, pp. 14–15). Yet when a foreign submarine was discovered in Pearl Harbor an hour before the bombing, it was not linked to an imminent Japanese attack. Kimmel did not go so far as to say that the mere *sighting* of a single hostile submarine in the defensive sea area might indicate the proximity of an enemy task force. The evidence, he said, would be "a single submarine *attack.*" Whatever the purpose behind this phrasing, Kimmel's warning was interpreted by his staff as applying to a situation prevailing *after* war had been declared.

To a large extent this is a problem intrinsic to an organization whose function is to produce assessments and predictions. The inherently precarious character of intelligence information frequently generates very cautious wording. For one thing, the area in which the intelligence analyst works is so speculative that he feels he must be vague in order to convey to the reader a sense of the inherent uncertainty surrounding the problem (Kelly and Peterson, 1971). For another, the analyst must be careful about staking his reputation repeatedly on predictions most of which are certain to be proved wrong by events. In most cases the analyst is not sure at all whether the available information—which by itself is often phrased vaguely and incompletely—points to the possibility of war; and even when the information clearly points to an imminent attack—which is quite rare—the analyst knows that enemy decisions are often subject to reversal on short notice. Before Pearl Harbor, for example, the Japanese were prepared to cancel their attack on American possessions in the Pacific up to twenty-four hours before the time set for that attack. "The fact that intelligence predictions must be based on moves that are almost always reversible makes understandable the reluctance of the intelligence analyst to make bold assertions" (Wohlstetter, 1962, p. 395). Finally, the need to reach a consensus throughout the intelligence community, whenever required, adds another constraint that reduces the phrasing of estimates to the lowest common denominator. As Hughes comments, "Especially amid controversy, estimators will reach for extra ambiguities in the search for interagency unanimity" (1976, p. 43).

Hence the peculiar phrasing used in intelligence predictions— terms such as *seems, may be, cannot be entirely ruled out, possible, strongly possible,* or *probable.* Frequently the analyst's rule is not to speak too clearly and precisely about the future unless he has to. When the analyst is pressed to make his estimate concrete and clear, the rule is to lower its probability.[4] Except for the alert order of June 14, 1940, none of Washington's messages used the word *alert.* "They said in effect, 'Something is brewing,' or 'A month may see literally anything,' or 'Get ready for a surprise move in any direction—maybe' " (Wohlstetter, 1962, pp. 167–168).

While cautious phrasing in warnings in understandable, ambiguous descriptions of contingencies such as "enemy future action unpredictable, but hostile action possible at any moment" do not guide the commander in the field to a specific decision, nor do they tell him of any change in the strategic situation. Prior to some surprise attacks, a general warning has been issued, but without creating a feeling that war is imminent. This suggests that a general, vague warning may not be sufficient and is likely to lose its effect over time. Since no army can be prepared for all possibilities at all times, it has to concentrate on the most probable ones at any given time; in other words, it tends to rely not on the warning but on its own expectations and conceptions. Thus Allied intelligence gave warning at the end of April 1940 that a German offensive westward was imminent and that, delivered anywhere except against the Maginot Line or in Switzerland, it could be launched with little or no notice. So general a warning was of no assistance, since the Allied High Command could not keep its forces on permanent alert (Hinsley, 1979, p. 135).

The problem is made more complicated by the fact that formal warnings issued by intelligence or the military command are often not the only ones around. They are usually accompanied by informal assessments and warnings, oral or written, communicated simultaneously among directors of intelligence agencies, military or political leaders, and commanders in the field. These assessments sometimes contradict the formal warnings, at least in some respects. Such inconsistencies also reduce the impact of the formal warning. Thus the Chief of Naval Operations, Admiral Harold Stark, counteracted some of the most impressive formal warnings in his personal letters to Admiral Kimmel in Hawaii. Written in a friendly and confidential tone, these letters explained that the outlook was not as bad as it might sound in the official message and thus added to the feeling of immunity in Pearl Harbor (Janis, 1972, p. 96).

The Timing of Strategic Warnings

The main function of intelligence warnings is to buy time in order to make the appropriate decisions and take the necessary countermeasures to face the threat. The chance that these decisions and measures will prove to be sufficient depends in part on the length of time between the warning and the attack. This warning span is determined to a large extent by the processes that take place from the moment the intelligence agency considers whether to issue a warning until the moment the warning reaches the troops in the field.

Only rarely has a strategic warning been issued in time. In most of our cases there was no clear warning at all, or it was issued at the last moment (see Table 2). The two outstanding cases are those of "Barbarossa" and the Yom Kippur War, when warnings were issued just a few hours before the attack. The timing was not accidental; it reflects a problem inherent to intelligence warning. Three main reasons seem to account for belated warnings. First, the enemy's decision to attack may be made a relatively short time before implementation—usually a matter of months or weeks and sometimes, as in the case of the Israeli decision to go to war in 1967, only days before. Consequently the victim is left with a short warning span, though it may be increased if the victim has properly anticipated the enemy's intention to go to war even before that decision is made. Then too an intelligence warning is based largely on the reading of early warning indicators that point to the possibility of imminent war. Yet since most of these indicators reflect the enemy's preparations for war, they usually do not appear until shortly before the attack, leaving an even shorter period of time to detect them. Last, the process of evaluating the information and making the decision to warn the policy makers and then alert the troops consumes time. When the analysts' dominant assumptions exclude the possibility of imminent war, it takes even more energy and time to change those assumptions.

The intelligence process, then, is itself a major obstacle to timely strategic warning; but it is not necessarily the final one. As Betts (1980b, pp. 552–553) notes:

Communications between intelligence officers and policymakers produce doubt and fluctuations of certainty; officials may have second thoughts and order more search, or they may declare alerts and then cancel them. Information processing may be slower than decision time or may be unsynchronized with the deliberations . . . The final tactical warnings that may congeal the consensus [that war is coming], as well as authorizations from the victim's leaders to their troops to move into wartime positions, can also be held up in the communication chain. This keeps the rates of speed in attack preparation and defense reaction in a ratio unfavorable to the victim.

Surprise and Military Preparedness

Military preparedness is the outcome of a series of measures—alert, mobilization, and redeployment—designed to counter an attack. In all our cases of surprise attack, the victim's state of military preparedness at the moment of attack was incomplete. The victim may have carried out only part of his readiness plan or may have taken inappropriate measures for that kind of attack. The state of preparedness is an index of the strength of the surprise. If we look on the process of the victim's response from the moment of warning to full preparedness as a continuum, then the point at which the attacker strikes determines the degree of surprise (Betts, 1980b, pp. 553–554; Brodin, 1978).

The state of military preparedness at the time of attack is the outcome of two main factors. First, the core of preparedness consists of those *basic measures* taken by any state as minimal precautions against potential future attack. These measures are determined by the basic perception of the potential war and its characteristics. This level of preparedness is different for each state; it may change, usually gradually, along with doctrinal or technological changes or with changes in budget constraints or in the perception of security problems. These basic measures involve the size of the regular army and its reserve forces, the purchase of weapon systems and the types of those systems, the deployment of formations and the level of their readiness, and so on. Second, these measures are augmented when needed by additional *emergency measures,* which are determined largely by the strategic warning itself. No army can keep its units in full readiness for a long period of time, and usually its basic preparedness is far from sufficient to face a massive attack. Thus the warning should enable the armed forces to bring their state of preparedness up to the required level. In this sense lack of preparedness at the moment of attack can be the result of either a failure to take the proper basic measures, a failure to issue a precise warning and take the required emergency measures, or both.

That the proper level of preparedness depends on a timely and clear warning poses several problems. As Betts claims, "response necessarily lags behind warning. Even if recognition crystallizes perfectly before the moment of attack, the victim may still suffer the costs of surprise if alert, mobilization, and deployment to defensive positions are still getting under way" (1980b, p. 553). Proper basic preparedness, however, will lessen the outcome of a failure to issue an appropriate warning. This was the case in Israel in 1973.

Then there is the problem of the warning span. The intelligence community is often required to assess the length of time before an attack can be expected, during which time it should be able to issue an advance warning of the actual attack. Such an assessment is very helpful, sometimes crucial, in planning and determining the desired level of basic preparedness. Sometimes, however, because of deep uncertainty the intelligence community is unable or unwilling to set this warning span. Thus on May 26, 1940, following its failure to issue warnings before the invasions of Norway and France, British intelligence warned the Chiefs of Staff that it could probably not provide advance notice of a German landing in Britain. It claimed that until it had firm evidence to the contrary, it would not depart from the assumption that invasion might come at any time and from any direction (Hinsley, 1979, pp. 167–168).

Sometimes the intelligence community is confident enough to project a warning span—usually a matter of days or at most a few weeks. Thus Israeli plans in 1973 were based on the assumption that there would be advance warning of more than twenty-four hours (indeed the assumption was that a warning would be given five to six days before the enemy opened fire, or two days in case of a disaster). The Director of Military Intelligence assured the General Staff that he would be able to give advance warning of any enemy intention to launch an attack in good time to allow for the orderly call-up of the reserves (Bartov, 1978, pp. 278–279; Agranat, 1975, p. 19). The assumption was that such a warning interval would guarantee that considerable reinforcements of mobilized reservists would already have reached the fronts by the time war broke out; consequently mobilization of reserve forces was not included among readiness measures until the last day before the war. Reliance on the promise of Israeli military intelligence to provide such a timely warning—which proved to be a grave error—was never questioned, and the Agranat Inquiry Commission concluded that there were no grounds for giving such an absolute undertaking (Agranat, 1975, p. 19; Herzog, 1975, p. 276; Dayan, 1976, p. 381; Bartov, 1978, pp. 278–279).

The problem is that nobody outside the intelligence community has the knowledge and experience to check the capability of intelligence agencies to issue a strategic warning. Morever, even within the intelligence community itself, the estimate of the warning span is to a large extent speculative. It is based on a capability—which rapidly changes—of collecting needed information at a given time and on an assumed capability of analyzing a developing situation, which can never be relied on.[5]

Furthermore, it is the clarity of warnings that determines to a large extent whether commanders in the field will take the appropriate countermeasures. Thus, during the night before the German invasion of Russia, Soviet field commanders received a relatively clear warning that a German surprise attack was possible along the front on June 22 or 23; the troops were ordered not to give way to provocative actions of any kind that might produce major complications, and to be at full combat readiness to meet a surprise attack. There was, however, no instruction to the commanders as to what they should do or how they might distinguish between war and provocation, or between not responding to provocation and responding to a surprise attack (Erickson, 1972, pp. 531–534; 1975, pp. 110–112; Sella, 1978, p. 561).

Even when the perception of the immediate threat starts to form, however, the main obstacles to sufficient and timely countermeasures are the political considerations involved in a decision to respond. In many of our cases of surprise attack political leaders were willing to take a risk and delay their decision to mobilize and put troops on alert. Countermeasures involve considerable external and domestic costs. The tendency of the decision makers is therefore to postpone a decision to take maximum measures as long as they have sufficient doubt about the imminence of war. This is especially so since "decision makers are used to living in an environment of *some* warning"; "the decision maker can appreciate the warnings, but suspend judgment and order stepped-up intelligence collection to confirm the threat, hoping to find contrary evidence that reduces the probability the enemy will strike" (Betts, 1980b, pp. 561, 564).

The problem, therefore, is how much readiness is enough. The fact that readiness implies taking diverse measures at several levels allows decision makers some maneuverability to gain time and save costs. Thus on October 5, 1973, the Israeli Defense Minister approved a "C" alert, the maximum for the regular army and the air force, but he did not approve mobilization of reserves. Partial mobilization of reserves was approved only a day later, following the arrival of additional information that war would break out that very day (Dayan, 1976, pp. 373–374). Similarly on June 21, 1941, the day before the German attack, Stalin ordered the antiaircraft defense of Moscow brought up to 75 percent of its operational readiness but apparently did not decide to bring the Red Army up to a state of full readiness (Erickson, 1972, pp. 530–531). Obviously the safer the leaders feel with basic preparedness and minimal additional measures to absorb the attack, the more willing they are to risk postponing further moves. Thus the Israeli decision to delay making additional readiness moves in 1973 was heavily influenced by the assessment that Israel's secure borders and strategic depth, especially in the south, as well as its regular army and second-strike capability constituted a viable alternative to frequent mobilization and thus would enable the country to absorb an Arab attack without excessive cost (Stein, 1980, p. 159; Brecher, 1980, p. 184).

There are various reasons for the tendency to delay readiness measures. The most important and most frequent reason is the fear that these measures will increase tension and cause deterioration toward war. Too often the victim forgoes any attempt to deter the enemy by increasing its level of preparedness, believing that these moves will increase the risk of war either by antagonizing the enemy or through miscalculation.

In all our cases this choice proved to be a mistake. The desire to prevent deterioration toward war was a major consideration in Stalin's decision to delay taking maximum countermeasures against a German attack. There are indications that shortly before the invasion Stalin grasped something of the danger; but since the Soviet Army was not sufficiently prepared for war at that stage, he tried to delay the conflict. Since he sought to prove that he had no intention of going to war with Germany, he reacted sharply against the notion of taking premature countermeasures. Up to the last minute he was preoccupied with the need to avoid provocation. On June 21, Commissar of Defense Marshal Semyon Timoshenko proposed sending an alert to all troops of the border military districts, but the draft order did not satisfy Stalin. He claimed, "It is too soon to issue such a directive—perhaps the question can still be settled peacefully. We must issue a short directive stating that an attack may begin with provocative actions by the German forces. The troops of the border districts must not be incited by any provocation in order to avoid complications" (Erickson, 1975, p. 110).

Similarly, prior to the Yom Kippur War the Israelis were careful not to overreact to the Arab military build-up. Defense Minister Dayan felt that any dramatic response by Israel to the Syrian build-up "would mobilize all Syria for war" (Nakdimon, 1982, p. 71). Even as late as the morning of October 5 the Israeli regular armored division in Sinai was ordered not to undertake any movements to forward positions that could arouse Egyptian suspicions of a planned Israeli attack (Herzog, 1975, p. 46). The same consideration played a role at Pearl Harbor as well. Describing the preparation of the November 27 warning Secretary Stimson claimed: "In Hawaii because of the large numbers of Japanese inhabitants, it was felt desirable to issue a special warning so that nothing would be done, unless necessary to defense, to alarm the civil population and thus possibly precipitate an incident and give the Japanese an excuse to go to war" (U.S. Congress, 1946a, p. 266-M). And in April 1940 the Norwegian government decided against immediate mobilization in the hope of avoiding any step that the Germans might construe as provocative. (Knorr, 1983, p. 23).

Another important reason for restraint in taking countermeasures is the desire not to make the first hostile move in the eyes of third parties. Before the Yom Kippur War Israeli decision makers feared that mobilization of the reserves would be perceived by world opinion as an aggressive act. After the war Dayan claimed, "If we knew *for sure* four days before the war, we would not have mobilized earlier . . . If we had started to mobilize the reserves, the whole world would have charged—'the Arabs opened fire because they saw that Israel was going to attack' " (Brecher, 1980, p. 185). The Israelis were also worried that escalating the crisis by making military moves would invite American pressure to renew the negotiations for a political settlement but on inconvenient terms (Bartov, 1978, p. 242).

Reluctance to make the first hostile move can also be an internal consideration. Before Pearl Harbor Washington feared that national support for a war effort could not be achieved unless Japan committed the first overt act. Accordingly the Army in Hawaii was put on an antisabotage alert, a defensive posture posing the least possible risk of an incident that Japan could call an overt act by the United States. Roosevelt's fear of isolationists at home influenced his decision on the eve of the Japanese attack not to call the Chief of Naval Operations away from a performance of *The Student Prince* because "undue alarm might be caused" (Sherwood, 1950, p. 434).

Last but not least among domestic constraints are economic considerations. On the local level, for example, U.S. forces at Pearl

Harbor had to take into account that in order to fly 360-degree reconnaissance with the planes available, it would have been necessary to reduce training, delay important shipments to the Philippines, exhaust crews, and run down the planes' airworthiness (Betts, 1980b, p. 560). On the national level the fear of incurring substantial expenditures and losing credibility sometimes causes decision makers to wait for unambiguous indications of attack, thus delaying countermeasures. As Defense Minister Dayan explained in 1973, frequent mobilization would have disrupted the fabric of daily life in a country dependent on a citizen army. Two days before the war Dayan was also concerned that a panic caused by overreaction would undermine the leadership's credibility (Stein, 1980, p. 159; Bartov, 1978, p. 316).

2

Information and Indicators

Analysis of surprise attacks suggests that the intelligence community seldom fails to anticipate them owing to a lack of relevant information. In most cases the victim possesses an abundance of information indicating the imminence of the attack. A study on warning intelligence sponsored by a U.S. Congressional Subcommittee on Evaluation examined the warning process during such crises as Pearl Harbor, Korea, the Cuban missile crisis, the 1968 Soviet invasion of Czechoslovakia, and the Yom Kippur War and found that in no case had lack of data been a major factor in the failure to anticipate the crisis (Latimer, 1979, pp. 50–51).

Nevertheless, intelligence analysts and decision makers do at times attribute intelligence failures to lack of information, especially regarding the enemy's intentions. In a report to the United Nations dated February 23, 1951, General Douglas MacArthur claimed that political intelligence had failed to penetrate the Iron Curtain and warn of Chinese intentions to intervene in Korea, and that field intelligence had been severely handicapped inasmuch as aerial reconnaissance beyond the Yalu River had been impossible. Since the Chinese avenue of approach to the battlefield was only "one night's march" from the sanctuary, MacArthur concluded, "no intelligence system in the world could have surmounted such handicaps to determine to any substantial degree enemy strength, movements and intentions" (DeWeerd, 1962, pp. 450–451). Yet even allowing for western intelligence services' difficulties in penetrating China, MacArthur could hardly complain of lack of evidence as to China's intentions, since these were repeatedly announced by the Chinese themselves but were not taken seriously by MacArthur. Nor did the

Chinese conceal from foreign diplomats in Peking that as of mid-September 1950 their troops were massing to reinforce the Chinese contingent in Manchuria. Even General Omar Bradley, then Chairman of the Joint Chiefs of Staff, later claimed that while he had no intelligence that the Chinese were going to enter the war, "we had the intelligence that they were concentrating in Manchuria . . . We had the information that they had the capability [of intervening in the war]" (U.S. Congress, 1951, p.759; see also Whiting, 1960, p. 111). In all the other cases no such complaints were even raised.

Usually although there is no quantitative lack of available information, there is a qualitative problem. Before Pearl Harbor, writes Wohlstetter, "our decision-makers had at hand an impressive amount of information on the enemy . . . [yet] they did not have the complete list of targets . . . They did not know the exact hour and date for the attack. They did not have an accurate knowledge of Japanese capabilities or of Japanese willingness to accept very high risks" (1966, p. 85). Kirpatrick adds, "Not one of the hundreds of [Magic] messages carried a clear statement of what the Japanese government intended to do if and when negotiations with the United States failed" (1973, p. 91).

The Pearl Harbor case is typical of the problem of the quality of information available to the intelligence analyst. There are almost no instances in which a single definite signal, one that would alert forces and tell them what to expect, arrives on time. Instead analysts usually receive a series of signals and try to combine them into a clear picture of what is going to happen. The point, as Wohlstetter argues, is that the puzzle is never complete. The data are ambiguous, and the signals viewed before the attack are muffled and fraught with uncertaintly. "The signals that seem to stand out and scream of the impending catastrophe are the ones learned about only after the event, when they appear stripped of other possible meanings" (Wohlstetter, 1962, p. 226).

Quality of Intelligence Information

The quality of intelligence information is determined by its reliability and its diagnostic value. The reliability of information is based on the extent to which it carries some inherent evidence that it correctly and objectively reflects the enemy's behavior, intentions, or capabilities. We can distinguish three levels of reliability with regard to intelligence information.

Nonreliable or *partly reliable* information is perceived as suspect usually because the source is problematic or subjective, or lacks adequate access to the relevant material or to subsources, or because the information is unclear, contradictory, or judged to have been manipulated by the enemy. A major portion of information derived from human sources falls into this category, as well as some non-classified information.

Information is judged to be *reliable but controlled* when it raises few doubts about the source's objectivity and access, yet this is information that we must assume the enemy knows we possess access to. Thus the enemy can partially modify his behavior in order to manipulate our perceptions and influence our conclusions. Aerial photographs can fall into this category: we have few doubts that the information they provide is factual; yet their utility is reduced since the enemy must be aware of our capability of acquiring them and may be camouflaging or altering his movements accordingly. The same is true for some nonclassified information.

Finally, *reliable noncontrolled* information is regarded as hard evidence because it is believed to disclose faithfully some important aspects of enemy behavior or intentions to which it is inextricably linked.[1] Analysis of the information is based on the assumption that the enemy is not aware of our access or is unlikely to realize that the information can be used as an indicator of his future behavior. Consequently the reliability of this kind of information stems from our belief that the enemy is not using it for deception and manipulation. The best examples of information in this category are intercepted messages and authentic documents.

To judge the diagnostic value of information we probe the data's capacity to confirm or reject any of the competing hypotheses or interpretations.[2] This depends, first, on the information's capability of resolution (that is, the ratio between the strength of its correct, clear evidence, or signals, and its confusing, misleading signs, or noise) and second, on the scope of the event reported in the information relative to the problem under consideration.

A short example might clarify the meaning of these two features. Suppose we have to estimate the enemy's intentions of launching an offensive. We obtain two pieces of information: an ambiguous Humint report to the effect that the enemy plans to go to war, and a reliable Sigint report about a state of alert planned in one of the enemy's brigades. The first report has a low resolution capability because of its ambiguity and questionable reliability, but it has a wide scope of occurrence because it relates directly to the core of the problem. The second report has a high resolution capability, since we have no doubt about its validity; but its scope of occurrence is narrow, since it refers to only one brigade, and it does not reveal much about the enemy's intentions. The diagnostic value of both reports is low, although owing to different reasons, since neither can determine whether the enemy's deployment is defensive or offensive. Information has a high diagnostic value if, for example, it provides clear-cut, reliable evidence that the enemy is going to war.

In general there is a negative correlation between the resolution capability and the scope of occurrence of the information. In order to achieve a greater resolution capability one has to narrow the scope of occurrence of the observed events. Technological improvements in the means of collection have generated better and more accurate information about the deployment and activity of the enemy's troops; but the scope of the observed events has not been broadened, and may even have been narrowed. Hence it is doubtful whether the diagnostic value of information is greater than it was before.

Given this background, one can distinguish two categories of intelligence information that are relevant for the prediction of possible attack. *Direct evidence* includes generally clear, reliable, noncontrolled information (and sometimes reliable controlled information as well) with high diagnostic value. Such evidence, if it originates with the enemy's leadership and includes a concrete warning, may tell us explicitly about the enemy's intended behavior or at least may leave little room for misinterpretation. The better the direct evidence, the better the chance to assess correctly the enemy's intentions and to issue a timely warning. Such evidence has the power to shake perceptions and prejudices and to change estimates. *Early warning indicators*, by contrast, include partly reliable or reliable but controlled information, and sometimes even noncontrolled information with relatively low diagnostic value. Some of these indicators may not be sufficently reliable; but even many of those indicators that are relatively reliable and exhibit great capability of resolution are no more than indicators. That is, they reflect a narrow scope of occurrence, they cannot adequately clarify the intentions behind the enemy's moves, and they cannot determine which of the various possible scenarios will prevail.

The main body of information available to intelligence analysts belongs to this second category. Information that belongs to the first category does exist, but it rarely concerns strategic offense, especially with regard to the enemy's intentions; its rarity is a central characteristic of intelligence information and a major cause of erroneous and distorted estimates. Undoubtedly one of the reasons why Churchill and the British intelligence agencies were more successful than Stalin in predicting the approaching German attack on the Soviet Union was their access to the Ultra material, the information derived from the interception and deciphering of secret German wireless communications. From that material, for example, Whitehall received the decoded message sent out by the Japanese ambassador in Berlin on June 4, 1941, giving an account of an interview he had just had with Adolf Hitler. Hitler had told the ambassador that he had decided that Communist Russia must be eliminated. The ambassador added that though no date was mentioned, the atmosphere of urgency suggested that an attack was close at hand. This information convinced the British Joint Intelligence Committee that Germany intended to turn against Russia. By June 10 Ultra had clarified that the attack would not come until after June 15. Between June 14 and June 22, the day of the attack, Ultra left no room for doubt about the imminence of the offensive (Hinsley, 1979, pp. 478-479).

Even when we do possess high-quality information, we still may not have a clue as to the enemy's future behavior. First, even high-quality information may leave significant room for doubt. Take, for example, the notorious piece of information that reached Israeli intelligence on October 6, 1973 at 2:00 A.M. and contributed to the decision to mobilize part of the reserve forces. It warned that the Egyptians and Syrians were going to attack that same day. Yet even that information was not unambiguous. It suggested that Sadat might postpone or cancel the offensive if he were informed in time that Israel anticipated an attack. Then too, the reported hour of the attack was questionable. Finally, this was not the first time that this kind of warning had come from this particular source. Defense Minister Dayan referred later to this report: "We had received similar messages in the past, and later, when no attack followed, came the explanation that President Sadat had changed his mind at the last moment" (Dayan, 1976, p. 375; see also Stein, 1980, p. 165). Similarly, several weeks before the 1968 Tet offensive the U.S. Army in Vietnam captured an authentic document, an attack order for a major offensive. Still U.S. intelligence concluded that the document was ambiguous as to the time fixed for the offensive. Moreover, it claimed that the document could not be taken as conclusive evidence that an attack order had been given; its writer was far removed from the highest levels of the Communist party organization, and thus his information might have represented not the actual policy of the party command but rather an internal propaganda version (Oberdorfer, 1971, pp. 117–119).

A second reason for the limited applicability of high-quality information stems from the dependency and blinding effect that it creates. Lewin calls this the Ultra Syndrome, "the assumption that because the intercepts on the table, so authentic and so eloquent, [tell] so much they must tell everything" (1978, p. 123). Analysts' preference for hard evidence leads them "to walk away from conclusions which would seem logical if all types and sources of data were considered equally relevant" (Graham, 1979, p. 31). Moreover, it is very difficult to maintain a consistently high level of collection effort. Even in the best intelligence agencies, the level of collection may drop, at least temporarily, from time to time. Whenever analysts are not fully aware early enough of the implications of such declines, their dependecy on reliable information may lead them to make grave mistakes. Levran (1980, p. 18) describes such an effect with regard to the Yom Kippur War:

> The main reason for the intelligence failure before the war stems from the fact that the analysts had had that reliable information to which they always aspire, that supported their assumptions. This information blinded them, just because it supported so convincingly their assessment; this information prevented them from examining properly the developments in the field, and from analyzing the information coming from other sources. The problem was that this high-quality, reliable information was not updated, and did not reflect the change of [Egypt's] intentions and its decision to go to war.

Early Warning Indicators

If direct evidence can be problematic, the problems are even worse with regard to early warning indicators. These are bits of information about the enemy's actions, movements, or future behavior, and statements made by the enemy that may point to a possible attack. Such indicators may refer at the strategic level to the enemy's long-range preparations and plans, while at the tactical level they may refer to an imminent attack. Warning indicators may have various degrees of reliability; usually their diagnostic value is low.

Early warning indicators must appear prior to an attack. Preparing a massive offensive requires many actions, including political preparations, which usually last days and more frequently weeks and months. This series of activities is the main source of warning indicators. To paraphrase a famous aphorism, the attacker might be able to conceal part of this activity all the time, or all of this activity part of the time, but he cannot conceal all of this activity all of the time.

Early warning indicators are generally produced by preparations for war. Hence they indicate the state of the enemy's military readiness and the build-up of its capability for war. At the same time early warning indicators should give some indication of the enemy's intentions—the nature of his military preparations, their direction and pace—and should implicitly point to the objectives and decisions behind them. Information about enemy behavior usually derives from three hierarchical levels within enemy ranks. The *top-level leadership* usually comprises a few political and military leaders who are active from the early stage in the decision to go to war. The *middle level* generally includes several dozen political leaders and military commanders who deal with preparations for the offensive. They may know about the decision to go to war at the second stage, weeks or even months before the attack; but sometimes they are familiar with only a part of the plan until shortly before the offensive. The *lowest level* includes the troops who have to carry out the preparations and the attack itself. This group comprises a large number of soldiers and officers who usually are unaware of the purpose of their preparations until a day or two before the attack.

Obviously the higher the level from which the information stems, the more valuable it is for strategic warning. Direct evidence comes mostly from the top level. "In the case of a highly classified decison, only the very center of the circle is relevant" (Gazit, 1980, p. 50). The problem is that this echelon is very small and very difficult to penetrate. It is easier to penetrate the middle level, and indicators stemming from it may still allow sufficient time in which to issue a strategic warning. Even if we do receive indicators from this level, however, they probably will not constitute conclusive evidence and will leave many doubts as to the enemy's intentions. We will surely get many indicators from the lowest level because of its breadth, and because the enemy will have to reveal part of his preparations in order to carry them out. But the quality and diagnostic value of the indicators coming from this level are low, since those who carry out the preparations are not aware of the larger war plan until the last moment. An Israeli survey of over eight thousand Egyptian prisoners following the Yom Kippur War found only one soldier who knew on October 3 that the preparations were for a real war; 95 percent learned only on the morning of October 6 that they were going to war on that same day; of the eighteen Egyptian colonels and lieutenant-colonels in Israeli captivity, four knew on October 4 that war would break out, one was informed on October 5, and thirteen were told only on the morning of the actual day (Herzog, 1975, p. 39). Such indicators leave a very short warning interval.

The quantity of indicators is a function of several factors. First, the higher the *level* of the enemy's basic military preparations, the smaller the extent of the final preparations left to be completed. Consequently a high level of basic preparation and predeployment in offensive positions will shorten the warning span. Second, the *size* of the enemy offensive determines the quantity of indicators. Preparations for a large-scale war or for an offensive in which the enemy's coalition includes more than one state will produce many more indicators than will a limited initiative (Levran, 1980). And third, there is the question of *time.* As time passes, the enemy's continuing preparations produce additional indicators. Meanwhile the number of leaders joining the inner circle familiar with the secret decision to go to war enlarges, thereby also increasing the volume of indicators.

The emergence of early warning indicators and their interception and analysis by the victim is demonstrated in the accompanying figure—which illustrates the activities taking place simultaneously within the camps of both attacker and victim. Let us assume that the attacker has decided to initiate a large-scale offensive six months in advance (1 in the diagram). During the coming months the attacker is engaged in preparations for war at the various levels of battle procedure (2), from the level of the general staff through the levels of army, corps, and division down to the level of the brigade and battalion. Toward the end of the six-month period this process is complete: the attacker, prepared, may launch his offensive (3) either immediately or after an interval.

The warning indicators (see curve) will not appear immediately after the decision to go to war is made. During the first months

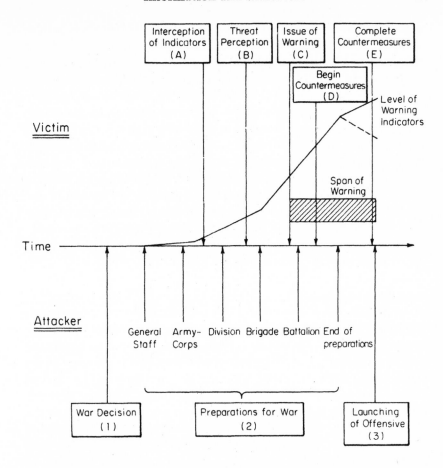

following the decision battle procedure is confined to the level of the general staff, and most of the preparations for the offensive are assimilated into the attacker's routine activity. In addition only a few leaders are familiar with the decision. Consequently only a small number of indicators will surface, and usually these are not recognized as exceptional. The quantity and quality of indicators gradually increase, especially as battle procedure reaches the level of the brigade and the battalion. The indicators may reach their peak a day or two before the attack, at which point the number of indicators will increase sharply, owing to both final preparations—especially those reserved for the last moment—and the fact that the troops are now aware of the imminent offensive. During this final stage the attacker is likely to make a major effort to conceal these preparations, especially the large-scale movements, in order not to arouse the victim's suspicions and to maintain surprise. Such an effort may even lead to a decline in the quantity of visible indicators.

The victim usually starts to intercept the indicators when battle procedure reaches the level of the forces (A). From this point on a process begins that should lead to the perception of the threat (B), to the issue of strategic warning to the decision makers and then to the troops (C), and to the taking of countermeasures (D-E). These stages were described in Chapter 1.

Obviously when the victim has both a relatively long warning span and sufficient time to complete countermeasures before the enemy launches the offensive, surprise attack can be prevented. This is the situation illustrated in the figure. When the victim's reactions are slow, however (stages B to E, in whole or in part, are not completed before the attacker's stage 3), surprise occurs.

Most warning indicators derive from the military arena. This includes activity designed to improve the operational capability of the troops and their redeployment, as well as activity involving logistics, command, and control. At the same time they comprise activity aimed at preparing the political background for the attack, such as high-level meetings and negotiations and actions preparing the civilian sector for war.

Here one must distinguish between major and minor indicators. Major indicators reflect those preparations that are essentially necessary for an overall offensive and are not typical of other kinds of military activity. In the days preceding the Yom Kippur War this category included steps such as accumulating bridging and fording equipment, clearing minefields, moving artillery into forward positions, and manning unoccupied surface-to-air and surface-to-surface missile positions. Minor indicators reflect activity that is not necessarily part of preparation for an offensive and might pertain to other kinds of military activity.

As an aid to analyzing evidence intelligence agencies may develop a list of possible warning indicators. Such a list can guide the analyst in deciding which indicators to look for when a threat of war is perceived.[3] Here the problem is that the existence of such a list may lead the analyst to make a technical count of indicators without understanding which accumulation of indicators is the significant one for that specific imminent attack (Levran, 1980, p. 19). Two additional characteristics of lists of indicators should be mentioned. First, the overall number of possible indicators grows steadily, since preparations for war today are much more complicated and diversified than they were thirty years ago (Agrell, 1979, p. 26). Second, the list changes constantly according to circumstance. For example, as early as 1969 Israeli Defense Minister Dayan rejected the use of a major indicator, the concentration of troops along the cease-fire lines, which had been a reliable indicator before the Six-Day War; but after 1969 the Egyptian Army was deployed regularly along the front line, and concentration of forces did not necessarily indicate imminent attack (Stein, 1980, pp. 156–157).

By and large a single warning indicator is not sufficient to determine that a strategic warning should be issued. Issuing a strategic warning requires an accumulation of indicators, some of which at least should be major. It is imperative to detect several indicators in specific spheres, such as redeployment or the enemy's air force, in order to make sure that some irregular activity is occurring; at the same time it is also necessary to find warning indicators in most spheres of the enemy's activity in order to ensure that the accumulation of indicators is not merely incidental or a local event with limited significance. This accumulation will first be analyzed qualitatively, according to the weight of the major indicators. Then it will be examined quantitatively, since the presence of a considerable number of indicators might be significant even if only a small number are major ones. Finally, the indicators will be analyzed according to their internal consistency and conformity and the extent to which they form a rational picture.

In practice the analysis of warning indicators faces severe problems. For one thing there will always be a gap between the indicators produced by the enemy's activity and the other side's capacity to locate and collect them. Consequently analysts may not recognize major indicators that might put them on alert, while at the same time they may collect scarce, partial, distorted, and ambiguous indicators that are likely to be misleading.

The analysis of warning indicators is also complex because it requires simultaneous estimates of developments in diverse sectors. There is always a serious danger of misunderstanding which accumulation and mixture of indicators is significant and which is not. In this respect the prior list of indicators is not very helpful. For example, before the Pearl Harbor attack the U.S. defense plan indicated that a single submarine attack might signal the presence of a considerable surface force, probably composed of fast ships accompanied by a carrier. Accordingly when on December 7 at 6:40 A.M.

the presence of a submarine was definitely established near Pearl Harbor, the entire Navy command should have been on full alert; in practice nothing was done (U.S. Congress, 1946a, p. 139).

Another basic criterion for judging indicators is the extent to which they are exceptional, that is, reflect a significant digression from existing routine. The accumulation of exceptional indicators that cannot be satisfactorily explained by the enemy's routine activity should call for a strategic warning. If, however, the indicators are found to conform to precedent and routine activity, they will cause no alarm, though they may suggest more cautious examination of the enemy's behavior.

One of the few cases in which indicators were correctly understood occurred prior to the German invasion of Russia. The British intelligence operatives who processed the Ultra decrypts became convinced that a new pattern was emerging. By late March 1941 they believed that a German invasion of Russia was possible, and by May 14, 1941, they decided it had become probable. They "had been especially impressed by two developments, the revelation of 5 May that a POW cage was being moved to Tarnow, which it felt to be inconsistent with a German plan for intimidating Russia, and the urgency with which Fliegerkorps VIII, the unit which had spearheaded the attacks in France, Greece and Crete, was being prepared for despatch to Poland" (Hinsley, 1979, p. 465).

Most indicators, even the major ones, have some routine precedents. Comparing present indicators to past ones considerably reduces their value as a source of warning. Thus during the years preceding the North Korean attack there had been innumerable minor border violations, as well as two limited invasions of South Korea. These border violations had become so regular an occurrence that Secretary of Defense Louis A. Johnson referred to them as "Sunday morning incursions." Their frequency led U.S. intelligence analysts to downgrade new indicators of a large-scale North Korean attack. "Nor was suspicion aroused by a sharp drop in the frequency of border incidents in the weeks before the attack; evidently no one thought this might signal the lull before the storm" (George and Smoke, 1974, p. 166). Similarly before the Yom Kippur War the deployment of the Egyptian Army in battle formations aroused little suspicion since it had been so deployed several times before. Its maneuvers in October 1973 were larger in scale, but they had been increasing for several years. When the Israeli Chief of Staff was charged with not having properly evaluated Egyptian improvements in the ramps descending to the Suez Canal in the three days preceding the attack, he responded that this kind of work had been done dozens of times during 1972 and 1973 (Stein, 1980, pp. 161, 164).

A related problem is that of the gradual appearance of indicators. Usually the enemy's preparation for the attack is a slow process, spread over weeks and months. Consequently the warning indicators also appear gradually, especially when the enemy is making an effort to deceive his victim by getting him accustomed to the preparation process. This gradual evolution makes it harder for the victim to identify meaningful indicators since they do not look exceptional in context. Thus the Germans took Allied intelligence by surprise with the arrangements they made for the timing of their attack on France. In January 1940 German orders for the offensive allowed six days for the approach march and final concentration of troops; but the Germans saw that these moves would offer the Allies effective advance notice that the offensive was imminent. After February 1940 they took the precaution of affecting the preliminary closing-up by gradual stages. "When the offensive was finally ordered on May 9 their troops were already near the frontier, in a position to move off on May 10 without affording the Allies an opportunity to observe or learn about their last-minute preparations" (Hinsley, 1979, p. 135).

Finally, there is the problem of inconsistency of indicators. We have already seen that one of the tests of the analysis of indicators is the extent to which they form a consistent picture. Yet often the indicators are not consistent, either because of an attempt by the enemy to deceive the victim or because of gaps in collection coverage. For example, before the Yom Kippur War the Egyptians were observed clearing mines at seventy points along the Suez Canal, but at the same time they were seen laying them at others; some descents to the canal were opened, but others were closed; unlike on previous occasions civil defense organizations in Egypt were not activated during maneuvers; and the normal daily routine of both soldiers and civilians continued without any change—Egyptian soldiers continued to fish and to wander along the banks of the canal without helmets (Herzog, 1975, p. 45; Stein, 1980, p. 161). Similarly on May 9, 1940, the French Deuxième Bureau was warned that a German attack was expected at dawn the next day. Yet on the same day the Bureau reported no sign of abnormal German movements beyond the frontiers of Holland and Belgium. Two reconnaissance flights of the British Air Force had been carried out there, and the pilots reported seeing nothing unusual (Shirer, 1971, pp. 602–603). Such inconsistencies are likely to appear when the enemy has not made a final decision to attack or is hesitating or changing its mind while nevertheless initiating preparations for war. Thus "for a certain period at least, then, two sets of contradictory, yet equally correct, signals can be emitted simultaneously . . . despite the apparent contradiction" (Handel, 1977, p. 464).

A final point concerns the state of tension. It is clear that the existence of military or political tension between two nations should be regarded as an important warning indicator that an attack may follow. Yet in most cases a state of tension cannot be a sufficient indicator. Most such periods of tension end without resort to military action. Furthermore, surprise attacks usually do not occur at the peak of tension, probably because the attacker is careful not to heighten the victim's suspicions. And in many cases the state of tension builds up gradually, making it difficult to perceive the process as one that will lead to war.

In most of our cases of surprise attack a prior state of tension did exist between the two parties. Yet the growing level of tension was not regarded as high enough to indicate that a critical point had been reached. Even when the state of tension was evolving, the victim interpreted the enemy's intentions as not requiring an advance warning or the taking of countermeasures. Thus Stalin recognized that the state of tension between Germany and Russia had increased, but he assumed that he would have time to take precautionary steps if they became necessary. American decision makers did not regard the state of tension with Japan as dangerous and so did not pay adequate attention to the signals from Japan. Prior to the Chinese intervention in Korea, MacArthur's headquarters described the situation on October 29, 1950, as "not alarming." And in 1973 tension with Egypt was not perceived by the Israelis as appreciably higher than it had been for some time.

Signal and Noise

The inherent difficulties in analyzing warning indicators are related to the larger problem of separating signals from noise. This distinction was introduced into the study of surprise attack by Wohlstetter, who borrowed it from communication theory. "By the 'signal' of an action is meant a sign, a clue, a piece of evidence that points to the action or to an adversary's intention to undertake it, and by 'noise' is meant the background of irrelevant or inconsistent signals, signs pointing in the wrong directions, that tend always to obscure the signs pointing the right way" (Wohlstetter, 1965, p. 691).

Wohlstetter's thesis has been criticized from several viewpoints. It has been argued that the thesis does not take into account evidence from psychological studies indicating that detection of a signal is not simply a function of its strength relative to background noise; rather, the effect of a signal's strength on the person's ability to identify it can be canceled out by the impact of that person's expectations and the rewards and costs associated with recognizing the signal (George and Smoke, 1974, pp. 572–573; George, 1980, p. 73). In addition some critics claim that ambiguity of information is not as important as uncertainty regarding some strategic assumptions, such as those concerning conditions under which an opponent might attack (Whaley, 1973, p. 242; Tanter and Stein, 1976, p. 9). Moreover, Wohlstetter's theory is considered incapable of explaining certain kinds of cases, for example those in which the role of deception by the enemy is dominant (Whaley, 1973). Last, it has been argued that the theory is of little use to decision makers processing ambiguous information in an uncertain environment, since a signal "can be distinguished from noise only after the sound" (Stein, 1977, p. 438).

As a result of this criticism there is now a tendency to expand the term *noise* to include various barriers and filters that separate signals from noise, such as an enemy's efforts to conceal his intentions or to deceive his victim; an enemy's hesitation and indecision; noise created by the international system; individual perceptions and expectations; and bureaucratic blocks to perception and communication (Handel, 1977, pp. 462–464). At this juncture a reference is in order regarding those aspects of noise that are related to information and indicators. In this sense almost every case of surprise attack yields evidence of the difficulty of hearing a signal against the prevailing noise of competing or contradictory signals, in particular when analysts are listening to the wrong signals or when they are inundated with a wealth of information. This evidence is supported by a series of psychological experiments conducted by Tversky and Kahneman (1975). They found that when subjects had to make estimates only on the basis of relevant information, their estimates were different from those made on the basis of both relevant and irrelevant information. In the latter case there was a consistent tendency toward erroneous estimates, although the subjects possessed all the information they needed to reach the right conclusion.

The issue of signals and noise presents at least three major problems pertaining to the quality of information and indicators. First, there is the problem of contradictory information stemming from unreliable or partly reliable sources. Often the analyst faces the impossible task of choosing between two contradictory reports without any solid basis on which to make a choice. For example, on May 4, 1940, the British military attaché in Berne sent in a report from a Polish intelligence officer stating that an offensive was imminent somewhere between Basel and Holland. But this report was only one of a large number of reports, most of which pointed in other directions. "At the time, moreover, it was impossible to distinguish which reports were genuine, which were guesswork and which were inspired by the Germans, for none of them came from sources that were known to be completely reliable" (Hinsley, 1979, pp. 130–131).

Another source of noise is the fact that many warning indicators stem from enemy activity that is not at all connected with preparations for an offensive. Even in times of absolute tranquillity, military units routinely engage in activities that may look like warning indicators. Indicators may in fact reflect regular military exercises and training, routine redeployment of formations, movements of units, and alerts associated with internal unrest or preparation for war against a third party. In most cases, on the surface the indicators look alike. Consequently, since most warning indicators may have interpretations other than preparations for offensive, separating the indicator from the noise is very difficult. As Stein remarks, "When the same indicator is consistent with competing interpretations, it is problematic as a guide to the interpretation of evidence and the estimation of likely action" (1980, p. 157).

Another problem is that in many respects preparations for an overall military maneuver or a full defensive posture resemble, or even duplicate, preparations for a real offensive. Many of the indicators produced by such activities look like real warning indicators, and it is easy to confuse them. This explains why the Germans chose the overall defensive posture as the main cover for their plan of deception prior to "Barbarossa," and this is also the reason why the Soviets chose the overall military exercise as a cover for their invasion of Czechoslovakia in 1968. In 1973 the Israelis were confused both by the Egyptian strategic maneuver and by their own assumption that the Egyptian-Syrian deployment was defensive. Despite their awareness of the similarity, analysts fail time and again to discriminate between such competing indicators.

Quantity of Intelligence Information

One characterstic of modern intelligence work is the extraordinary increase in the quantity of information monitored by collection agencies. By and large this increase reflects improvements in the means of intelligence collection. The greatest successes achieved in technical collection have been brought about by improvements in overhead reconnaissance and signal intelligence. At the same time this increase is partly due to the fact that collection agencies simply have an interest in collecting more information; this bureaucratic interest is prompted by analysts' requests for additional information, which are based on the belief that one missing piece of information might provide the solution to a problem. Pressures for greater collection efforts increase especially following a failure—not a rare phenomenon in the intelligence business. After each significant intelligence failure, a major effort is begun to improve the collection of data (Szanton and Allison, 1976, p. 196; Freedman, 1977, pp. 62–63; Latimer, 1979, pp. 50–51).

The increasing amount of information creates significant problems for analysis. Analysts find it difficult to contend with large quantities of information, and this difficulty affects their estimates. For example, before the attack on Pearl Harbor "no single person or agency ever had at any given moment all the signals existing in this vast information network" (Wohlstetter, 1962, p. 385). And in 1973, in a typical noncrisis week, hundreds of Sigint reports on the Middle East crossed the desk of the area specialist in a production office of the U.S. intelligence community; the intercepts of Egyptian-Syrian war preparations were so voluminous "that few analysts had time to digest more than a small portion of them" (*Pike Papers*, 1976, p. 20).

Part of the problem, in the words of the Church Committee—the Senate Select Committee established in 1975 to investigate the intelligence activities of the U.S. government—is that "analysts naturally attempt to read all the relevant raw data reports on the subjects they are working on, for fear of missing an important piece of information . . . Analysts, perhaps for fear of being accused of an 'intelligence failure,' feel that they *have to* cover every possible topic, with little regard for its relevance to U.S. foreign policy interests" (U.S. Congress, 1976, Book 1, pp. 274–275).[4]

In addition, the more information that is collected, the more difficult it becomes to filter, organize, and integrate it into an estimate. There are limits on analysts' abilities to process information and to aggregate estimates from multiple indicators. Several experiments show that judgments become more inconsistent as the amount of information increases, probably because of information overload. One experiment suggests that accuracy of judgment does not increase significantly with increasing information, but confidence increases steadily and significantly (Heuer, 1978a; Oskamp, 1965).

This is not to say that no effort should be made to obtain additional information. There are circumstances in which additional information does contribute to better analysis and sharpens an analyst's skepticism regarding his own judgment. Heuer distinguishes four types of additional information that an analyst may receive. One involves additional details about variables already included in his analysis. Such information should not affect the overall accuracy of the judgment. A second is information on additional variables. Since judgments are based on a very few variables rather than on the entire spectrum of evidence, such information does not improve predictive accuracy unless there are known gaps in the analyst's understanding; in that case a single report concerning some previously unconsidered factor will have a major impact on his judgment. A third type is information concerning the value to variables already included in the analysis. New facts affect the accuracy of the analyst's judgment when they deal with changes in variables that are critical to his estimates. A fourth type of information indicates which variables are most important and how they relate to one another. Such assumptions make up the analyst's mental model and tell him how to analyze the information. Since the accuracy of judgments depends primarily on the accuracy of the mental model, additional information of this type will have a significant impact on the analyst's judgments.

Hence, Heuer (1978a, 1979) concludes, additional information improves the accuracy of estimates to the extent that it helps bring the analyst's mental model into greater conformity with reality. But to fulfill this requirement information must meet two criteria: it must specify the level or strength of a key variable or identify which variables are most important and how they are related; and it must be authoritative, unambiguous, and relatively complete.

While Heuer is right in his characterization, it is difficult to translate his suggestion into practical terms. Analysts are provided with information that can be readily collected, not information that is most needed. Marginal returns on increased collection efforts tend to diminish because increased efforts become bigger, more expensive, more difficult and dangerous, with no direct relationship between the additional data and improved analytical ability. Moreover, the more information collected, the more noise it contains. Thus an intensified collection effort does not necessarily lead to better analysis and more accurate estimates; when the additional information contains a large proportion of noise, the risks of another intelligence failure leading to surprise may even increase (Freedman, 1977, pp. 62–73; Gazit, 1980, pp. 41–42; Levran, 1980, p. 18).

3

Intentions and Capabilities

In evaluating the enemy's future behavior, and in particular the possibility that he will launch an attack, intelligence agencies attempt "to gauge the technical limits within which he is operating, to determine his usual ways of behavior, under what conditions he will probe, push or withdraw" (Wohlstetter, 1965, p. 692). They evaluate the enemy according to two main categories: first, his capabilities—a "state's ability to achieve a given objective expressed in time and force requirements" (Kent, 1949, p. 62); and second, his intentions—his objectives and how he means to use his capabilities in order to achieve them.

Undoubtedly the enemy's perceived capabilities and intentions are the key to predicting his future behavior. But there is a long-standing debate over whether the enemy should be evaluated mainly in terms of his capabilities or in terms of his intentions.[1] On the one hand it can be argued that concentrating on the enemy's capabilities is more sound, since it produces an evaluation based on facts and measurable data rather than guesses as to what the enemy has in mind. On the other hand, "if we always went by capabilities, how would we ever keep our own arms below our own maximum capability?" (Greene, 1965, p. 133).

Estimates of intentions differ from those of capabilities in terms of both the data and the material involved as well as the difficulties those estimates entail. Estimating capabilities is based in part on hard evidence that is relatively easy to obtain, whereas estimating intentions is based mainly on more ambiguous evidence. Both intentions and capabilities change, but intentions are apt to change more abruptly than capabilities. Consequently intentions are more difficult to follow, and estimating them may result in total failure, while estimating capabilities may lead to only partial failure. Still, the fact remains that estimates of capabilities deal with prolonged processes which themselves undergo gradual change. This in turn leaves room for incremental mistakes that are sometimes more difficult to detect. Moreover, the enemy's actual capability of launching an attack is often unknown, even to himself, until the moment of the attack and the test of war; but his real intention is always known, at least to the enemy's leadership, prior to the attack.

Thus the claim that "the most difficult and most crucial element in the intelligence craft lies in estimating the enemy's *intentions*" (Shlaim, 1976, p. 362) seems unjustified. Without diminishing the extreme complexity of estimating intentions, one must admit that estimating capabilities seems to be almost as complicated and fragile. As a matter of fact, most cases of surprise attack reveal an erroneous estimate of capabilities (see Table 3).

Moreover, any attempt at making a clear-cut distinction between estimates of intentions and estimates of capabilities is irrelevant for all practical purposes. Intentions and capabilities are not separate elements; there is a dialectic connection between them. Intentions are a major factor in building up capabilities, while limitations on capabilities and their potential impose a major constraint on intentions (Harkabi, 1975, pp. 118–119).

Table 3.   Erroneous estimates of enemy intentions and capabilities*

Case	Intentions	Capabilities
Norway, 1940	+	+
France, 1940	−	+
Holland, 1940	+	−
Russia, 1941	+	−
Pearl Harbor, 1941	+	+
Singapore, 1941–42	+	+
North Korea, 1950	+	−
China-Korea, 1950	+	+
Egypt, 1956	+	?
China-India, 1962	+	−
Egypt, 1967	−	+
Israel, 1973	+	+

Note: Plus (+) indicates an erroneous estimate concerning the enemy's capability and/or intention to go to war. Minus (−) indicates no failure in estimate. Question mark (?) indicates insufficient data.

Estimates of intentions and capabilities are thus interdependent. An erroneous estimate of the enemy's intentions may lead to an erroneous estimate of his capabilities, and vice versa, resulting in a failure to predict a forthcoming war. If the analyst assesses the enemy's capabilities as insufficient for launching a successful attack, he will tend not to take seriously the enemy's intentions, even when the latter are explicitly declared. In 1973 Israel assumed that Egypt lacked the military capability to launch successfully a massive attack across the Suez Canal, and therefore did not pay much attention to Sadat's threats of war. In the Israeli view, since the enemy was purportedly unable to cross the canal, why worry about his intentions?

Conversely, once the analyst assesses that the opponent has no intention of going to war, he will tend to pay less attention to his capabilities. Thus in 1950 U.S. intelligence determined that North Korea would exert pressures on South Korea and might even try subversion but that it had no intention of staging an invasion. Consequently, less attention was paid to the question of whether the North Koreans *could* invade South Korea, and insufficient countermeasures were taken to face such a possibility. General MacArthur remarked later that even if he had been supplied with an authentic copy of the North Korean attack order seventy-two hours in advance, it would not have made much difference, for it would have taken three weeks to get a sizeable body of troops to Korea from Japan (DeWeerd, 1962, p. 441).

Thus the question facing the analyst should not be whether to rely on an estimate of either intentions or capabilities alone. Since the two kinds of estimates are interdependent, the analyst should rely on both. At times the analyst faces no problem in estimating the enemy's capabilities: he is convinced that the enemy has the capability of launching a successful offensive. In such a case the main problem lies in evaluating the enemy's interests and intentions. Nevertheless the overall assessment may prove wrong even then, as was true, for example, in the German invasion of Holland and the Soviet invasion of Czechoslovakia. In most cases of surprise attack any uncertainty regarding the enemy's capability further complicates the problem. In order to estimate capabilities the analyst has to take into account the enemy's assumed intentions and willingness to take risks. Otherwise his evaluation would consist of an indiscriminate list of the enemy's capabilities and options with no sense of the probabilities that might be attached to those options (Freedman, 1977, p. 184).

At the same time, the higher the estimate of the enemy's capabilities, the more seriously his intentions must be taken. Otherwise the analyst is bound to repeat the American and Israeli mistakes. In October 1950 the Americans did not relate the growing Chinese military strength in Manchuria to Peking's possible intention of intervening in Korea; and in October 1973 the Israelis did not relate the growing military capability on the Syrian and Egyptian borders to possible Arab aggressive intentions.

In this sense the apparent change of emphasis in U.S. military doctrine during the last thirty years seems justified. Stech (1980b, pp. 38–39) found that in the early 1950s, U.S. military doctrine held that military intelligence should estimate only enemy capabilities, not intentions. *Field Manual 30-5, Combat Intelligence* instructed commanders in 1951 to "be certain that they base their actions, dispositions, and plans upon estimates of enemy capabilities rather than upon estimates of enemy intentions." Twenty-five years later *Field Manual 100-5* states that "enemy intentions must be considered along with capabilities and probable actions," and that commanders must seek to detect indicators of enemy intentions as well as capabilities.

Inference and Difficulties in Estimating Intentions

The opponent's intentions consist of his objectives and expectations as well as the way he plans to use his capabilities in order to achieve those objectives. Hence his intentions include three main elements: (1) his *basic objectives and expectations*, which are what he would like to achieve in the absence of internal and external constraints;[2] (2) *plans and designs* to achieve his goals, which are the courses of action he considers in order to advance his objectives, taking into account the various constraints involved in each of these courses; and (3) his *determination on some action*, which includes his resolution and willingness to take risks. These three elements can be viewed as stages in a process in which the opponent starts with a definition of objectives, moves on to the planning stage, and finally ends up with a decision on a selected course of action.

Any estimate of the opponent's intentions should take account of a number of factors, beginning with his ideology and his long-range as well as immediate political and military objectives. The opponent's perception of his own military and political capabilities is also relevant, since it limits his choice of objectives. As Pruitt (1965, p. 402) suggests, having a certain capability sometimes encourages the development of goals. A nation that has the ability to wage war will be more likely to solve its problems by force than a nation that does not have such a capability. The opponent's image of our intentions and capabilities is an additional factor. For example if the opponent believes that we have underrated his strength and thus have developed aggressive intentions toward him, he may choose to take preemptive action (Handel, 1977, pp. 477–478). We must also look at the enemy's conceptual framework and behavioral style, his expectations, his mode of calculating utility, and his willingness to undertake risks (George and Smoke, 1974, pp. 582–583).

It is relatively easy to perceive the opponent's basic objectives correctly at the first stage; often he describes them explicitly. Hitler defined his strategic objectives in *Mein Kampf*, and German writings on naval strategy explained a decade before the invasion of Norway that the Germans would feel compelled to occupy it (Holst, 1966, p. 36). Prior to the Chinese intervention in Korea, Peking had clearly defined the casus belli as the entry of U.S. forces into North Korea and its own response as military intervention on behalf of North Korea. This had been communicated through neutral diplomatic channels and was indicated in official public statements as well as in the controlled domestic press (Whiting, 1960, p. 110; Appleman, 1961, pp. 758–759). In 1973 the Israelis held few doubts as to the long-range goals of the Arabs.

Failure to understand the enemy's goals in a broad perspective is not, however, a rare phenomenon. Thus in 1950 U.S. officials may have underestimated the desire of the Soviets to strive for hegemony in Northeast Asia, and thereby failed to understand the role they would assign to a North Korean attack as furthering this objective. Similarly U.S. policy makers did not recognize early enough Peking's desire to maintain the existence of a communist state in North Korea (George and Smoke, 1974, pp. 169, 211).

While in most cases analysts have no doubt about the enemy's basic hostile intentions, they often fail to believe that he has decided to act in the near future to achieve his goals. They may be reluctant to believe that the enemy has the capability or resolve to launch a risky offensive. Furthermore, it is easy to interpret public statements and threats as bluffs and attempts at blackmail; one must always take into account that the enemy tries to achieve by threats what he is unable to achieve by force. In any case such statements or writings do not provide any basis for judging the certainty, timing, or location of an attack (Betts, 1980b).

Within this logical framework, an enemy's capability is a clue to his intention. Capability is often developed in the pursuit of goals; thus a nation that wants to invade its neighbors is likely to build a war machine. Yet the extent to which building a capability produces a sense of threat depends in part on the perceived type of capability. Sometimes a nation's reasons for arming are seen as legitimate and nonthreatening. Since there are various reasons for building military capability, most of which could be defensive, capability as evidence of intention is especially ambiguous (Pruitt, 1965, pp. 402, 405). Consequently in some of our cases (Egypt in 1967 or the October 1973 war), although the victim knew that the enemy was fully mobilized for imminent war, this signal did not have the effect of an alert.

It is even more difficult to detect an enemy's intentions at the second stage, when he considers the various courses of action prior to making his decision. The enemy might not foresee his future moves. Events may lead him to rethink his goals and values; he may not act as planned if the new environment, external or internal, differs from what he had expected. Moreover, when a military move is possible, he may act on the basis of multiple options, proceeding with the attack only on certain contingencies (Jervis, 1976, pp. 54–56; Knorr, 1979, p. 75).

Indeed in only a few cases is the opponent determined to go to war come what may, with the main remaining question being one of timing. Hitler's offensives fall into this category. But by and large the opponent decides on a military move only after reaching the conclusion that he cannot defend or achieve his vital interests by other means; his decision therefore concerns not only the question of when to attack but essentially whether to attack at all. While he is considering his options, intelligence analysts are faced with a twofold task, as described by Gazit (1980, pp. 51–52): "They must highlight developments that will call for decisions by the other side, and they must try to anticipate the opponent's responses . . . There is practically no information that would help intelligence to predict events. Even if we did have an intelligence source capable of reaching the decision-makers of the other side and asking for their possible reactions, their answers would have to be considered with great reservations."

Lacking direct information about the enemy's intention at this predecision stage, the analyst must estimate the enemy's alternative courses of action in terms of probabilities and their outcomes. The analyst is then expected to point out the course that seems to him most likely to be adopted by the enemy, being either the most beneficial to the enemy or the most dangerous for the analyst's state. At the same time the analyst should be able to alert decision makers to a developing threat early enough to take countermeasures, even if he cannot determine whether the enemy has made up his mind to attack. Obviously any assessment of this kind is speculative by nature and limited in reliability.

The analyst's most complicated undertaking comes in the third stage, which occurs once the enemy has made a strategic decision to go to war. Here the analyst's main problem is twofold: to find out whether such a decision has been made and if so to discover its details (Gazit, 1980, p. 45).

Identifying the enemy's strategic decision poses inherent difficulties. In Chapter 2, I discussed the problem of achieving direct evidence of the enemy's decisions and the unreliable nature of indicators. The analyst is always faced with the problem of identifying the indicators that are to be considered reliable evidence of the enemy's decision to go to war. There is also the problem of the analyst's unremittingly following the process of decision making within the enemy's leadership, a process that poses enormous difficulties in a retrospective analysis, let alone at the time when events are actually taking place.

The analyst's job is further complicated by a number of stumbling blocks. Strategic decisions constitute the most closely guarded of national secrets. Often they exist in the mind of one man alone, as in the case of Hitler; or else they are shared by only a few top officials. Under democratic governments the number of leaders participating in such decisions is small; under autocratic governments it is even smaller. To identify secret strategic decisions the analyst may have to discover what goes on in the minds of certain enemy leaders and, even more difficult, he must decide what those leaders would do under a variety of different circumstances. Thus in 1956 Gamal Abd el-Nasser rejected all hints concerning British-French-Israeli collaboration. He "just could not bring himself to believe that [British

Prime Minister Anthony] Eden, with all the knowledge he claimed of the Middle East, would jeopardize the security of all Britain's friends and Britain's own standing in the Arab world by making war on an Arab nation alongside Israel" (Heikal, 1973, p. 107). Similarly the Israelis found it hard to believe that President Sadat would personally lead Egypt into war. "In pre-war Israel, Sadat was thought to be the antithesis of Nasser, a leader without pan-Arab ambitions, a man who intends to devote efforts and resources to Egypt itself" (Bar-Lev, 1975, p. 262).

Then too, as Knorr notes, "the foreign actor is not a unitary person; he speaks with separate and often distinct voices". Such discrepancies are usually "the normal result of different people speaking in divergent contexts . . . Foreign statements may be ambiguous or misleading because their authors have not settled on their own plans" (1976, p. 111).

Moreover, a state's intentions relate to given circumstances. They may change between the time when the decision is considered or even made and the time of the intended act. Strategic decisions, including those relating to war, are reversible on short notice and can change very rapidly. They may alter as a result of new domestic constraints, the appearance of new leaders, changes in relative capabilities, the opening of new alternative options for achieving the goal, or the loss of surprise. Even after a final decision is made, the enemy may leave room for reversing it.

In addition, as I have said, any failure in evaluating an enemy's capabilities may result in an erroneous assessment of his intentions, even when these have been explicitly declared: for if the enemy is incapable of going to war, why worry about his intentions? At worst he will launch an attack that amounts to nothing more than banging his head against the wall. This was the feeling in France prior to the German invasion, as described by General André Beaufre: "Since Hitler would not defeat us, why should he want war with us?" (1965, p. 150). And in an interview given in April 1973 the Director of Israeli Military Intelligence, General Eli Zeira, explained that the intentions of Arab leaders frequently exceeded their capabilities; if these statements of intention were to be treated as valid indicators, "the rhetoric could lead to frightening miscalculations" (Stein, 1980, p. 156).

Furthermore, an enemy's intentions and decisions are often dependent on the future acts of the analyst's own government. In the case of Pearl Harbor the effects of the American embargo on Japan were multiple and mounting, but the degree of pressure was not easy to calculate. In order to interpret a danger signal to the United States—a specific military or diplomatic move by Japan—it was absolutely essential to know the latest American move, and to know it within a matter of hours. Yet few intelligence analysts are familiar with changes in their own government's policy and intentions. Thus the chief intelligence officer in Hawaii, who had access to all the information available there, claimed that he had no knowledge of U.S. government policy in the event of a Japanese attack on the British; he was not on that "level of high policy" (Wohlstetter, 1962, p. 57).

Last but not least, from the moment the enemy decides to go to war the other side's analysts are working against the clock. The time between the decision and its implementation is limited; within this interval intelligence has to identify the decision and issue a warning early enough to enable its forces to take the necessary countermeasures. Yet often the victim is not aware that he is working against the clock, since usually he does not know or even suspect that the enemy has already made a decision to go to war. Consequently he may fail to concentrate his collection efforts on identifying the enemy's decision and is bound to lose precious time. Under these circumstances the analyst is not likely to come up with reliable estimates of the enemy's intentions. Nevertheless he is expected to evaluate the possible courses of action that the enemy may consider, pointing out the most probable as well as the most dangerous ones, and try to determine how close the enemy is to making a decision.

The Enemy's Conceptual Framework

A logical evaluation of the enemy's intentions is not enough. The enemy may evaluate his own capabilities and options according to different criteria, and he may reach different conclusions and act in unexpected ways. Thus the analyst's evaluation must be made from the enemy's perspective. As Wasserman suggests, "the only satisfactory basis for intelligence prediction is the universalizable or objective standard of estimating the actions of other states *rationally in terms of their assumptions*" (1960, p. 168). Yet explaining an enemy's behavior as rational on his own terms is difficult because it involves understanding his different conceptual framework. The actions and intentions of the enemy are likely to appear strange, irrational, and unpredictable in terms of one's own conceptual framework; any rational explanation therefore requires considerable knowledge and imagination and sound intuition.

It is much more difficult to understand the enemy's viewpoint and assess his intentions when his system is politically and culturally alien. In fact all cases of surprise attack since 1939 have involved states with different sociopolitical systems and ideologies. The analyst's beliefs about his own political system have a considerable influence on how he understands the enemy's way of thinking and acting. In some cases, such as that of the Soviet Union, the analyst's concepts are tied to a political ideology that explicitly provides a frame of reference for viewing the opponent. This may prove a serious handicap to intelligence. Kennan (1958, p. 22) claims that when it comes to analyzing western motives, the entire Soviet system of intelligence gathering breaks down seriously. This is so because over many years the Communist party has made it impossible for those who collect factual information to interpret it through an objective analysis of western society. The analysts have no choice but to cast their report in terms of Marxist-Leninist ideology, whether this is applicable or not.

Even where ideology is not an obstacle, the analyst's experience with his own system will partly determine what he knows and what he is apt to perceive. Thus, misunderstanding the internal strength of the new communist regime in China, the U.S. government determined that the Chinese would not intervene in Korea; thinking in terms of a democratic administration, it assumed that the internal control of the Chinese government would be weakened by such an act and that China stood to gain no real advantage from war (U.S. Congress, 1951, p. 2101; DeWeerd, 1962, p. 446). As it turned out, both assumptions proved wrong. Participation in the Korean War strengthened the internal control of the Communist party in Peking, and China emerged from the war as one of the great military powers.

Another aspect of this problem involves states that are relatively closed in terms of communications and contacts with other societies. Several cases of surprise attack belong in this category. Here the problem is twofold: intelligence services find it difficult to penetrate such societies and collect relevant information; and there is a greater chance that analysts and decision makers will fail to understand the values, assumptions, and expectations on which leaders of such societies base their decisions.

The main reason for the failure to understand the enemy's frame of reference is the tendency to attribute to the enemy our own way of thinking and mode of calculation. We are prone to believe that the enemy looks at reality the way we do and will never act as we ourselves would not. If we are interested in maintaining the status quo, we tend to assume that the enemy shares our feeling and therefore will not change the status quo by going to war. This bias is also related to the perception of our own image. We tend to assume that other people see us the way we see ourselves and that our intentions are as clear to others as they are to us. Thus the crossing of the Thirty-eighth Parallel in Korea was not considered by U.S. decision makers as an act that would arouse strong anti-American sentiment in Peking. The Americans, who traditionally regarded themselves as the protectors of the Chinese, found it inconceivable that they could be perceived as a serious threat to a nation with which they had so long been friendly. Since they harbored no aggressive intentions toward China, they judged an assurance of good will to be a sufficient guarantee (Spanier, 1965, p. 97; Williams, 1973, p. 226; George, 1980, p. 69).

Looking at reality through the enemy's eyes means not only understanding his ideology but also studying his *operational code*. The notion of an operational code, as developed by George (1969), refers to the degree of control the enemy believes he has over the course of events, his concept of conflict, his view of effective political means, and his approach to calculating action. Perceiving the enemy's frame of reference means also understanding the background of his experience, motivation, expectations, and fears, as well as the dynamic of internal bargaining and bureaucratic pressures within his system. It is against these factors that the enemy will interpret information, develop intentions, and make his decisions. As George suggests, "An incorrect image of the opponent can distort the appraisal of even good factual information on what he may do" (1980, p. 68). Understanding those factors that form the enemy's conceptual framework is a major task.

Many estimates assume that the enemy can be counted on to behave rationally. Analysts usually define rationality in terms of the enemy's value system; that is, the enemy will choose a course of action that he expects will further his values. When there is no good information about the enemy's intentions, or when the enemy is still in the predecision stage, there is no choice but to estimate his intentions according to the rationality criterion. Yet, since rationality is defined in terms of the enemy's values, the assumption that he is rational does not provide any guide to estimating what he will decide to do. Thus judging the other side as rational according to our own values brings us back to the problem of understanding the enemy's value system.

George (1980, pp. 67–68) describes an additional problem in this context:

> Foreign-policy issues are typically complex in that they raise multiple values and interests that cannot easily be reconciled. Even for the rational actor, therefore, choice is often difficult because he faces a value trade-off problem. How the opponent will resolve that dilemma is not easily foreseen, even by those close to him let alone by those in another country who are attempting to predict his action on the basis of the rationality assumption . . . The opponent's attempt at rational decision-making is likely to be affected by uncertainties that render problematical his efforts to calculate expected outcomes of various courses of action . . . How the opponent will deal with these uncertainties is not easily foreseeable, and once again this limits the ability to predict his behavior by applying the general assumption of rationality to his behavior.

The conceptual framework of the enemy, though it is powerful in shaping his behavior, does not by itself determine it. Behavior depends on the information that informs the enemy's actions. The victim's estimate may go wrong not because he failed to understand the opponent's conceptual framework but because he was not aware of the information on which his opponent has acted, forgetting that this information might have been different from his own.

The decision of King Hussein of Jordan to go to war in June 1967 illustrates these difficulties. Hussein's decision was based on Israel's reaction to the Egyptian military moves in Sinai; yet Israel's decision to launch an offensive against Egypt was unknown to Jordan until June 5. During the two weeks before the war Hussein probably thought of his options as bad, worse, and worst: if Israel struck against Egypt and he did not intervene, he would be labeled a traitor and might lose his throne; if Israel struck at Egypt and he did intervene, he might lose his territory (this in fact happened); if Israel did not move, the crisis would bring about a tremendous victory for Nasser—until then Hussein's adversary in the Arab world—who would then be better able to undermine the king's regime from within. Facing these unhappy choices, Hussein decided to join Nasser's camp, sign a defense treaty with Egypt, and accept an Egyptian general as the commander of his front with Israel. Hussein had the impression that Israel was reluctant to use force. This, coupled with the defense treaty and the immediate entry of Iraqi troops into Jordan, probably caused him to assume that he would not have to decide whether to go to war. Eventually Hussein made his decision to open fire on the morning of June 5, within an hour of receiving Nasser's dispatch that Israel was attacking, unaware that by that time the Egyptian Air Force was being destroyed (Kam, 1974, pp. 15–17, 60–61).

From the intelligence viewpoint the problem was to identify the king's decision, made hastily and under stress and affected by uncertainties and lack of crucial information. According to Israel's values a Jordanian decision to go to war was irrational, since Israel assumed that it could defeat both Egypt and Jordan. Had Hussein decided not to open fire, although Egypt was beaten, the king would still have had a fair chance of keeping his throne. Yet the king's values were different, and Israeli analysts had to consider his fear that he would not be able to face probable internal unrest unless he helped Egypt by opening fire. This consideration was given appropriate weight in the Israeli assessment, and no intelligence failure occurred.

The case of King Hussein illustrates the main considerations that an analyst must take into account in estimating an opponent's intentions: the opponent's attitudes and predispositions, which in turn strongly affect his behavior; his evaluation of costs, risks, and gains; the value he places on the outcome of alternate courses of action; his fears and expectations; his estimate of the other side's intentions and capabilities and of the overall balance of power; and the personal characteristics of his leaders. It also demonstrates the importance of the information received by the enemy at the time of making his decision and serves to remind us that the other side may make its decisions under highly stressful conditions.

Finally, misunderstanding the enemy's frame of reference may lead a state to misjudge the threat it poses to the attacker, which may force the latter to go to war. Thus U.S. policy makers did not understand in 1950 that the new communist government in Peking, still in the process of consolidating its position, might have felt that the presence of American troops on its frontier constituted an intolerable threat to Chinese security. In Peking's view U.S. policy in Asia had started to assume an increasingly threatening posture with the outbreak of the Korean War; the Chinese perceived an ominous reversal in U.S. policy toward China. Yet U.S. policy makers believed that China's national interests were not seriously threatened or affected by the U.S. intervention in Korea (Spanier, 1965, p. 94; Rees, 1970, p. 113; George and Smoke, 1974, pp. 214–215).

Risk Taking by the Enemy

The difficulty of seeing things through the enemy's eyes gives rise to further problems in assessing a central factor of his intentions—his willingness to take risks. What are the criteria by which analysts can measure the risks an enemy is likely to take? Since analysts are likely to perceive a reality somewhat different from that of the enemy's government, it is very difficult for them to anticipate these risks. Even when there is a common view of an important aspect of reality, the difference in perspective may lead to different conclusions. Wohlstetter (1962, p. 354) notes about Pearl Harbor: "Japanese and American estimates of the risks to the Japanese were identical for the large-scale war they had planned, as well as for the individual operations. What we miscalculated was the ability and willingness of the Japanese to accept such risks. As Ambassador [Joseph] Grew had said, 'National sanity would dictate against such an event, but Japanese sanity cannot be measured by our own standards of logic.' "

The analyst tends to assume that the enemy will try to reduce risks in making his decision; but this assumption does not solve any analytical problems, since the question of how much risk is too much is a matter of subjective preference. Reduction of risk is not always the preferable strategy (Dror, 1971, p. 17), and the enemy's willingness to take risks relates to specific circumstances: he may decide to take risks in a certain case but refuse to do so in another. Thus even a good understanding of the opponent's conceptual framework does not ensure a correct estimation of his behavior in any given situation.

There are other difficulties in judging the enemy's readiness to take risks. If we estimate his capability as extremely insufficient for launching a successful attack, we are bound to rule out the possibility that he will take that risk. Thus Israeli intelligence assumed that the Arabs would not risk an attack that they knew would be suicidal, and MacArthur estimated that with America's largely unopposed air force, and given American nuclear potential, no Chinese military commander would hazard the commitment of large forces on the Korean peninsula (Willoughby, 1956, pp. 361–362). Underestimating the enemy's capacity for taking risks can also happen at the political level. Speaking about the North Korean invasion of South Korea, Secretary of State Dean Acheson remarked: "It was thought, or perhaps hoped, that the danger of alienating world opinion in the 'cold war' and the risk of invoking our striking power with atomic weapons in a 'hot war' would deter any use of armed forces in aggression" (DeWeerd, 1962, p. 440).

The enemy, for his part, may regard the risks involved in the military option from a different viewpoint. For one thing the enemy may not see the move as a very risky one. The Soviets, for example, probably did not regard the invasion of South Korea by the North Koreans as a high-risk strategy; the absence of a U.S. commitment to defend South Korea might have encouraged Soviet leaders to reduce their estimate of the risks of the invasion (George and Smoke, 1974, p. 168). Or the enemy may count on the time factor, hoping to control risks by manipulating intervening events. This was the mistake made by U.S. analysts prior to the Cuban missile crisis: they assumed that the Soviets would regard missile deployment in Cuba as a high-risk strategy, even though the risks were some steps removed in time. In fact Soviet leaders evidently believed that missile deployment was a calculable and controllable low-risk strategy (George and Smoke, 1974, pp. 489, 584–585).

Then too, when analysts regard the risks as too high for the enemy, they ascribe too little weight to the substantial advantages that might tempt the enemy to undertake the risks.[3] Smoke (1977, p. 277) found evidence that policy makers tend to underestimate the dissimilarity in wartime expectations between opponents. They understand that the opponent's objectives are radically different from their own, but they tend to underestimate how much their opponent's expectations also differ from their own.

Furthermore, the enemy may share the other side's view that his own capabilities are insufficient for going to war but may rely on some advantage, such as surprise, to offset his disadvantages. Thus before the invasion of Norway both the British and the Norwegians had underestimated the degree of risk the Germans were prepared to accept. "It was perhaps not sufficiently recognized that the nominally inferior actor may overcome some of his alleged strategic disadvantages by audacious and swift performance aimed at a maximum exploitation of the factor of surprise" (Holst, 1966, p. 35).

The enemy, moreover, may actually appreciate the high risks

involved in his military move but still may believe that he has no other choice, or that his move is the least costly course of action. It is particularly difficult for a victim to recognize the enemy's feeling that war is inevitable because all other options for averting the threat to his security have been exhausted. Thus in 1941 Japanese leaders believed that they had no choice but to attack the United States since war was inevitable, and they had a better chance to win at that time than in the future. Later Secretary Acheson (1969, p. 36) remarked:

> No one in Washington realized that . . . [Tojo's] regime regarded the conquest of Asia not as the accomplishment of an ambition but as the survival of a regime. It was a life-and-death matter to them. They were absolutely unwilling to continue in what they regarded as Japan's precarious position surrounded by great and hostile powers . . . [On December 1] at the meeting of the Privy Council which decided on war, General Tojo had described the consequences of submission: . . . "Should Japan submit to [U.S.] demands, not only would Japan's prestige be entirely destroyed and the solution of the China Affair rendered impossible, but Japan's existence itself would be endangered."

The enemy may also assume that he could lose the battle but still win the war because military balance is not the critical issue. This was the reason for Israel's failure in 1973 to perceive the Arabs' willingness to accept high risks in order to change the political status quo.

While the analysts may correctly evaluate the enemy's capabilities, the enemy may evaluate them wrongly. There is some evidence suggesting that the Pearl Harbor surprise owed something to an irrational disregard by Japanese planners of the overwhelming American superiority in war potential (Wohlstetter, 1962, pp. 350–357). Estimating an enemy's mistake in judgment is a difficult task. In about half the surprise attacks since 1939 the attacker eventually lost the war, despite the advantage of surprise. It is clear that surprise is not a sufficient condition for winning a war. These cases demonstrate that in the final analysis those who had claimed that an attack by the enemy would be an error proved to be right; yet this correct analysis failed to prevent an incorrect estimate of the enemy's intentions. As Stech notes, "Intelligence failure is likely to be followed by strategic failure because the most surprising plans are those which are assessed as likely to fail and, in fact, such plans do surprise because they will eventually fail" (1979, p. 41).

This last aspect is again related to the problem of "irrational" behavior with regard to risk taking. The opponent may act irrationally even according to his own values—for example as a result of acting under unusual stress—or in a way that seems to be irrational to the other side's analysts. Churchill (1950, p. 603) describes that difficulty:

> A declaration of war by Japan could not be reconciled with reason. I felt sure she would be ruined for a generation by such a plunge, and this proved true. But Governments and peoples do not always take rational decisions. Sometimes they take mad decisions, or one set of people get control who compel all others to obey and aid them in folly. I have not hesitated to record repeatedly my disbelief that Japan would go mad. However sincerely we try to put ourselves in another person's position, we cannot allow for processes of the human mind and imagination to which reason offers no key.

Churchill pinpoints the issue. Irrational behavior is extremely difficult to predict precisely because it follows a course that makes no sense to the rational mind. Surprise attack often works because it violates the rules of rationality. Moreover it is difficult for the analyst to overcome his natural tendency to build a model of events that overrationalizes the other side's actions. This tendency is a particularly vexing problem for the intelligence analyst, since his information is sparse and since he is dealing with a society that is in competition with his own. Competition almost forces him to assume that the enemy is rational. The problem is that this assumption of rationality may confuse the analyst's perception of the real situation (De Rivera, 1968, p. 28).

Estimating Capabilities

Evaluating the enemy's capabilities is also a critical problem. In most of the surprise attacks since 1939 incorrect assessment of capabilities was a central factor in the ultimate failure to predict the coming of war. The problem is indeed complicated, and there is no adequate and tested formula to solve it.

To begin with, we must ask how we can define the enemy's capabilities. According to an accepted definition, capabilities are considered in time of war to be *unopposed* capabilities. For example, to say that Cuba has the capability of landing an invading force of one infantry regiment in the United States means that Cuba has one regiment properly trained and equipped for invasion, and that it has the shipping necessary for transporting and landing the regiment; the underlying assumption is that there would be no opposition whatever (Platt, 1957a, p. 64; Stech, 1979, p. 17).

Such a definition is inadequate. It causes confusion and misunderstanding on the part of the intelligence consumer. Using the same example, the consumer may understand that Cuba actually has the capability of landing a regiment in the United States, while in fact under most circumstances Cuba could not do so (Platt, 1957a, pp. 64–65). At a meeting of the General Staff on September 17, 1973, the Israeli Director of Military Intelligence announced that for the moment, because of Israeli air superiority, the Arabs were unable to go to war. Yet at a Cabinet meeting two weeks later on October 3 his deputy said that from the operational viewpoint the Egyptians were capable of launching an attack. Prior to the Yom Kippur War Israeli decision makers were evidently more impressed by the first statement; a day before the war Defense Minister Dayan said in an interview that the Egyptians would not go to war in the near future because they were not prepared (Bartov, 1978, p. 287; Nakdimon, 1982, pp. 68, 81).

Moreover, this definition states only that the enemy has the physical capabilities for carrying out a specific operation unopposed. Yet what should interest intelligence analysts is not the enemy's absolute capabilities for launching an attack but rather his relative ones as compared with their country's own capabilities for blocking that attack. The problem is not whether the enemy's army can launch an attack but rather whether it can launch one successfully, the success depending on one's own army's capabilities no less than on the enemy's. Few intelligence analysts, however, are in a position to evaluate both the enemy's and their own army's capabilities. This problem might be dealt with by the operations branch, but this group is oriented primarily toward its own army and is therefore not in a good position to follow developments in the enemy camp. The problem of a comprehensive evaluation of the enemy's capabilities thus tends to suffer from a lack of clearly defined authority; even the development of net assessment is still problematic in this regard.

Furthermore, the enemy's military capabilities may differ from one situation to another. The enemy's army may have the capability of defending its territory but not of launching an offensive against another country, and it may therefore behave quite differently and display different degrees of motivation in the two situations. Similarly the enemy may have the capability of launching an offensive but may be incapable of fighting simultaneously on two fronts.

Estimates of capabilities are nonetheless often required to state whether the enemy can or cannot go to war, and to distinguish between various contingencies and intermediate stages. In 1967 the Egyptians probably assumed that Israel would not be able to go to war, since this would mean fighting on two or even three fronts; this assumption proved wrong. And in 1973 the Israeli Chief of Staff believed that the Syrians were capable of occupying a limited expanse of territory in the Golan Heights, though they could not occupy settlements or all of the heights (Bartov, 1978, p. 306). It is extremely difficult for the analyst to define accurately what is within the range of enemy capability and what is beyond it.

Furthermore, intelligence analysts tend to ignore the fact that their own army may be strategically surprised by the enemy. Consequently they evaluate the enemy's overall capabilities under "normal" conditions rather than in conditions following a surprise attack, when its chances would be much improved. While most armies have contingency plans for a possible enemy attack, probably only a few have such plans for a surprise attack. The Israeli Commission of Inquiry found that the Israeli General Staff, with the experience of twenty-five years of wars and military actions, had no such plan in 1973 (*Agranat Report*, 1975, p. 40).[4]

In the light of these difficulties the enemy's capabilities should be analyzed according to a variety of basic contingencies, taking into account such factors as the enemy's military strength; the terrain; the timing of a possible attack and its likely circumstances; and the constraints imposed on the enemy (and his victim) with regard to the attack.

Yet even if some solution to this problem is found (for example a way to integrate into the estimate those assumptions that concern both capabilities and a variety of contingencies), the problem of evaluating the enemy's capabilities still entails complications. As a result capability estimates are often erroneous either because of mistakes in evaluating the enemy's strength or because of wrong assumptions about one's own capabilities—or both.

An analyst may start with the problem of data. Usually the available information about the enemy's military strength and capabilities is inaccurate, incomplete, obsolete, or ambiguous. The intelligence agency may sometimes lack absolutely vital information. For example, before Pearl Harbor U.S. intelligence was seriously lacking in information regarding the progress and state of Japanese military and naval preparedness and equipment, and it was unaware of the degree to which the Japanese were equipped to attack Pearl Harbor. It estimated Japanese aircraft output at two hundred per month, although it actually exceeded four hundred. Japanese pilot training was considered inferior even though Japanese pilots averaged far more flying hours than their American counterparts. No wonder U.S. intelligence underestimated Japanese capabilities and the State Department labored under the impression that the United States could defeat Japan in a few weeks (U.S. Congress, 1946b, p. 29). Moreover, it is virtually impossible to assess the effectiveness of new weapons whose existence is hardly known. Before Pearl Harbor the range, speed, and invulnerability of the Zero fighter were underestimated; the sonar gear of Japanese destroyers was considered inferior to that of American destroyers when actually it was five times more powerful; and the aircraft capacity of Japanese carriers was also underestimated (Wohlstetter, 1962, p. 337; Morgan, 1983, p. 55). The nature of enemy technology is not usually the problem, since information about that technology is often available. The problem is that "wartime capabilities of weapon systems cannot automatically be deduced from their technical characteristics, but depend on the operational concepts, strategy, and tactics that would direct their use" (Betts, 1980a, p. 123; see also Handel, 1980, pp. 94–95). In peacetime estimating particular military uses of technology might be an even more complicated problem since data are rarer and intelligence analysts are less alert in evaluating the enemy's capabilities.

The difficulty of data collection and analysis leads to the essential problem of estimating, or measuring and comparing, military capabilities. Knorr puts the problem well: "There are neither theoretical guidance nor empirical apparatus for measuring and comparing, and essentially predicting, the combat strength of the mobilized forces of different states. The only known measurement test which is accurate is the test of battle . . . The main problem arises from the fact that the presence of qualitative factors makes quantitative comparisons often inconclusive" (1970, pp. 22–23). Most attempts at estimating the balance of power between states are mere quantitative comparisons of various sorts: order-of-battle data, the number of men under arms and the potential of mobilization, the quantities and types of weapon systems and their performance, some aspects of logistic capacity, and military budgets. Capability estimates concentrate on these quantitative aspects both because they are more visible, assessable, and open to continuous survey and because, thanks to modern technology, they can be identified with far greater precision than in previous years. Yet even quantitative comparisons—if information is sufficient—create problems. We may be faced with different quantitative components: how much, for example, will superiority in the air compensate for inferiority on land? (Knorr, 1956, p. 28; Agrell, 1979, pp. 27–32; Colby, 1981, p. 92).

Comparing weapons inventories, then, is not the same as comparing capabilities of achieving a given objective, and it says very little about the actual capabilities of the enemy to cope with one's own armed forces. More specifically a whole series of factors is significant to the outcome of a war, and these factors are almost impossible to estimate or measure in advance. They include the motivation and morale of the forces; the quality of military leadership and the tactical ability of commanders on various levels; the flexibility of the command structure in unexpected situations; the training and discipline of troops; the quality of military intelligence, control systems, and communications; the quality of maintenance and the performance of arms under wartime conditions; the use of doctrine; staff organization and performance; the geographical relationships of countries and the availability of bases and logistic supply conditions; the ability to absorb casualties; and finally economic and technical capacity, administrative skill, and potential foundations of military power.

Sometimes analysts can draw conclusions about some of these factors, since there are several criteria that the intelligence community may use in assessing aspects of the enemy's capabilities. For example, it can partly estimate troop training, the quality of military leadership, or maintenance and logistic capability: but most of these estimates are general and inaccurate, and many factors cannot be measured at all. Most important, we have no practical method of defining the relationships among these factors (Knorr, 1970, p. 23; Marshall, 1966, p. 2). Nor can we sufficiently compare the enemy's capabilities to ours. This means that we have no practical method of integrating these diverse factors—the analysis of each is so incomplete—into an accurate, comprehensive statement that will define the enemy's capability of achieving a given objective in various contingencies. If this is true with regard to the present, it is even more so when we attempt to project the estimate into the future, about which we have almost no information.

This is not to say that analysts do not attempt to provide estimates of the enemy's capabilities; but lacking the ability to measure and compare qualitative factors accurately, they turn to two other methods that tend to distort the outcome. The first I mentioned earlier: they concentrate on quantitatively assessable factors. As a result comparison of elements such as order-of-battle and weapons inventories may achieve a prominence relative to other components of military capabilities that does not entirely jibe with their intrinsic importance. Comparison of weapons inventories partly explains why Egypt was surprised by Israel in 1967. Standing before the military tribunal, Egyptian War Minister Shams Badran explained that nobody had expected Israel to attack since the Egyptian Air Force and Armored Corps were believed to have overwhelming superiority over Israel's. The mistake was that Egyptian intelligence had not taken into account three hundred Mirage combat aircraft which had ostensibly been delivered to Israel (*Al-Ahram*, Cairo, February 25, 1968). As it turned out, the Egyptian mistake was not in ignoring the additional Mirages (which did not in fact exist) but in attributing dominance to Egypt's quantitative superiority.

The second method is an attempt to draw a more general conclusion with regard to the enemy's capabilities on the basis of his past performance. Here we see a distorting effect of the enemy's past military actions on the estimate of his current capabilities. In 1973 Israel partly based its assessment of Arab capabilities on the poor performance of the Arab armies between 1967 and 1970. "The Six Day War and the various postwar clashes between Israeli and Arab units in the air and on the ground led us to the judgment that if war broke out it would not be difficult for Israel to win," wrote Defense Minister Dayan (1976, p. 509). Yet these same Arab armies surprised Israel by manifesting a higher degree of motivation and an improved combat capability in the 1973 war. For another example, before the fall of Singapore the British military attachés in Tokyo had for many years written accurate reports showing that the Japanese Army was a most efficient one. Yet Malaya Command consistently underrated the efficiency and skill of the Japanese, possibly because their inability to subdue the poorly equipped Chinese forces led to the belief that the Japanese armed forces were inefficient.

Underestimating the enemy's capabilities leads to overconfidence and decreased alertness, which in turn increases the difficulties of assessment, as in the case of Singapore. "It was perhaps because of these factors that very little effort had been made by headquarters staffs from 1939 onwards to study either enemy methods or the art of war in jungle" (Kirby, 1957, pp. 457, 166).

At times a third method is employed in estimating the enemy's capabilities—relying on the enemy's own evaluation of his relative military capabilities. Obviously to know or assess reliably the enemy's self-evaluation requires extremely good information, which is not often available. This method was employed by Israel prior to the Yom Kippur War. The Deputy Director of Israeli Military Intelligence reported in an informal Cabinet meeting on October 3, "The possibility of an Egyptian-Syrian war does not seem likely to me, since there has been no change in their assessment of the state of forces in Sinai so that they could go to war" (Agranat, 1975, p. 22; Stein, 1980, pp. 155, 162). The problem with such a method is that analysts who strongly believe that they can rely on the enemy's own evaluations may develop an overconfidence in these evaluations; when a change occurs in the enemy's evaluation without being detected by the other side's analysts, their entire structure of assumptions may go wrong. This was one of Israel's gravest mistakes in 1973.

The inadequacy of capability estimates seems to account, at least in part, for one of the major causes of strategic surprise: the failure of the victim continually to reconfirm axioms pertaining to the enemy's capabilities. Analysts and decision makers tend to accept axioms that purport to explain what the enemy can or cannot do, axioms that may have been true in the past, without rechecking their validity. For example, the French war plan in 1940 neglected the central sector of the Ardennes, where, it was said, "the terrain would defend itself." This assumption had not been seriously questioned in France even though the British military analyst Sir Basil Liddell Hart had stated as early as 1928 that it was "based on a delusion" and that "the impassability of the Ardennes has been much exaggerated." Moreover, the concept of the Maginot Line, which had originated in strategic studies undertaken in the early 1920s, assumed that military technology continued to favor defense over offense, as it had during the First World War. This assumption was not revised when improved tanks and aircraft made it obsolete in the 1930s. As a result German capabilities were grossly underrated

(Goutard, 1959, pp. 84–85; Shirer, 1971, pp. 166, 627; Knorr, 1979, p. 81).

Malaya and Singapore provide an even more striking case. Before the Japanese attack a British senior officer in Singapore explained, "Malaya is the easiest country in the world to defend. There's one main road running roughly from north to south and a railway line. So long as we can hold these, the country stays ours." When asked about the beaches, he replied that they were unimportant. The military maps showed blank space between the beaches and the main road. Two-thirds of the country had been ruled out as impenetrable jungle. In fact, because too many senior officers had never penetrated the jungle, they assumed that no one else could and did not realize that the jungle was riddled with animal and native tracks. The Japanese came through these tracks or floated along the rivers or cycled down the minor roads to Singapore. They managed to outflank strong defensive positions on the trunk road by advancing along the coast or by making seaborne landings behind them. Ironically they had only school atlases for maps, so they did not know that the British considered the jungle such a serious barrier to their progress (Leasor, 1968, pp. 18, 117–118; see also Kirby, 1957, pp. 344–345).

The persistence of axioms contributes to the belief in military superiority. Sometimes analysts and decision makers believe that the military superiority of their state over that of the enemy is so overwhelming that it overshadows all other considerations. Such a feeling of invulnerability often leads to underestimating the enemy's capabilities and ignoring changes in his military strength. This is the case especially when analysts and decision makers believe that their state's superiority is long lasting, and when they assume that the enemy is aware of it. Dayan expressed such a belief two months prior to the Yom Kippur War: "The overall balance of power is in our favor, and this fact is overwhelmingly decisive in the face of all other considerations and prevents the immediate renewal of war . . . Our military advantage is the outcome of both the weakness of the Arabs and our increasing strength. Their weakness arises from factors that I do not suppose will quickly disappear . . . Our superiority can, in my opinion, be maintained in the coming years as well" (*Ma'ariv*, Tel-Aviv, August 10, 1973).

Among the various reasons contributing to a feeling of military superiority three should be especially emphasized. The first is the feeling of invulnerability behind secure borders and an impenetrable barrier. The Israeli self-image of invulnerability was closely linked to the notion of secure borders, which were believed to have been attained in 1967. The front lines were thought to be well-fortified barriers that would not easily be pierced (Dayan, 1976, p. 509). Similarly the French felt secure behind the Maginot Line. "The confidence that these fortifications would stop the Germans the next time with little loss of life to the defenders responded to a feeling deep in the consciousness of the French people, still exhausted from the bloodletting of the Great War" (Shirer, 1971, pp. 166–167).

Second, the belief in military superiority has an especially distorting effect when it relies on the concept that the other side has deep-rooted, permanent deficiencies. Dayan expressed a widespread feeling in Israel that one of the sources of Israeli strength was the low standard of the Arab soldier in terms of education and approach to technology.

Third, the belief in superiority is often associated with confidence in second-strike capability that will ensure eventual victory even if the enemy attacks first. The Israel Defense Forces' belief in their second-strike capability relied on assumptions such as these. The IDF held that the aerial superiority of the Israeli Air Force over the Arabs' air forces guaranteed the failure of any Arab offensive; that no meaningful loss of ground would occur that could not quickly be regained; that once the enemy's advance was blocked, Israeli offensive moves would be immediately decisive; and that the IDF would penetrate deep into Syria if it tried to seize the Golan (Brecher, 1980, pp. 54–55, 67; Bartov, 1978, p. 287). On October 15 and November 9, 1950, MacArthur claimed that the Chinese could get no more than fifty to sixty thousand men across the Yalu River; should they intervene in full force, his air force would destroy them and "there would be the greatest slaughter." This reliance on air power was perhaps the crucial factor in MacArthur's miscalculations: at that very moment 120,000 Chinese soldiers either had already crossed, were in the act of crossing, or were moving from their assembly and training areas to the crossing sites (U.S. Congress, 1951, p. 1835; Truman, 1956, p. 366; Appleman, 1961, pp. 760, 765, 767).

The belief in military superiority is closely linked to the belief in deterrence. When decision makers believe that their armed forces have an overwhelming superiority, or when they underrate the enemy's capabilities, they tend to be overconfident about their deterrent posture. If deterrence is believed to be strong, the danger of surprise attack is higher. As their confidence in deterrence rises,

decision makers tend to ignore early warning indicators of impending attack and assume that the enemy does not wish to commit
suicide and hence will not start a war. Consequently their reaction
is delayed and their warning span becomes shorter. Moreover, as
George and Smoke note, the impression that deterrence is successful
may be illusory, since "as long as deterrence is not openly challenged, the defender is inclined to assume that deterrence is working" (1974, p. 567).

Thus within the Israeli leadership in 1973 nobody questioned the
assumption that the IDF's overwhelming superiority over the Arab
armies guaranteed, at least in the short term, that the Arabs would
be deterred from indulging in military adventures (Bartov, 1978, p.
279). French generals recalled similar feelings in May 1940. General
Maurice Gamelin, Chief of the French General Staff, confessed: "I
believed in victory. I felt sure we could stop the Germans." General
Beaufre wrote: "We had the finest Army in the world based upon
the most modern defensive system in existence; its leaders were
interviewed and, confident in their doctrine, assured their question-
ers that any German attack would be smashed at the frontier" (Shirer,
1971, p. 602; Beaufre, 1965, p. 150). Similarly in 1941 the American
fleet at Pearl Harbor was regarded as a deterrent against Japanese
aggression. Moreover, the development in 1940 of the B-17 Flying
Fortress, designed to threaten the crowded Japanese islands, further
strengthened the belief that Japan would be deterred from challenging the United States directly. U.S. policy makers ignored the possibility that a deterrent could also be a tempting target (Ben-Zvi,
1976, p. 385; Williams, 1973, p. 224).

The question of what the enemy can do in order to achieve his
objectives depends not only on military capabilities but on political
ones as well, such as constraints imposed by international conditions, domestic politics, or a third party. These too are a source of
grave miscalculation, since international conditions or the interests
and actions of a third party may be too complex to predict. Three
examples will illustrate this point. In 1940 the strategic assessment
of the Norwegian leadership was based on the unqualified assumption that the British Fleet controlled the North Atlantic and the
North Sea and would be able to prevent any attack from Germany.
This view of the strategic situation influenced the Norwegians' judgment of warning signals about German preparations (Koht, 1941, p.
57; Holst, 1966, p. 34). In 1967 Nasser assumed that Israel was so
isolated politically that it could not act militarily against Egypt. He

probably assumed that Israel, lacking American support for a military action, would be deterred from acting by fear of a Soviet reaction. What Nasser did not perceive was that the prolonged crisis and the inability of the United States to solve it created an implicit American interest in an Israeli action, which was enough to neutralize possible Soviet threats and give Israel sufficient time to act without political pressures. Finally, in 1973 Israel did not give much weight to the possibility that the Arab countries could agree on a coordinated military move in the absence of real political unity (Harkabi, 1975, p. 116).

PART TWO

Judgmental Biases and Intelligence Analysis

4

Conceptions and Incoming Information

The pattern of surprise attack by and large repeats itself. The victim's analysts[1] believe that the enemy cannot or does not intend to launch an attack. Incoming information about the enemy's behavior can be interpreted in several different ways, and it is precisely this ambiguity that analysts seize on to prove their hypotheses and reinforce their belief that attack is not imminent. That is to say, they read and interpret the information in a manner that suits their hypotheses and beliefs, ignoring other possibilities. Only after the surprise occurs do they find out that the information did in fact indicate the coming attack. The relation between this incoming information, on the one hand, and the analyst's set of conceptions about the enemy's behavior, on the other, reveals some of the basic problems in intelligence and analysis.

My examination of this intellectual process at the level of the individual analyst basically assumes that the process is consistently biased, and that this bias is the cornerstone of intelligence failures. I place relatively heavy emphasis on these shortcomings and biases— perhaps more than a balanced survey of any individual's judgments would justify. After all, man's judgmental strategies can deal quite effectively with a wide range of problems. Moreover, even if man's cognitive processes are consistently distorted, not all of the judgmental biases appear in each of these processes; in addition, some of these biases may offset others, and some biases are less significant than others. Yet, since we are dealing with an analytical process fraught with mistakes and difficulties of such great magnitude, it seems worthwhile to focus attention on those biases that are relevant to explaining the errors of the intelligence process.

The term *judgmental biases*, in our context, refers to the tendency to make mental errors, often systematic rather than random, in a certain direction. Such errors lead analysts to create and maintain incorrect assumptions and misinterpret events. A variety of biases exists in the processing and interpreting of information.

The Set of Conceptions

The job of lifting out the significant signals from the confusion of noise and correctly interpreting the ambiguous early warning indicators requires a background of wide knowledge and a variety of hypotheses to guide observation. Without a very large and complex set of beliefs and attitudes, theories and assumptions, images and expectations, the stream of information would not speak to the analyst at all. This unavoidable set of conceptions simplifies and gives structure to the external world of the observer and enables him to identify relevant variables and to organize and interrelate them into meaningful systems.

Interpretation is partly based on preexisting systems of knowledge, which include beliefs, theories, propositions, and schemas. These knowledge structures categorize objects and events quickly and for the most part accurately, and define a set of expectations about objects and events. Some of this knowledge may be represented as beliefs and theories, which are in a sense propositions about the characteristics of objects; yet people's generic knowledge also seems to be organized by a variety of less "propositional," more schematic cognitive structures (Nisbett and Ross, 1980, pp. 7, 28).

The belief system includes "all the accumulated, organized knowledge that the organism has about itself and the world" (Holsti, 1962, p. 245). It represents "all the beliefs, sets, expectancies, or hypotheses, conscious and unconscious, that a person at a given time accepts as true of the world he lives in" (Rokeach, 1960, p. 33). The belief system includes *theories* and *images*. Theories are general rules of thumb that explain or relate different facts or phenomena. Images are sets of beliefs about the nature and characteristics of an object; they may be defined as "the organized representation of an object in an individual's cognitive system" (Shlaim, 1976, p. 357). Images usually contain a small set of sharply defined elements on which the attention focuses, along with many more peripheral elements only dimly and sketchily perceived.[2]

Belief systems, and especially images, screen the selective reception of new messages and often control the perception and interpretation of these messages. They determine which information we deal with, how we organize it, how we store and retrieve it, and what meaning we attribute to it. There is considerable variation among individuals in the richness and complexity as well as the validity of their beliefs (George, 1980, p. 75; Heuer, 1979, p. 5).

In addition, because of limits in mental capacity the human mind cannot cope directly with the confusing reality of the physical and social environment. In order to deal with the complexity of the world, the individual has to form simplified, structured beliefs about the nature of the world. One theory holds that in order to simplify reality, individuals filter their perceptions through clusters of beliefs, or "cognitive maps" of different parts of the environment. The beliefs that make up these maps provide the individual with a relatively coherent way of organizing and making sense out of what would otherwise be a confusing array of signals picked up by the senses (Holsti, 1977, p. 12).[3]

The very usefulness of belief systems increases the dangers generated by incorrect systems. The accuracy of the individual's judgment depends on the accuracy of both his belief system and the values attributed to the key variables in that system. Yet some beliefs, theories, and images are relatively poor and inaccurate representations of reality. Images, for example, become distorted by emotions, biased information, and cultural tradition. Moreover, objects and events are not always labeled accurately and sometimes are processed through an entirely inappropriate knowledge structure. By controlling the selection of facts and the way in which they are processed the belief system tends to reinforce itself by encouraging reinterpretation of information that does not fit the image and by explaining away all contradictory evidence that cannot be ignored in terms that stem from the same premise. Since individuals do not respond to "objective" facts but do respond to their images of reality, unless the content of the image coincides in some way with reality, their assessments and decisions based on these images are likely to be incorrect (Nisbett and Ross, 1980, p. 7; Finlay, Holsti, and Fagen, 1967, p. 30).

The system of theories and beliefs is a more or less integrated set of ideas and images about the environment. It may include tacit global theories as well as more specific ones. It may comprise ideological preconceptions and beliefs about the nature of man and the causes of human behavior, the structure of society or economic processes, military and political strengths, and technological development. Or it may include theories about the nature of and cause-and-effect relations in international politics.

In our specific case the analyst's set of beliefs and images hinges on one focal point: the behavior of the opponent. This set of conceptions includes beliefs and images about some of the topics discussed in Chapter 3. It may include beliefs about the opponent's long-range interests and foreign-policy objectives, his immediate aims and intentions in the present crisis, the strategy he is following, his diplomatic style, his military and political capabilities, his determination to use force and his willingness to take risks, his image of the other side's intentions and capabilities, and his trustworthiness or deceptiveness.

In this context Snyder and Diesing (1977, p. 291) distinguish between two levels or components of the image:

> a background or long-term component, which is how the parties view each other in general, apart from the immediate crisis, and an immediate component, which comprises how they perceive each other in the crisis itself. The opponent's ultimate aims, over-all military potential, and alignments are included in the background component, and his objectives in this crisis as well as the intensity of his interests, loyalty of his allies, and his available military power at the crisis locale are included in the immediate component. Before the crisis starts, only the background component exists, but when the initial moves of the crisis occur the immediate component, the definition of the crisis situation, is worked out. On the basis of this definition of the situation some expectations about how the opponent will react are deduced.

The set of conceptions in the case of intelligence analysts is based mainly on a professional knowledge of political and military structures, processes, and leading personalities in the enemy camp. It is sometimes quite different from, though affected by, what is called "the national image" that one society has of another. Intelligence analysts are products of their society and are likely to be affected by its values and images; but as they acquire professional experience through intensive and prolonged study of an enemy's behavior in

many situations, these specialists learn to apply tests of validity to
these images and values. As a result they can be expected to rise
above stereotyped views.

The Persistence of Conceptions

The root of the problem is the persistence of that inevitable and
indispensable set of conceptions that guides the analyst in selecting
and interpreting information. Psychologists have found that people's
theories, beliefs, and images exhibit an extraordinary persistence,
despite a wide range of evidence that should invalidate or even reverse them. Once formed or adapted, initial beliefs will structure
and distort the processes through which subsequent evidence is interpreted. New evidence will appear reliable if it is consistent with
one's initial beliefs; contrary evidence is dismissed as unreliable,
erroneous, or unrepresentative. In general people are more apt to err
on the side of resisting a change in their beliefs than to make the
opposite error of too quickly altering them; and people are too quick
to reject discrepant information.[4]

Perseverance of beliefs is inherent in all spheres of life. There are
many examples in science. Copernicanism made few converts for
almost a century after Copernicus' death. Newton's work was not
generally accepted for more than half a century after the *Principia*
appeared. "The source of resistance is the assurance that the older
paradigm will ultimately solve all its problems, that nature can be
shoved into the box the paradigm provides," writes Kuhn (1970, pp.
151–152). In science perseverance of beliefs has a useful role. As
Kuhn has shown, the paradigm—the accepted body of concepts and
theories that sets the framework for research—helps determine what
phenomena are important and require further research and which
should be ignored.

Perseverance also guarantees that scientists will not be too open-
minded and distracted and that "anomalies that lead to paradigm
change will penetrate existing knowledge to the core" (Kuhn, 1970,
pp. 52, 65). Yet at the same time the paradigm leads scientists to reject
evidence that is not compatible with their theories. The outcome
is that major discoveries may be missed while the paradigm survives
even in the face of discrepant information that should discredit it.

Nisbett and Ross (1980, p. 169) suggest three hypotheses about
perseverance of beliefs:

1. When people already have a theory, before encountering any genuinely probative evidence, exposure to such evidence . . . will tend to result in more belief in the correctness of the original theory than normative dictates allow.
2. When people approach a set of evidence without a theory and then form a theory based on initial evidence, the theory will be resistant to subsequent evidence . . .
3. When people formulate a theory based on some putatively probative evidence and later discover that the evidence is false, the theory often survives such total discrediting.

Certain kinds of beliefs and images are more difficult to change than others. One feature of an image is the number of beliefs, hypotheses, past experiences, and other images supporting it. The more supporting cognitive elements there are, the harder it is to change an image; and the more frequently an image has been supported in the past, the greater its strength. A second feature is that the more consistent the elements supporting an image, the less flexible the image. For our purpose it is important to note, as Pruitt suggests, that "images that are based on the evaluative dimension are likely to be relatively inflexible, since the elements supporting them are likely to be fairly consistent" (1965, p. 411). Moreover, the smaller the number of alternative images held at a given moment—that is, the closer to monopoly an image is—the greater its strength. At the same time images tend to be self-reinforcing: once established they generate more and more supporting cognitive elements and may be strengthened by virtue of their agreement with the images of other individuals (Withey, 1962, p. 107). Finally, as Rokeach (1960, pp. 196–197) describes, closed-minded persons betray more difficulty than open-minded persons in integrating new beliefs into a new system. One of the reasons for this difficulty is that closed-minded persons recall new beliefs poorly; and the less they remember, the less they integrate (see also Rokeach, 1960, pp. 286–288).

Various explanations have been put forth to account for perseverance. People apparently persevere in their beliefs because it is quite natural for them to maintain them, and because many beliefs embody strongly held values (Nisbett and Ross, 1980, p. 180). In addition, reviewing a belief in the light of new evidence confronts the individual with the thought that he may have been wrong and threatens a return to an earlier state of uncertainty. Perseverance of conceptions can also be explained by people's beliefs about the consistency of the environment and by their efforts to make sense out of the world by viewing various bits of information as part of a larger pattern. Thus the need to impose structure on the environment causes people to make premature commitments as to the nature of those things they are observing (Dixon, 1976, pp. 30–31; Jones and Nisbett, 1971, p. 90).

A great deal of research has focused attention on the primary effect in impression formation, in which the earliest presented information has an undue influence on final judgment. "Early-encountered information serves as the raw material for inferences about what the object is like. These inferences, or theories about the nature of the object, in turn bias the interpretation of later-encountered information" (Nisbett and Ross, 1980, p. 172).[5] Thus people may form an image on the basis of relatively little information; but once they have this image, they find it very difficult to change it, because it governs their perception of additional information. After an image has been formed, new information will not have the same impact it would have had at an earlier stage. The result is that images do not reflect the totality of the available information. The problem is especially relevant for intelligence analysts: since they are under pressure to reach quick, even instantaneous conclusions, their images are formed on the basis of little information.

When conceptions are formed under stress, as during a crisis, people do not compare a large number of theories to see which best explains most of the evidence. Rather they adopt the first one that provides a satisfactory explanation. Yet despite the fact that such theories are not formed under optimal conditions of information processing, they tend to persevere: changing the original theory implies admitting a mistake made at a crucial moment (Vertzberger, 1978b, p. 198; Jervis, 1976, p. 191). This is especially so when those who believe in the theory feel that it is supported by events.

The search for causal explanations also accounts for the reluctance to abandon initial impressions. Individuals "do more than merely aggregate information consistent with their self-perceptions and social perceptions. They also search for antecedents that cause and account for events . . . Once an action, outcome, or personal disposition is viewed as the consequence of known or even postulated antecedents, those antecedents will continue to *imply* the relevant consequence even when all other evidence is removed" (Ross, 1977, p. 371).[6]

Another reason for the consistency of beliefs has to do with the nature of the learning process. As Heuer (1979, pp. 7–8) describes it, this is especially relevant to intelligence analysis:

> Learning to make better judgments through experience assumes systematic feedback concerning the accuracy of previous judgments, and an ability to link the accuracy of a judgment with the particular configuration of variables that prompted an analyst to make that judgment. In practice, however, intelligence analysts get little systematic feedback, and even when they know that an event they predicted has actually occurred or failed to occur, they typically do not know for certain whether this happened for the reasons they had foreseen. Thus, an analyst's personal experience may be a poor guide to revision of his mental model.

An additional explanation has to do with the reality-simplifying process that comes into play during intense international crises. Researchers have found that people tend to protect cognitive consistency more when they are in threatening situations. "The stress accompanying such situations imposes a need for a simpler kind of consistency. Tolerance of ambiguities and complications drops markedly. Under high stress individuals simplify their perceptions of reality; they fail to observe features that in more relaxed states they would readily notice and recognize as important" (Smoke, 1977, p. 284).

Examples of the refusal to change established beliefs about the enemy's expected behavior are found in each of our cases of surprise attack. The Agranat Commission of Inquiry, for instance, stated explicitly that such persistence was the root of the Israeli failure in October 1973. The Israeli error began with a basic concept that the Arabs would not attack during the next two to three years, and every new development was adapted to this concept. In some cases even a clear indication of imminent attack was not enough to change the established view. Before Pearl Harbor the popular hypotheses in the United States held that Japanese aggression would be directed against Russia, Southeast Asia, or both, and that Japan would not risk a conflict with the United States. The second hypothesis collapsed, of course, with the attack on Pearl Harbor, yet this drastic change was perceived too slowly in the Philippines. General MacArthur had a minimum of nine hours' warning between his knowledge of the Pearl Harbor attack and the initial Japanese assault on his forces.

The news of the attack clearly did not tell him to take adequate countermeasures in the Philippines; his planes were found by the Japanese attackers still in formation, wingtip to wingtip, at the bases (Wohlstetter, 1965, p. 694).[7]

There are three specific circumstances in which analysts and decision makers tend especially to stick to the idea that war is not imminent. In the first instance the analyst, and particularly the policy maker, is committed to the established view or to a policy connected with it. Psychologists have found that to the extent that a person is emotionally committed to a belief, he will probably cling to it by whatever cognitive tricks are necessary. A strong commitment to a hypothesis may make people unwilling to change their stated level of confidence even though their opinions may change. Thus people require more information to change their minds about a previous decision than they did to arrive at that decision in the first place. Public statements and organizational pressures against dissenting from the established view may strengthen such a commitment and therefore reduce the flexibility of images (Nisbett and Ross, 1980, p. 180; Slovic and Lichtenstein, 1971, p. 705).

A second instance occurs when the enemy provides analysts and policy makers with what appears to be clear support for their views. Thus Sadat's failure to go to war as he had asserted he would by the end of 1971 convinced Israel's leadership that threats by the Egyptian president need not be taken seriously. His expulsion of Soviet advisers was also read as a crucial indicator of Egypt's military weakness and as proof of Sadat's determination not to become involved in a war with Israel, at least for several years (Brecher, 1980, pp. 53–54).

Third, we can expect strong resistance to changing an established view when that view is not confined to the small group of intelligence analysts but is shared by the majority of policy makers and the public. This occurs quite often. In estimating the enemy's behavior the intelligence community is not alone; it has plenty of feedback from outside. Once a national consensus about the opponent's behavior becomes settled, it is very hard to dislodge it. It affects the analysts' conceptual framework, information processing, and treatment of evidence. In some cases such a consensus may contribute to cognitive closure and reduce the perception of an external threat.

For example, during 1972–73 the prevailing view throughout Israel was that the Arabs were unable or unwilling to go to war. "The government and the opposition alike—followed by a growing majority within Israeli society—reached the wrong conclusion based on the situation in the occupied territories. Gradually, people came to believe that a satisfactory situation in the occupied territories would endorse peace, that our improved image among the Arab population there would bring peace. And intelligence analysts would inevitably find it very difficult to divorce themselves from such common perceptions" (Ben-Porat, 1973, p. 71).

Assimilating Information

The persistence of conceptions causes one of the most difficult problems in intelligence work. Since views are not likely to change easily, people tend to fit incoming information into preexisting images and to perceive what they expect to see. This assimilation in turn perpetuates inaccurate beliefs and images.[8]

In the early stages, when the individual is trying to make sense out of the evidence, he will be relatively open to a variety of views and hypotheses. But once he believes he understands the situation, he is not likely to change his view easily, and his initial organization of the stimuli strongly structures later perceptions. Heuer describes this process: "Despite ambiguous stimuli we form some sort of tentative hypothesis about what it is we are seeing. The longer we are exposed to the ambiguous data, the greater confidence we develop in this initial and perhaps erroneous impression, so the greater the impact this initial impression has on our subsequent perceptions. For a time as the picture becomes clearer, there is no *obvious* contradiction; the new data are assimilated to our previous image, and the initial interpretation is maintained" (1982, pp. 39–40).

An established way of perceiving evidence is hard to break, not so much because the new perception is difficult to grasp but because the established one is hard to lose. The stronger a view, the smaller the amount of appropriate information necessary to confirm it and the larger the amount of contradictory information necessary to disprove it. Consequently an early view tends to persist because the quality and quantity of information necessary to disprove it is significantly greater than that required to form an initial hypothesis. Furthermore, Ross (1977, p. 371) suggests that once misleading information is assimilated, it becomes independent of the assimilation process and becomes part of the overall perception. The erroneous perception may survive the discrediting of its original evidential basis because the impression is supported by additional evidence that is independent of the discredited basis.

Moreover, as Jervis (1976, pp. 162–163) explains, beliefs influence the way incoming information is categorized and filed in the individual's memory. The label placed on an event or idea influences the way it is seen, and the individual is encouraged to see further resemblances between these and other events or ideas in the same category. By the same token, the availability of a piece of information depends on whether it has been filed under the categories for which it is later seen as relevant. Since the individual files information in terms of the concepts and categories he holds at the time the information is received, new hypotheses are hard to develop.

Consequently analysts preserve their images and conceptions despite what seems in retrospect to have been clear evidence to the contrary. Information that is consistent with their images is perceived and processed easily, but they ignore information that does not fit, or they twist it so that it confirms, or at least does not contradict, their beliefs, or they deny its validity. The treatment afforded any given piece of information is directly connected to its quality. Definite evidence is very difficult to obtain; less reliable information is likely to be interpreted in a way that reinforces existing beliefs. Much incoming information is immediately filtered out as irrelevant, is rejected, or is referred for further study and disappears. Analysts use different standards for criticizing opposing evidence than for criticizing supporting evidence: they are more sensitive to information that confirms their images than to information that contradicts it. In many cases discrepant information is simply not noticed. When analysts do not perceive information as conforming to their beliefs, they often nonetheless interpret it as compatible with their beliefs, and they ignore the possibility that evidence seemingly consistent with their views may be irrelevant or tainted. Consequently data considered subsequent to the formation of an impression will appear to offer considerable support for that impression (Jervis, 1976, p. 143; Ross, 1977, p. 370).

Thus before the Chinese intervention in Korea, Far East Intelligence interpreted all information in the light of its belief that this was a bad time for the Chinese to intervene; when aerial reconnaissance failed to find masses of Chinese troops, it took this as evidence supporting the hypothesis and did not consider the possibility that masses of troops were well hidden in small groups (De Rivera, 1968, p. 55). Similarly, despite the possession of the Enigma machine that gave them access to secret German communications, not all British intelligence agencies agreed that Germany was going to attack Russia until close to the event. Whitehall intelligence organizations judged the Sigint evidence on the assumption that Germany was negotiating with the Soviets, and in light of the fact that this assumption was still receiving support from diplomatic sources, they put a different interpretation on the Enigma clues. For them additional proof of the scale and urgency of Germany's military preparations was also proof of Germany's determination to get its way in the negotiations (Hinsley, 1979, p. 475).

Several features of incoming information influence its assimilation into existing conceptions. For one thing the more ambiguous the information, the greater the tendency to assimilate it. "Since ambiguity is defined in terms of the ease with which the evidence can be interpreted in a number of ways, the greater the ambiguity the less likely that the evidence will embarrass the established image" (Jervis, 1976, p. 195). The less ambiguous the information, the more difficult it is to ignore, since it is less susceptible to distortion. Then too the weight of a piece of information may be related to its scale of value. It was found that neutral information receives less weight than more polarized information; yet (and more relevant to our case) information with too great a surprise value has less import (Slovic and Lichtenstein, 1971, pp. 690–691). Thus when a piece of information pointing to imminent attack is received, it may draw attention to the threat and lead analysts to seek further information; when this piece of information seems too far-fetched, however, its influence on the assessment is smaller, since it may be perceived as exceptional and not reflective of the real situation. Furthermore, a single piece of information may have a smaller distorting effect than many such pieces; a series of information items increases the probability of misperception or distortion of each individual piece, since its correct interpretation depends on the overall perception of the series. In addition, when information about an impending attack is repeated, especially when a threat begins to be perceived, it becomes more difficult to ignore it or to assimilate it to existing views.

The timing of the receipt of information is also important. Because of the primacy effect, information received at an early stage of the analytical process will have a greater impact on the estimate than information received later.

Last but not least, the way in which information is received by intelligence analysts makes it difficult for them to change their conceptions and facilitates its assimilation to their views. Information is received gradually, bit by bit, and usually the analysts do not go back to reconsider all the evidence together or restudy the whole series of signals. As a result, when analysts are examining information in small doses, superficially comparing it with earlier information and hastily confronting it with their existing hypotheses, they lose the cumulative alerting effect inherent in the whole body of information. Thus a retrospective study of the list of warnings available to analysts in the cases of Pearl Harbor, "Barbarossa," and the 1973 war indicates that in each case some extraordinary development was going to take place. But probably few, if any, analysts ever looked at these reports combining information in the way commissions of inquiry do with the aid of hindsight.

According to Jervis (1976, p. 308),

> when discrepant information arrives gradually, the conflict between each bit and what the person believes will be small enough to go unnoticed, be dismissed as unimportant, or necessitate at most slight modifications . . . each piece of evidence will be considered to have been adequately accounted for, and the actor will not perceive that discrepant information is accumulating. If his explanation for any single event is questioned, a defender of the image can reply, and believe, that while this one explanation is not completely satisfactory, the image still is surely correct because it accounts for such a wide range of data. In this way one questionable interpretation will be used to support an image that in turn can be used to justify other dubious explanations. This is an especially great danger in judging other states' intentions since interpretations of past events often quickly become enshrined.

This way of treating information explains why the information provided by the Magic intercepts did not alert top American analysts that war was impending. Security was so tight that no one was allowed to keep a complete file of the messages. Instead intercepts were sent to officials one at a time and returned to the intelligence office as soon as they were read. Most readers scanned the messages rapidly while the officer in charge of delivery stood by to take the copy back again. Thus no one ever reviewed the entire series of messages (Wohlstetter, 1962, p. 180), and no single intercept was striking enough to change the established views.

Information and Expectations

The interpretation of incoming information is affected not only by the belief system but by expectations as to the enemy's behavior as well. Initial expectations are deduced from the belief system, and they are influenced by past experience, personal tendencies, and organizational and national norms, as well as by the definition of the situation. Different circumstances evoke different sets of expectations.

Initial expectations tend to be inaccurate. If incoming information so strongly contradicts expectations that it cannot be ignored or assimilated, expectations are adjusted, albeit as little as possible (Snyder and Diesing, 1977, p. 494). Since expectations are rooted mainly in beliefs and images, however, they tend to persist even in the face of disconfirming information. Furthermore, they predispose the analyst to pay particular attention to certain kinds of information and to organize and interpret this information in certain patterns. Snyder and Diesing describe this process: "Since the influence of expectations and interpretation is unconscious, the interpreter does not realize at first that he has read his own ideas into the message; he thinks the ideas are objectively there in the message. Consequently he treats the fit between message and expectations as an objective confirmation of his diagnosis, which increases his confidence in the diagnosis. This makes it easier unconsciously to read his expectations into the next message, and so on" (1977, p. 287). Expectations tell the analyst what objects to look for, how these objects are likely to appear, what is important, how to draw inferences from what is noticed, and how to interpret what he sees. In this sense expectations, like beliefs, also play a positive role. They may prevent too early a change of mind on the basis of possible misleading information and provide more time for additional information. Assimilating considerable amounts of information to existing beliefs and expectations is necessary for rational decision making (Jervis, 1976, pp. 145, 154, 172).

Yet this guiding and simplifying role of expectations is also misleading. Many psychological experiments have confirmed that the more familiar a phenomenon is, the more quickly it will be recognized. If an analyst expects a signal, he is much more likely to perceive ambiguous evidence as if it were that signal. Mere noise or other signs will be mistaken for the expected one (De Rivera, 1968, pp. 40–41, 53; Jervis, 1976, pp. 146–147, 153). Similarly if an analyst thinks he knows how the enemy is going to behave, he will interpret ambiguous information as confirming his predictions. Information and events that are inconsistent with his expectations tend to be ignored or distorted in perception; it takes more information to recognize an unexpected event than an expected one. An analyst often forgets that information will seem in many cases to confirm a certain hypothesis only because he already believes that hypothesis to be correct. For example, if he believes that war is not imminent, it is only natural for him to ignore little clues that, in a review of the whole, might collectively add up to a significant war warning. As Schelling noted, "There is a tendency in our planning to confuse the unfamiliar with the improbable. The contingency we have not considered seriously looks strange; what looks strange is thought improbable; what is improbable need not be considered seriously" (Wohlstetter, 1962, p. vii). Since incoming signals that constitute a challenge are much less readily accepted than those that confirm existing expectations, warning signals may not be perceived at all in the flow of contradictory information. When the head of Army Intelligence at Pearl Harbor received a warning from Washington about the Japanese message ordering the destruction of codes, he simply filed it away; he could not sense any hidden urgency because he was not expecting immediate trouble, and his expectations determined what he read (Wohlstetter, 1962, pp. 388–390).

Of the many examples illustrating the tendency to integrate information into prevailing expectations, two stand out. The first is the attack on Pearl Harbor. From late November 1941 the Pacific Fleet Intelligence assessment was that the outbreak of war with Japan was to be expected at any moment, but not at Pearl Harbor; highest probability was still assigned to a Japanese attack in Southeast Asia or the Russian Maritime Provinces. Consequently the message sent by Naval Operations on November 27, warning against the possibility of Japanese attack on the Philippines or Southeast Asia, was assimilated into that view. As Colonel Edwin Layton, the Fleet Intelligence officer, later described his reaction to the message: "It certainly fitted the picture up to date, and that we would be at war shortly if Japan would decide not to leave her Philippine flank open and proceed southward . . . It made me feel that the picture we had was a good picture, and perhaps complete." In early December Fleet Intelligence had two reports that Japanese carriers had left home ports and were moving south. These reports were compatible with the hypothesis that Japan was going to attack southward, and since war was not expected at Pearl Harbor, they were treated accordingly. As Layton explained: "I did not at any time suggest that the Japanese carriers were under radio silence approaching Oahu [the island on which Pearl Harbor is located]. I wish I had . . . My own personal view, and that is what we work on, when making estimates to ourselves, was that the carriers were remaining in home waters preparing for operations so that they would be in a covering position in case we moved against Japan after she attacked, if she did, in Southeast Asia" (Wohlstetter, 1962, pp. 43–46).

Norway provides another example. The British intelligence agencies tended to adapt their incoming information to their expectation that Germany would attempt an invasion of the United Kingdom. When the German Air Force attacked the British Fleet Air Arm base at Hatston in the Orkney Islands on March 16, 1940, British Air Intelligence thought that the attack might indicate a German decision to work up gradually to an all-out attack on Britain. It missed the fact that Hatston was the British air base nearest to Bergen and Trondheim in Norway. Moreover, the strategic assessment shared by the Norwegian and British navies—when it at last became obvious that some move was afoot—was that the most likely action by the Germans would be an attempt by their battle cruisers to break through one of the northern exits to the Atlantic. The signals received in Oslo and Scapa Flow, the main anchorage of the British Home Fleet, during the first week of April were interpreted as indicators that this strategic prediction was in the process of being vindicated. As a result of this miscalculation the Home Fleet set out on April 7 on a course that would enable the fleet to intercept ships attempting to break out into the Atlantic but left the central North Sea uncovered (Hinsley, 1979, pp. 119–120; Holst, 1966, p. 34).

One final factor related to expectations is wishful thinking. Psychologists have noted a general disposition in individuals to exaggerate gratifying features of their environment and to overestimate the possibility of desirable events. In conditions of great uncertainty people tend to predict that events that they want to happen actually will happen. They have a tendency to increase the subjective probability of those events that are regarded as more desirable. In this way the individual may change his beliefs in accordance with his desires and interpret incoming information as conforming to those desires (Knorr, 1964a, p. 462). A typical related claim is that the party seeking to maintain the status quo rarely perceives a threat as immediate, since the enemy's aggressive intentions appear somewhat remote; this was the case with Stalin in 1941 and Israel in 1973 (Handel, 1977, p. 472).

Yet interpretation of information is influenced more by expectations than by desires. Although examples of what seems to be wishful thinking were instrumental in many cases of surprise attack, their net influence may not be great. Jervis (1976, pp. 365–369, 380) maintains that the common claim that people tend to perceive what they want to perceive is not adequately supported by evidence. Desires may have an impact on perception by influencing expectations, but this is only one of many such factors. In our case there is no evidence that a nation that wishes to maintain the status quo will consequently misperceive threats. Of course a nation that desires to keep the status quo may indeed be more vulnerable to surprise attack, but only because it might be more reluctant and fearful to mobilize too early lest it generate a deterioration toward war.

Treating Discrepant Information

The persistence of conceptions, together with the tendency to assimilate information to existing beliefs, raises the question of how analysts explain the wealth of discrepant information that they encounter. As I noted earlier, most of this information can be easily fitted to, or somewhat twisted to fit, the established hypothesis. But there are other psychological mechanisms for treating discrepant information that may reduce the receptivity to warning.

First, an analyst may fail to see that incoming information contradicts his beliefs; he may misunderstand the message or misjudge its relevance. In this case the information is immediately ignored or dismissed. Obviously this requires no alteration of hypotheses and causes no strain of reconciling the information with existing beliefs (Jervis, 1976, p. 29; Janis and Mann, 1977, pp. 125–126). Thus on December 3, 1941, Admiral Kimmel in Hawaii was advised "for action" that Japanese diplomatic posts had been ordered to destroy most of their codes and secret documents. In retrospect this was the most significant information received during the ten days before the attack on Pearl Harbor. Kimmel and his staff agreed that this information appeared to fit in with the information they had received about "Japanese movement in South East Asia." Consequently nothing was done; the Commander of the Hawaiian Department of the Army was not even informed of the existence of this report (U.S. Congress, 1946a, p. 130).

If a message is too clear to dismiss or ignore, analysts may rein-terpret it to conform with their views rather than to contradict them, or they may at least reduce its salience to the point where it is no longer uncomfortable to live with the incongruity (Finlay, Holsti, and Fagen, 1967, pp. 33–34). In this manner contradictory infor-mation may be written off as unimportant or incorrect, and incon-sistency is denied. When during September and October 1941 the United States intercepted several messages in which the Japanese consul in Honolulu was instructed by Tokyo to obtain information concerning the exact location of all ships in Pearl Harbor, no one attached the right significance to this order. Admiral Harold Stark, Chief of Naval Operations, testified later: "We knew the Japanese appetite was almost insatiable for detail in all respects. The dispatch might have been put down as just another example of their great attention to detail." And Commander Arthur McCollum, Chief of the Far Eastern Section of the Office of Naval Intelligence, explained that beginning in 1935 the Japanese Navy was not satisfied with the type of intelligence forwarded by the consular agents and in consequence undertook to set up an observation net of its own, particularly on the West Coast of the United States (U.S. Congress, 1946a, p. 185).

In yet another instance the analyst may admit that the infor-mation is discrepant but will reject its validity, or at least treat it as if it were of little consequence. It is relatively easy for analysts to discredit contradictory information, since they often demand of discrepant information that it meet higher standards of evidence. It also must have a higher degree of clarity than supportive information in order to gain acceptance (George and Smoke, 1974, p. 574; Nisbett and Ross, 1980, p. 169). Thus in June 1941 Admiral Royal Ingersoll, Assistant Chief of Naval Operations, informed Navy headquarters in Hawaii that ships in shallow water might be vulnerable to tor-pedoes. Ingersoll stated that no minimum depth of water in which naval vessels might be anchored could arbitrarily be assumed to provide safety from torpedo plane attack. Yet Ingersoll also wrote that deep-water attacks were much more likely, and this reassur-ing statement caught the eye of the recipients. After receiving this letter Admiral Kimmel said, "All my staff, Admiral Bloch and I considered the torpedo danger negligible" (Janis, 1972, p. 90; Wohl-stetter, 1962, p. 370).

Another fairly uncommon way of treating such information is to evade the conflict or pretend that there is no such problem. This mode of defense enables a person temporarily to ward off psychological stress by maintaining an illusion of invulnerability, despite information that, if perceived correctly, would alert him to the impending threat. The consequence of this unrealistic approach is that decision makers can remain unaware that a problem exists until they are surprised. Thus when estimates of the North Koreans' strength indicated that they would not be strong enough to invade *unless* furnished with much Russian equipment, it was simply reported that North Korea did not have adequate strength for a successful invasion, and estimates to the contrary were overlooked (De Rivera, 1968, pp. 79–82; Janis and Mann, 1977, p. 129).

Far more common is the tendency to discredit the source of discrepant information, thereby rejecting its validity or relevance. Discrediting a source is easier when the information is ambiguous, especially when the recipient has additional doubts as to the source's reliability. Thus Stalin rejected all the British and American warnings about the coming of a German attack as sheer capitalist provocation designed to disrupt relations between Germany and the Soviet Union. Similarly in early June 1950 the American ambassador to South Korea reported a heavy North Korean arms build-up along the Thirty-eighth Parallel and pointed out that the North Korean forces had an overwhelming superiority over the South Korean forces. Yet since the ambassador had shortly before requested tanks and heavy equipment for the South Korean Army, his report was perceived as merely a supportive argument for this request (De Rivera, 1968, p. 19).

Analysts may even recognize the potential importance of the discrepant information, and admit that they cannot either explain it or fit it into their hypotheses, yet still refuse or hesitate to change their views (Jervis, 1976, pp. 294, 188). Two days before the October 1973 war Israeli intelligence found that the families of Soviet advisers in Egypt and Syria were being airlifted out. This fact, against the backdrop of the Arab army build-ups, could hardly be explained by prevailing views; but Israeli analysts did not conclude that they should solve the contradiction by changing their conception about Arab capabilities and intentions. Rather they simply lived with this puzzle until the outbreak of the war.

Analysts may also try to deal with discrepant information by *bolstering*—that is, by seeking new information and considerations that strengthen the challenged beliefs. They may increase the collection effort and wait for additional information to confirm or disconfirm the threat, in the hope that further evidence will support the existing view. Jervis adds that bolstering can refer "to the rearranging of attitudes in order to decrease the impact of the discrepant information. Thus a person can admit that, while one aspect of a valued object is associated with something negatively valued, other aspects of it are more important than he had thought previously" (1976, pp. 294–295). Thus the Navy command in Hawaii invented a series of new arguments and rationalizations that enabled it to avoid thinking about the losses that might ensue from its policy of continuing to devote all resources to training and supply functions, without taking special precautions to protect Hawaii from a surprise air attack (Janis and Mann, 1977, pp. 126–127).

Another mechanism for treating discrepant information is *undermining*, whereby the analyst searches for new evidence in an effort to weaken the discrepant information, including discrediting the source (Jervis, 1976, pp. 294–295; Bonham, Shapiro, and Trumble, 1979, p. 11). Alternatively, when the information is too clear to ignore, the analyst may reject the overt message and look for a hidden meaning that does not contradict his views. Deception is common in international relations, and many aspects of the enemy's behavior that contradict the analyst's accepted image can be interpreted as attempts to deceive. In January 1940 a German aircraft made a forced landing in Belgium. Its passenger was carrying a copy of certain highly secret parts of Hitler's order for the offensive in the West. The British and the French, who were shown the plan, wrestled with the question of its authenticity and finally concluded that it was a deliberate German plant. They could not believe that any German officer would have dared to defy security instructions by carrying these plans in an aircraft that might have to pass over enemy territory (Strong, 1968, p. 61; Whaley, 1969, p. 186). Similarly, in his memoirs Chief of the Soviet General Staff Marshal Georgi Zhukov quoted Soviet Military Intelligence conclusions as saying, "Rumors and documents to the effect that war against the USSR is inevitable this spring should be regarded as misinformation coming from the English or perhaps even the German intelligence service" (Whaley, 1973, p. 196).

When the incoming information is too discrepant to be disposed of by any of these means, the analyst may have to modify some of his concepts or restructure his views. One mechanism for achieving consistency while minimizing the adjustment is *differentiation*— that is, the analyst splits the information into two or more parts and adjusts only his beliefs concerning the part that is causing attitudinal conflict. The opposite of differentiation is *transcendence*: here the analyst may combine his concepts into a superordinate concept at a higher level, consistent with other beliefs, thereby enabling him to reconcile the conflict (Jervis, 1976, pp. 295–296; Snyder and Diesing, 1977, p. 314; Bonham, Shapiro, and Trumble, 1979, p. 11).

The October 1973 war provides an example of differentiation. The unprecedented Egyptian build-up was explained by Israeli intelligence as part of a major maneuver taking place at the time; the Syrian build-up was not considered sufficiently significant, since it was assumed that Syria could not go to war without Egyptian participation, and this was considered unlikely. Yet Israeli intelligence could not explain the transfer of Syrian Sukhoi-7 aircraft to an airfield closer to the front, which indicated offensive intentions. Consequently, while the assessment that war should not be expected on either front was not changed, the Israelis thereafter took into account the possibility that the Syrians might attempt a limited raid on or occupation of two or three settlements in the Golan Heights (Bartov, 1978, pp. 296, 300).

A final point concerns the analyst's choice of mechanism for dealing with discrepant information. The analyst may choose his technique unconsciously, sometimes even irrationally. He may use these mechanisms separately or in combination. His choice of mechanism may depend on the nature of the problem, on the ambiguity of the information, on the reliability of its source, and on individual preferences. But generally he will look for that technique by which he can best fit the discrepant information into his beliefs without drastically changing his conceptions.

Cognitive Biases and Overconfidence

Persistence of conceptions is not the only source of biased judgment. According to modern theory of perception and memory, people reach conclusions about what they have seen or what they remember by reconstructing their knowledge from fragments of information. "During reconstruction, a variety of cognitive, social, and motivational factors introduce error and distortion into the output of the process" (Slovic, Fischhoff, and Lichtenstein, 1976a, pp. 14–15).

Biases of judgment have several common characteristics. They are often systematic and consistent rather than random; and since they result from the inherent fallibility of human judgment, many biases are difficult to correct. Moreover, many such biases are shared by experts and laymen alike. And most important, "the error remains compelling even when one is fully aware of its nature. Awareness of a perceptual or cognitive illusion does not by itself produce a more accurate perception of reality" (Kahneman and Tversky, 1979, p. 314). Consequently such biases may persist even though people are warned against them and rewarded for correcting them. Finally, there is a process of accumulation and feedback among judgmental biases. Thus the accumulation of biases creates a structure of distorted conceptions and assumptions, which makes it more difficult to locate and correct errors.

Here I shall focus on some of the cognitive biases that distort the logical processes by which fragments of information are molded into conclusions. Some of these biases are caused by faulty application of knowledge or information in making estimates, inferences, and predictions. I shall deal mainly with biases that affect the estimation of probabilities, as well as with the causes and implications of overconfidence.

The Use of Judgmental Heuristics

Psychological research on judgment under uncertainty has concentrated on the methods that people use to evaluate evidence and the procedures they rely on to assess subjective probability.[9] Collecting different types of information from various sources and integrating them into an overall judgment is a difficult cognitive process. When it is compounded with the fact that no individual is capable of making optimal use of available information, this difficulty causes one to resort to simplification strategies. Recent research has identified a number of general inferential rules, known as *heuristics,* which reduce difficult mental functions into simpler ones and solve a variety of inferential tasks. People rely on heuristic rules when faced with the difficult task of assessing the probability and frequency of events and predicting values.[10]

The use of heuristics is relevant to the issue of intelligence failure: analysts are constantly assessing probabilities with respect to the outcome of events and developments, the enemy's intentions and capabilities, the meaning of early warning indicators, and the credibility of sources. The problem is complicated since analysts have to examine many pieces of information that have different degrees of reliability and are related with varing degrees of probability to several potential outcomes (Heuer, 1981b).

Usually heuristics are quite useful and effective; but in some circumstances they lead to systematic and severe errors with serious implications. They may lead to distorted assumptions, which in turn serve as a basis for further misconceptions. New incoming information, which might have clarified the uncertainty without the use of heuristics, will no longer correct the conceptions, for once conceptions are accepted as valid, their logical basis is not reexamined, and the uncertainty inherent in such information is ignored to some degree anyway.

Tversky and Kahneman identify three judgmental heuristics that are employed to assess probabilities and to predict values: availability, representativeness, and adjustment and anchoring.

Availability. The availability heuristic is used in judging frequency, probability, and even causality. Tversky and Kahneman have suggested that people assess the likelihood or frequency of an event by the ease with which relevant instances or occurrences can be brought to mind (1973, p. 208; 1974, p. 1127; see also Taylor, 1982, pp. 191–197). Another cue that people use when judging the probability of an event is the number of other such instances that are readily remembered.

In general availability is a useful clue for assessing probability or frequency because frequent events are usually recalled better and faster than less frequent ones. The ease with which things come to mind, however, is affected by many factors unrelated to actual probability. Availability is also influenced by factors such as emotional saliency, recency, vividness, and imaginability. These may but need not necessarily be correlated with the event's frequency and its correct probability. Consequently the availability heuristic can be a fallible guide for such judgments; reliance on it may result in systematic overestimation of probabilities and perceived frequency with regard to familiar, recent, vivid, or otherwise memorable or imaginable events.

The use of the availability heuristic and that heuristic's biases have important implications for intelligence analysis and the perception of approaching attack. Availability "points up the vital role of experience as a determinant of perceived risk. If one's experiences are biased, one's perceptions are likely to be inaccurate. Unfortunately, much of the information to which people are exposed provides a distorted picture of the world of hazards" (Slovic, Fischhoff, and Lichtenstein, 1980, pp. 184–185).

In addition, the analysis of an enemy's intentions and the interpretation of early warning indicators are based to a large extent on comparing instances from past experience. Recent occurrences are likely to be relatively more available than earlier events and will have more influence on the analyst's estimate than less available instances. Availability also implies that any factor that makes a traumatic event or hazard highly memorable or imaginable could seriously distort the perceived risk of that hazard (Slovic, 1978). This explains in part the impact of the last war on the failure to anticipate surprise attacks.

Then too analysts assign inferential weight to information in proportion to its salience and vividness. Yet "this strategy of evidential weighting is dangerous because the vividness of information is normally related only obliquely at best to its true value as evidence" (Nisbett and Ross, 1980, p. 8).

Imaginability also plays an important role in the evaluation of probabilities. The risk of coming attack may be underestimated if some possible dangers are difficult to conceive of or simply do not come to mind. Thus on December 7, 1941, at 7:02 A.M. a radar unit detected a large number of planes approaching Hawaii at a distance of 132 miles. The aircraft-warning information center was advised of the approaching planes, but an Army lieutenant at the center took the call and instructed the radar operators, in effect, to forget it. His estimate was that the flight was either a naval patrol, a flight of Hickam Field bombers, or possibly several B-17s from the mainland that were scheduled to arrive in Hawaii that morning (U.S. Congress, 1946a, p. 66). Since he had never experienced war, the possibility of an attack did not cross his mind; he interpreted the indicator according to his expectations.

Finally, as Heuer suggests, intelligence analysts often have difficulty in estimating the likelihood of events that have a low probability of occurrence but, if they did occur, would have very serious consequences. Since it is difficult for analysts to imagine such developments, they assign them an even lower probability. We have already noted that imaginability is often irrelevant to an accurate assessment of the probability of such events (Heuer, 1980c; 1982). Indeed in most cases surprise attack is a typical case of the low-probability, high-risk category; the availability bias can explain why analysts are likely to underestimate its true probability.

Representativeness. This heuristic enables one to estimate the likelihood of one state of affairs given the knowledge of another state of affairs by judging the similarity between the two. It allows the estimator to reduce many inferential tasks to simple similarity judgments. According to Kahneman and Tversky's definition, "a person who follows this heuristic evaluates the probability of an uncertain event, or a sample, by the degree to which it is: (1) similar in essential properties to its parent population; and (2) reflects the salient features of the process by which it is generated. Our thesis is that, in many situations, an event A is judged more probable than an event B whenever A appears more representative than B" (1972, p. 431).

The use of the representativeness heuristic may lead to serious errors because similarity, or representativeness, is not influenced by several factors that should affect judgments of probability. Mere similarity is an unreliable guide to likelihood. Representativeness is sometimes used as the only judgmental strategy when it alone cannot provide an accurate judgment. People tend to predict the outcome that appears most representative of salient features of the evidence while ignoring other criteria such as reliability, validity, and amount of available evidence (Nisbett and Ross, 1980, p. 7; Ross, 1977, p. 363).

One of the factors that does not influence representativeness but should affect it is the prior probability, or base-rate frequency, of outcomes. Prior probability, which summarizes what people know before receiving evidence of the case at hand, is relevant even after specific evidence is obtained. When required to predict the outcome of an event, however, people seem to rely almost exclusively on specific information and ignore prior probabilities (Kahneman and Tversky, 1973; Tversky and Kahneman, 1974; Slovic, 1982).

Moreover, people have little understanding of the importance of the size of the sample of events that they can recall, and of that sample's freedom from biases. They are insensitive to the instability and unreliability of the characteristics displayed in a small set of events. Such biases create distortions in characterizing the sample. Yet people seem to be willing to generalize from samples known to be biased in crucial parameters (Tversky and Kahneman, 1974; Nisbett and Ross, 1980, pp. 9–10).

In addition, people often make predictions by selecting the outcome that they assume will be most representative of the input. "The confidence they have in their prediction depends primarily on the degree of representativeness (that is, on the quality of the match between the selected outcome and the input) with little or no regard for the factors that limit predictive accuracy" (Tversky and Kahneman, 1974, p. 1126). Such unwarranted confidence, which is produced by a "fit" between the predicted outcome and the input information, is called by Tversky and Kahneman "the illusion of validity." They claim that this illusion persists even when the person is aware of the factors that limit the accuracy of his predictions.

Last, the internal consistency of input is a major determinant of people's confidence in predictions based on that input. Highly consistent patterns are most often observed when input variables are highly redundant or correlated. Hence people have greater confidence in predictions based on highly redundant predictor variables, since these tend to agree with one another in their implications. Yet a principle of prediction asserts that the accuracy of prediction decreases as redundancy among input variables increases. Thus the effect of redundancy on confidence is contrary to what it should be (Tversky and Kahneman, 1974).

The use of the representativeness heuristic and its biases have important implications for intelligence analysis. Analysts may neglect base-rate data. They may also reject data about the distribution of the outcome in similar situations. Instead they may overemphasize specific information about a case under consideration. As a result, unique events or extreme indicators may be perceived as representative, thereby distorting the estimate. A single piece of information may cause a false alarm, with all its damaging implications, even when most of the earlier indicators do not suggest a threat.

The evidence on the basis of which analysts draw their conclusions about the enemy's intentions and capabilities is usually very limited. Sometimes analysts receive warning indicators concerning only a small portion of the enemy's units; sometimes the signals are minimal in comparison to noise. Yet analysts are prone to forget this fact, believing instead that small samples are as good as large ones. Consequently they tend to be overconfident of conclusions drawn from a small body of evidence, neglecting the possibility that this evidence may not be representative of the entire body of potential evidence. Similarly, because there are only a few relevant events, analysts and policy makers tend to rely on too small a sample of historical precedents, assuming that if an event has happened even a few times, it might repeat itself.

Thus in 1940 Halvdan Koht, the Norwegian foreign minister, who dominated his country's foreign policy, did not expect Germany to strike without first raising an issue of conflict or at least an ultimatum and presenting negotiable demands. This expectation was based on observation of Hitler's behavior during the preceding crises over Austria, Czechoslovakia, and Poland (Holst, 1966, p. 39). A year later Stalin made the same mistake, assuming that any German attack would be preceded by an ultimatum, giving him an opportunity to take the initiative. The sample of three cases was too small for Stalin to rely on. Nor was it representative: the more recent preludes to war in Norway, Denmark, and France had shown that the delivery of an ultimatum by Hitler was not a precondition to his initiating war.

Analysts usually adopt the hypothesis or explanation that encompasses the greatest quantity of evidence within a logically consistent scenario. Yet when information is consistent, analysts may ignore the fact that it represents a small and unreliable sample. Moreover, information may be consistent only because it is highly correlated or redundant, in which case several related reports may be no more informative and meaningful than any single one (Heuer, 1981a, pp. 305–306; 1981b, pp. 47–48).

Finally, a good deal of evidence indicates that people have a very poor conception of the uncertainty contributed by randomness. In particular they do not recognize randomness, and they offer deterministic explanations of random phenomena. This tendency to ignore random errors creates several difficulties. When analysts formulate hypotheses using uncertain signals, they keep searching for deterministic rules that will account for all the signals. Moreover, when analysts are convinced that a signal comes from a reliable source, they may assume it contains no element of error. Last, analysts may hold a discredited hypothesis too long because certain noisy data seem to support it and reject a correct hypothesis because noisy data seem inconsistent with it (Fischhoff, 1976, p. 431; Stech, 1979, p. 315).

Adjustment and anchoring. A third heuristic that seems useful in describing how people ease the strain of integrating information is a process called adjustment and anchoring. In this process some natural starting point or anchor is used as a first approximation of the judgment. This anchor is then adjusted to accommodate the implications of the additional information or analysis. Typically, however, the anchor tends to reduce the amount of adjustment demanded, so that the final judgment remains closer to the starting point than need be. The adjustment factor, therefore, is imprecise and fails to do justice to the importance of additional information.

Adjustment is also insufficient. Different anchors yield different estimates, each biased differently toward the initial values. The reason for this insufficiency is either that people tire of the mental effort involved in adjusting or, possibly, that the anchor point takes on a special significance and people feel that it is less risky to make estimates close to it than to deviate far from it (Tversky and Kahneman, 1974, pp. 1128–1129; Slovic, Fischhoff, and Lichtenstein, 1976b, p. 172).

The implication for intelligence failures is clear. Analysts have to review and update their estimates from time to time, either because they have received important new information or because of a changing situation. A natural starting point for such an adjustment can be a basic belief system, the initial definition of the situation, or the previous estimate on that subject. The bias created by the anchoring and adjustment heuristic suggests that analysts may not change their estimates sufficiently. Their judgment is affected by the initial anchor, and their review of estimates may lag behind their receipt of incoming information and perception of changing situations.

Thus before the Second World War the strategy of the defense of Singapore was to deploy a skeleton garrison; it was understood that if any danger arose in that area, part of the British fleet would be dispatched to prevent enemy attack. Once the war in Europe began, it became clear that the British fleet could not be sent to the Far East. Also in 1940 Japan occupied Indochina and gained use of its airfields. Yet the old strategy of the defense of Singapore was adhered to, and the British continued to believe that it could not be conquered (Leasor, 1968, pp. 15, 123–126).

Overconfidence

Philosophers and psychologists have long noted that people are often much too confident of the accuracy of their judgments. Overconfidence, which can be defined as an unwarranted belief in the correctness of one's assumptions, is manifested in most stages of the process of judgment formation. People are insufficiently critical of the knowledge, information, hypotheses, and reasoning they use to form judgments and often believe that they have a much better picture of reality than they do. As a result they exhibit greater certainty about their assessments, theories, and conclusions than closely reasoned analysis would justify. Overconfidence also results from neglecting evidence that contradicts the chosen assumption and relying more heavily on considerations consistent with a chosen assumption than on considerations contradicting it. Overconfidence appears to be typical in judging the probability of events that are treated as essentially unique. Empirical research has provided evidence of this overconfidence and of the alarming extent to which confidence is often unrelated to accuracy. Research shows also that experts seem as prone to overconfidence as lay people.[11]

Obviously some of the judgmental biases described earlier contribute significantly to analysts' overconfidence, but there are additional reasons and explanations. For one thing people have a desire for certainty. Psychologists explain that one way to reduce the anxiety generated by confronting uncertainty is to deny that uncertainty. This denial is one of the sources of overconfidence (Slovic, Fischhoff, and Lichtenstein, 1979, pp. 17–18).

Then too our environment is often not structured to show the limits of our predictions. Errors in estimation are hard to detect, and sometimes we receive little or no feedback. Even when feedback is received, we may distort its meaning to convince ourselves that what occurred agrees with our estimate. We can usually find some reason for our failures other than our inherent inadequacies. In other instances the criterion for judging our assessments is so vague that we cannot tell how poorly we are actually doing (Slovic, Fischhoff, and Lichtenstein, 1977, p. 6).

In addition psychologists claim that people commonly view their memories as accurate reflections of their experiences and believe that they can answer questions directly from memory without making inferences. Considerable research has demonstrated, however, that memory is more than just a copying process. Thus if people are unaware of the reconstructive nature of memory and cannot distinguish between assertions and inferences, they will not critically evaluate the inferred knowledge and will be overconfident of their conclusions (Fischhoff, Slovic, and Lichtenstein, 1977, pp. 562–563).

A related cause of overconfidence is oversensitivity to the consistency of available information. People tend to draw more confidence from a small body of consistent evidence than from a much larger body of less consistent evidence. "The effect of consistency indirectly contributes to overconfidence. In their search for coherence, people often see patterns where none exist, reinterpret data so as to increase their apparent consistency, and ignore evidence that does not fit their views. In this manner, people are likely to overestimate the consistency of data and to derive too much confidence from them" (Kahneman and Tversky, 1979, pp. 323–324).

Overconfidence has played a part in all cases of surprise attack, among analysts and decision makers alike. In fact a successful surprise attack can be regarded as a reflection of the victim's overconfidence: inevitably intelligence agencies and policy makers were surprised because they were so confident that war was not imminent.

The implications of overconfidence for surprise attack can be viewed on two levels. On the conceptual level, if an analyst is confident that war is not likely, he will not easily recognize signals and warning indicators that contradict his belief. The higher the degree of confidence, the slower the analyst will be to accommodate discrepant evidence, and the less willing he will be to accept alternative hypotheses about the enemy's intentions.

On the operational level, the more confident a nation is that no attack will be launched, the less willing it is to take precautions and countermeasures against possible attack. When Nasser moved his armed forces into Sinai in May 1967 Israel was far from confident either of Egypt's intentions or of its ability to predict the Arabs' future actions; as a result it took full countermeasures. Six years later, beginning in late September 1973, when warning indicators accumulated, Israel was much more confident both of its conception that the Arabs were not going to war and of its ability to predict the outbreak of such a war. Thus the risk threshold that Israel was willing to accept in 1973 was much lower than in 1967.

5

The Process of Analysis

The discussion of judgmental difficulties and biases serves as an introduction to this chapter, where I divide the process of intelligence analysis and estimation into its main components and examine the difficulties and distortions involved in each of them, especially with regard to surprise attack.

Prediction and Intelligence Analysis

To understand how analysts reach a conclusion about the enemy's future behavior, one must first examine the essence of prediction. According to Toch (1958, p. 58):

> A prediction is the statement of a belief regarding the future, based on a subjective appraisal of the immediate past and an evaluation of experiences in the remote past: it is an extrapolation from past experience . . . Successful prediction would thus be contingent on the reliability of significances assigned to the world and on the ability to select from these significances those relevant to what has not yet occurred . . . Successful prediction also depends on an ability to anticipate novelty and to not assume permanence or undistorted sequences.[1]

Prediction is heavily influenced by many of the difficulties and biases described in the last chapter. To the extent that the factors of uncertainty and human judgment are significant, the accuracy of prediction is adversely influenced. Obviously perseverance of conceptions, neglect of evidence, and simplification strategies bias the process of prediction.

According to McGregor (1938), a prediction is influenced not only by objective factors and the stimulus situation but also by subjective factors. The individual's attitudes, wishes, and knowledge provide a frame of reference that influences the formation of the hypothesis on which his prediction will be based. The influence of such subjective factors on prediction is determined by two major variables: the *degree of ambiguity* inherent in the situation (the more ambiguous the situation, the more significant is wishful thinking in the determination of prediction), and the *importance* that the predictor attributes to the issues involved. In addition, various personality traits influence the predictive process. An *optimist's* predictions tend to accord with his wishes; an event is less probable for the *cautious* predictor than for the average one; and the *skeptical* predictor is likely to be more influenced than the average predictor by his contact with objective conditions and less ready to accept his friends' expressions of opinion.

Certain errors are common to most predictions and introduce a systematic bias in their outcomes. Forecasters may underestimate or completely neglect certain crucial factors or fail to strike the proper balance between diverse factors, thereby possibly rendering the prediction invalid. They may also put a priori emphasis on certain variables that appear critical in certain contexts, without adequate validation or reality checks (Martino, 1972, pp. 561–576; Choucri, 1978, p. 14; Washburn and Jones, 1978, p. 97).

The most severe error in making predictions—and the most relevant to the failure to anticipate surprise attack—is the common assumption that a trend will continue in a straight line. Abrupt changes in the development of processes occur time and again. A successful prediction should therefore be able to forecast potential sources of change, to determine the timing of the change, and to describe what will happen after the change takes place.

The psychological difficulties of anticipating novelties and changes are significant. This is due in part to the fact that people strive toward consistency within themselves and therefore are unlikely to predict events that break sharply with their perceptions. In addition predictors are aware of the danger in deviating, however slightly, from past patterns, since the deviation may turn out to be no more than an insignificant temporary change in the pattern. Also relevant is the fact that the predictor's imagination might be too limited. Consequently the natural tendency of predictors is to believe that those things that have remained unchanged up to a certain point will continue to remain unchanged. They are aware that future changes are possible and might even occur abruptly; but they are alert to the possibility of change only with regard to those aspects in which past changes have already made them aware of the potential for instability. When predictors think in terms of possible changes, they believe that these changes will take place both in the same direction and at the same rate as in the past; their natural perception of change is that the future will differ from the present in the same way that the present differs from the past (Jouvenel, 1967, p. 61; Rothstein, 1972, pp. 172–178; Chuyev and Mikhaylov, 1975, pp. 40–41, 190; Ascher, 1978, p. 203).

Prediction is extremely difficult and is likely often to be erroneous, particularly when it refers to international relations and military affairs.[2] Many kinds of uncertainty are at work in these areas. The number of variables that should be taken into account in predicting international and military behavior is large, while information about the future is scarce, incomplete, and sometimes misleading. Unlike in many other fields it is extremely difficult, sometimes even impossible, to reduce this level of uncertainty by means of tests and experiments. An opponent can alter and control certain conditions and influence the other side's observations, for example by deception.

Many events in the international arena are unique, devoid of precedent. Also the frequency of events may vary to an extreme degree. Consequently prediction, being based to a large extent on observed regularities, becomes more difficult. Short-term unique events are the most difficult to predict because they may not have any precedents. Yet this type of event is often of the greatest concern to the intelligence community. While methods such as generating alternative scenarios do exist for dealing with unique events, they cannot produce the clear-cut, concrete predictions that are required. Unfortunately enemy attacks in general, and surprise attacks in particular, fall into this category of unique events. Minor wars occur once every couple of years, major ones every decade or two; but from the viewpoint of a specific state, only a few of these wars, if any, are relevant as precedents for predicting surprise attack.

Processes and trends in international relations and military affairs are also becoming more complex than in the past, and hence more difficult to predict. Most strategic issues, including the decision to go to war, now involve an assortment of disciplines—political, military, technological, economic. Consequently it becomes more difficult to understand the strategic implications of complex situations. Thus, although in 1941 Washington expected a Japanese attack on Thailand, the Kra Peninsula, or Dutch holdings, most American policy makers did not understand that a Japanese attack on these targets would mean war with the United States and that, in view of the strategic principle that the flank of an advancing force must be guarded, Japan would have to destroy the U.S. fleet in Hawaii before advancing too deeply into southeastern waters. Similarly in 1962 Prime Minister Jawaharlal Nehru did not perceive the implications for India of the Sino-Soviet rift. He assumed that India's special relationship with the Soviets would guarantee its position vis-à-vis China. He did not understand that China might regard an attack against India as a means of undermining Soviet leadership within the socialist camp and that Soviet ability to support India would be limited (U.S. Congress, 1946b, pp. 29, 44; Vertzberger, 1978b, p. 25).

Last but not least, many political and military conditions can change within a short period of time, even quite abruptly. The hypotheses on which a prediction is based may be initially correct; but as the situation changes, new factors that should change basic assumptions may be ignored or unknown. The opponent's pattern of behavior or intentions may alter suddenly as a result of changes in leadership or technological development. The intervention of surprising events is not a rare occurrence. Military capabilities and methods of armed conflict change too, though more gradually. Furthermore, as changes in many factors that influence international relations have become more rapid and pervasive than in the past, the probability of discontinuity has increased. This is partly explained by the growing number of exogenous and uncontrollable variables that disrupt continuity and can lead to explosive situations—for example, new weapons technologies and increased military capabilities, Third World emergence, energy problems, and a worldwide propensity toward terrorist and other radical aggressive movements. Sometimes changes develop gradually until, after a period of time, the cumulative results may bring about a drastic change. As a result predictors in international relations cannot rely on the constancy of conditions or on their ability to forecast both the course and intensity of change.

The analyst's hypotheses and beliefs, though realistic in the past, may not register such changes quickly and correctly. This is particularly true since certain beliefs are always slightly out of date because they are based on recent history rather than on current events. Again to a large extent the problem is with the analyst's set of beliefs. Without this set he would not be able to say if change had taken place, but with it he is less likely to see the evidence of change. In other cases the basic change is noted, but its implications for particular kinds of behavior may not be immediately clear.

During the last week before the Six-Day War the Egyptians did not perceive the implications of two new rapid developments that heavily influenced Israel's decision to go to war. On June 1, 1967, an emergency Cabinet was formed in Israel, including Moshe Dayan as Defense Minister. While the Egyptians felt that this development increased the probability of war, they did not go so far as to suspect that it would mean war within four days. More important, on May 30 Nasser had concluded a military treaty with Jordan and Iraq that put Jordan under an Egyptian commander and called for the entry of an Iraqi division into Jordan. Nasser apparently did not understand the severity with which Israel, with the Egyptian and Syrian armies already concentrated on its borders, would regard this development. Nasser did not perceive that Israel was now forced to act quickly to forestall the Jordanian and Iraqi armies before being surrounded on all sides.

Perceiving the implications of a change is especially difficult when the victim has lived in peace for a long time, so that a state of effective war readiness requires an increasing exercise of imagination and alert. Such a standard is difficult to maintain indefinitely, especially when the victim feels geographically immune from surprise attack, like the United States before Pearl Harbor, or when a state has traditionally not been involved in international conflicts, like Norway before 1940. Prediction can also be distorted when the predictor strongly believes that the overall situation is inherently stable. This was the belief in Israel in 1973. Israeli forces were well established on the cease-fire lines, and these positions seemed to be gaining a measure of legitimacy. The Arab armies appeared to be too impressed by Israel's military strength to risk an offensive. The Arabs in the West Bank and Gaza seemed reconciled to prolonged Israeli control. The impression of stability became even stronger when Moscow and Washington agreed to define their relationship in terms of détente, whereby it was held unlikely that the Soviet Union would provoke American resentment by actively inciting the Arabs to war (Eban, 1977, pp. 485–487; Bartov, 1978, pp. 279–280).

It is also difficult to trace such a change when it involves a slow development rather than a sudden event, especially when the surprised side had grown accustomed to certain behavior on the part of its opponent. Thus the gradual and progressive commitment of the North Koreans and later the Chinese forces in Korea acted to blind U.S. analysts to the proper conclusions (DeWeerd, 1962, p. 457). They simply did not perceive in time that the communists were increasing their intervention beyond local border clashes.

Stages of Intelligence Analysis

A typical intelligence production consists of all or part of three main elements: *description* of the situation or event with an eye to identifying its essential characteristics; *explanation* of the causes of a development as well as its significance and implications; and *prediction* of future developments. Each element contains one or both of these components: *data*, provided by available knowledge and incoming information, and *assessment*, or judgment, which attempts to fill the gaps left in the data. An ideal intelligence production would contain only data with no gaps left for assessment; yet this happens only rarely. Usually data are far from complete, and we need to use our judgment in order to proceed beyond the available information.

The process of intelligence analysis and assessment is a very personal one. There is no agreed-upon analytical schema, and the analyst must primarily use his belief system to make assumptions and interpret information. His assumptions are usually implicit rather than explicit and may not be apparent even to him. Sometimes the analyst himself finds it difficult to explain clearly why he understands reality in a certain way. Often there is no guide to tell him that his analysis is correct until it is proved or disproved by actual developments. Some of his beliefs concerning the enemy's behavior are vulnerable only to specific events that occur when it is too late to alter his assessment. As a result no two analysts will agree on all issues, even if they have the same base of knowledge and information (which is rare); and when they do reach the same conclusions, their analytical structure is usually different (Jervis, 1976, p. 312; Heuer, 1979, p. 7).

The process of intelligence analysis is a continuous one. It has neither starting point nor end. It has no clear stages, and the analyst himself will find it difficult to tell where he is in the process at any given time. In essence the process is an interaction among beliefs, hypotheses, and information. While it is possible to point out some vague procedural stages, this does not mean that the analyst is necessarily progressing from one stage to the next. Sometimes he works simultaneously on several stages; sometimes he even reverts to an earlier stage. Yet the entire process is characterized by one feature that is important for the understanding of surprise attack. As Heuer suggests, "The progression from one step in the analytical process to the next is essentially a process of increasing specificity of hypotheses and of increasing selectivity in the information considered by the analyst" (1980b, p. 6).

Few attempts have been made to outline the steps of the analytical process. Clauser and Weir (1975, p. 75) describe a simple model that concentrates on the generating of hypotheses and comprises five steps: making observations directly or vicariously; postulating initial alternative hypotheses; screening initial hypotheses; selecting the best hypotheses and subjecting them to further tests or postulating new hypotheses; and choosing the hypothesis best supported by available data.

Heuer (1980b) expands this model by adding the element of incoming information. His model, while still a simplified one, represents a way in which the analytical process should function ideally. It includes eight steps: defining the problem; generating preliminary hypotheses; selectively acquiring data; refining hypotheses; selectively acquiring additional data; interpreting and evaluating data; selecting a hypothesis; and continuing to monitor new evidence that might invalidate the selected hypothesis.

In both models it is apparent that the process of intelligence analysis includes three main components: generating and evaluating alternative hypotheses; evaluating incoming information; and selecting the best hypothesis.

Generating and evaluating hypotheses comprises the first four steps described by Heuer. The process commences by transforming the open-ended issue into a set of better-defined problems so as to delimit the range of information that must be collected and evaluated. Then the scope of potentially relevant information is narrowed further by the development of tentative hypotheses. This leads to a process in which data are collected on the basis of their usefulness in evaluating the hypotheses. The development of hypotheses and collection of information to test them "is an iterative process that may go through many cycles. Each time the hypotheses may become more specific and the data collection more narrowly focused" (Heuer, 1980b, pp. 4–5; see also Stech, 1979, pp. 312–313).

The second component—evaluating incoming information—is a central part of the analytical process. The analyst asks three main questions: How reliable is the information? What is the significance of the information compared to other available information? To what extent does the new information confirm or refute existing hypotheses, and how should it be interpreted?

The third component—choosing among competing hypotheses—is the aim of the whole process. Alternative hypotheses are compared with the interpreted information, and the analyst selects the hypothesis that seems best supported by the information. Yet this is not the end of the process. Even after a hypothesis is chosen, the constant stream of information and the changing situation force the analyst to reexamine his hypothesis and test it further against accumulating new evidence.

Approaches for Generating and Evaluating Hypotheses

During the analytical process analysts employ various approaches to generating and evaluating hypotheses. The first is *deduction*, or reasoning from general rules or theories to particular cases. "A theory is a generalization based on the study of many examples of some phenomenon. It specifies that when a given set of conditions pertain, certain other conditions will follow" (Heuer, 1980b, p. 7). Deducing from theories helps the analyst to look beyond current developments, to recognize which trends are superficial and which significant, and to predict future developments for which there exists no concrete evidence. Deduction has two weaknesses relevant to intelligence analysis. In intelligence research, conclusions may be drawn correctly but the premises from which they are drawn may be false, thus rendering the conclusions false. Hence deductions should be used carefully, with an awareness of their limitations and of potential errors in the premises. Then too, since deductions are usually based on established theories, they may encourage the persistence of false beliefs and provide the basis for rejecting evidence that might otherwise indicate future events (Heuer, 1980b, pp. 7–10; Clauser and Weir, 1975, pp. 82–83).

One of the theories prevailing among analysts and decision makers is that, since war is such a risky course, an opponent will not resort to a military move unless he has first exhausted all other means of achieving his aims. The implication is that as long as the analyst is able to see less risky ways by which the opponent can defend his interests, war should not be perceived as imminent. While this rule is applicable in many cases, it may prove inadequate when the enemy believes that war is not too risky to his interests or that other means are futile. Thus in 1950 the Central Intelligence Agency (CIA), the Department of the Army, and the Far Eastern Command did not believe that the North Koreans intended to attack immediately. Secretary Acheson explained later that "the view was generally held that since the Communists had far from exhausted the potentialities for gaining their objectives through guerrilla and psychological warfare, political pressure and intimidation, such means would probably continue to be used rather than overt military aggression" (U.S. Congress, 1951, III, p. 1991; see also Spanier, 1965, p. 22).

Similarly the American intelligence community believed in 1973 that war made sense for the Arabs only in the absence of a viable political alternative for recovering their territory. Top U.S. officials were aware that Secretary of State Henry Kissinger in his talks with Israelis and Egyptians at the United Nations had arranged for preliminary talks on a settlement to begin in November 1973. Hence the existence of a political alternative, in addition to Israel's military superiority, made an Arab-initiated war seem implausible (Quandt, 1977, p. 168).

The second approach, *induction,* is the analytical process by which generalizations and judgments are made on the basis of observation. Intelligence estimates are largely the result of inductive processes. Induction commences when the analyst examines specifics and attempts to understand a situation in terms of its unique logic. Then he looks at the causes of the situation or its possible outcomes. He begins to perceive certain relationships in the data. For example, by looking at the enemy's behavior during periods of tension the analyst may generalize as to the necessary early warning indicators that should appear prior to a possible attack. Observing a number of such cases enables the analyst to progress from judging individual patterns to forming a more abstract concept. Obviously in the inductive process the analyst also draws heavily on general rules, yet these rules refer not to the entire situation but only to a small portion of it (Clauser and Weir, 1975, pp. 81–82; Heuer, 1980b, pp. 10–15; Stech, 1979, pp. 309–310).

The inductive process has its own weaknesses. It requires of the analyst an ability to understand the enemy's conceptual framework; it deals with a large number of uncertainties and ambiguous information; and it requires the analyst to cope with many unique events. A case in point is the formation of the American conception regarding Arab military capabilities, which exemplifies how a few observations may lead erroneously to a far-reaching generalization. According to the CIA's postmortem of the 1973 war, one reason for the U.S. analysts' belief that the Arabs would not initiate war was a passage in the *Arab-Israeli Handbook* of July 1973; the book, a joint effort of the CIA, INR, and the Defense Intelligence Agency, included a passage, reiterated and reinforced in discussions within the American intelligence community in early October 1973, that claimed that the Arab fighting man "lacks the necessary physical and cultural qualities for performing effective military services." The report commented:

> No preconceptions seem to have had a greater impact on analytical attitudes than those concerning relative Arab and Israeli military prowess. The June war was frequently invoked by analysts as proof of fundamental and perhaps permanent weaknesses in the Arab forces and, inferentially, of Israeli invincibility . . .
>
> There was, in addition, a fairly widespread notion based largely . . . on past performances that many Arabs, as Arabs, simply weren't up to the demands of modern warfare and that they lacked understanding, motivation, and probably in some cases courage as well. (*Pike Papers*, 1976, p. 20)

Induction and deduction complement each other. The analyst may use both approaches at various stages of the process. Each one forces the analyst to examine the evidence from a different perspective, and both are necessary if all relevant data are to be exploited. While induction is preferable for forming hypotheses concerning short-term developments, deduction is required for estimating long-range developments (Heuer, 1980b, p. 21A).

Analogies and Learning from History

A third kind of strategy used in the analytical process is *analogy*. In Chapter 4 I discussed some aspects of the use of analogies in the context of heuristics. Here we shall look at that strategy from a wider perspective, with emphasis on the process of learning from history. Analysts use analogies to form conceptions, to interpret information, to choose among hypotheses, and to understand the causes of a development and predict its outcome. Looking for analogies is perhaps the most natural procedure that comes to mind during the process of analysis and prediction. When analysts face unfamiliar developments they look around for a similar situation about which they already know something. If the two situations are sufficiently similar, the analysts may bypass the stage of analyzing the causes and identifying the variables of the new development and assume that its outcome will resemble that of the familiar situation.

When intelligence analysts seek analogies for international and military problems, they naturally draw on the lessons of the past. According to Jervis (1969, p. 246), three main sources contribute to an actor's conceptions of international relations and of other states and influence the level of his perceptual thresholds: his conceptions about his own domestic political system, his previous experience, and international history. I have already discussed aspects of the first source in terms of seeing with the eyes of the enemy. Personal experience will be touched on later in this chapter. The third and most important element is learning from history.

For the analyst history seems to be the main source of conceptions. As Jervis puts it, "What one learns from key events in international history is an important factor in determining the images that shape the interpretation of incoming information . . . Previous international events provide the statesman with a range of imaginable situations and allow him to detect patterns and causal links that can help him understand his world" (1976, p. 217).

In drawing historical analogies analysts make some implicit assumptions. They assume that the future will in some way resemble the past and that events that occurred in the past will occur again in the future. They assume also that the same factors and processes that caused an event in the past would bring about a similar outcome in the future, and that a trend that exists now will continue to exist at least for the foreseeable future. More specifically they assume that since the opponent has behaved in a certain manner in the past, he can be expected to behave in the same way under similar circumstances in the future (Clauser and Weir, 1975, pp. 297–298).

With these implicit assumptions the analyst starts by attempting to place the new situation within the context of his experience and knowledge in order to understand it. Then he specifies key elements in the current situation and seeks out historical precedents containing the greatest number of similarities to the current situation in order to shed light on it. When a past situation seems analogous, the analyst compares it item for item with the current situation; and if he finds the degree of correspondence satisfactory, he forecasts an outcome similar to the earlier one.[3]

There are significant problems inherent in the use of historical analogies. Learning from history is superficial and overgeneralized. According to Jervis, "People pay more attention to *what* has happened than to *why* it has happened." Because of a lack of sensitivity to the causes of past events and their restricted nature, "the lessons learned will be applied to a wide variety of situations without a careful effort to determine whether the cases are similar on crucial dimensions." The search for causes is usually quick and oversimplified. "When the decision-maker thinks he knows the causes of a previous outcome, he rarely takes the next steps of looking for other cases in which this variable was present to determine its influence in other situations or of trying to locate additional instances of the same outcome to see whether other causes could produce the same result" (1976, pp. 228–229). The analyst may observe a few similarities between a historical event and the present situation, and instead of making a thorough and systematic comparison he may end his investigation and assume that the two situations are analogous. In this way analysts ignore differences between present and past situations and apply analogies to a wide range of events far beyond any real justification. In some cases the points of similarity that seem convincing are not necessarily the ones that are relevant to producing the expected outcome. Even when the similarities are relevant, a difference that seems to be irrelevant may inhibit the anticipated outcome (Platt, 1957a, p. 153; Jouvenel, 1967, p. 85; Martino, 1972, p. 66; May, 1973, p. xi).

There are other reasons why learning from history can often be oversimplified and overgeneralized. We saw in Chapter 4, in regard to the availability heuristic, that learning takes place from major, dramatic events. Events that have made a strong and vivid impression can lead the analyst too quickly to perceive a new situation primarily in terms of its similarity to the historical precedent. Often analysts "see the present as like recent and dramatic events without carefully considering alternative models" or "trying to see what smaller and often less dramatic aspects of the past case can be used to help understand contemporary events" (Jervis, 1976, pp. 281–282).

Moreover, the analyst usually assumes that since the past event has had a certain outcome, it must in some way represent the normal behavior of the participants. With this assumption of normality, he can forecast an analogous outcome to the present situation. But the behavior of the participants in the past event was not necessarily "normal"; often there are many other outcomes that could just as plausibly have arisen from the initial conditions (Martino, 1972, p. 67).

Overgeneralization is also caused by the complexity of the subject matter and the biased sample of cases available for study (Jervis, 1976, p. 235). The complexity of international relations and of the internal political and military processes involved in a decision to go to war poses a serious stumbling block to the analyst. The sample of cases from which he learns is necessarily small, biased, or unrepresentative, and it is difficult to make the numerous comparisons required for a balanced analysis.

An additional factor pertains to the process by which analysts learn from history. Analysts, and especially policy makers, do not ordinarily examine a variety of analogies before selecting what seems to be the appropriate one to learn from. Rather they tend to seize on the first analogy that comes to mind and satisfactorily fits the present case. Yet it is difficult to distinguish a proper historical analogy from a poor one without an empirical test of its inference, and analysts and policy makers have few if any occasions to verify the appropriateness of lessons drawn; they rarely receive unambiguous evidence about its validity (Fischer, 1970, p. 257; May, 1973, p. xi; Jervis, 1976, p. 236).

Furthermore analysts, and particularly policy makers, tend to draw on events that they have experienced firsthand or that are particularly important to them. Involvement in a past situation will lead the person to see other cases as similar. An analyst who participated in a former intelligence failure or success can be expected to be overly influenced by that experience in making future estimates. Cases with which he is personally familiar will be recalled more easily. Yet lessons drawn from firsthand experience tend to be overgeneralized. The sample of such events is biased owing to the accidental or limited nature of personal experience (Jervis, 1976, pp. 235, 239, 270). As a result of these difficulties and biases, the analyst often runs the risk of drawing the wrong conclusions from historical analogies. He may see the world as more constant than it actually is. "Change is often regarded as incremental and, therefore, as something that can be handled by precepts based on the past; even rapid change is expected to follow lines regarded as normal in terms of the past" (Dror, 1971, pp. 4–5). This view makes a poor basis for anticipating such an abrupt change as an enemy attack.

Historical analogies, then, may have several distorting effects on the perception of an imminent attack. They tend to reduce alertness to early warning indicators. Perceiving a growing threat depends in part on observing extraordinary warning indicators. Yet very often the victim concludes that there is nothing new in the appearance of these indicators, since in the past they proved insignificant. For example, prior to the invasion of South Korea, North Korea moved its regular divisions close to the Demilitarized Zone and positioned them for attack. This development was not regarded by the Far East Command as a cause for alarm, since movement following this pattern had been observed in 1947, when the North Koreans had initiated an annual rotation of completely equipped units between the Thirty-eighth Parallel and rear areas (Ridgway, 1967, p. 14).

Analysts also attempt to understand the enemy's intention by looking at its history. Yet past behavior is often a misleading guide to future intentions. Thus in April 1941 the British Joint Intelligence Committee concluded that Germany would not have forgotten that its occupation of western Russia in 1918 had become a liability, and concluded that Germany must therefore know that another occupation of Russia would severely reduce the number of forces available for offensive use elsewhere (Hinsley, 1979, p. 456). Similarly Secretary Stimson assumed in late 1941 that American economic pressure would not bring Japan to initiate war because in 1919 President Woodrow Wilson had "got his dander up and put an embargo on all the cotton going to Japan and a boycott on her silk, with the result that she crawled down within two months and brought all her troops out from Siberia like whipped puppies" (Ben-Zvi, 1979, p. 101).

Analysts seek to learn not only from an enemy's history but also from their own, especially from constant historical factors. Until recently its physical separation from strong neighbors gave the United States the luxury of relative invulnerability to direct attack. America had never been attacked at home by an external enemy and had never been at war with Japan before Pearl Harbor. Yet Japan had been in a war with Russia in 1905, a fact that gave greater weight to the possibility of a Japanese attack on the Soviet Union in 1941. The case of Norway, a neutral country in a war-stricken continent, is even more striking. Before 1940 Norway had not been involved in a war for 125 years. In particular it had avoided participating in the First World War, relying on the policy of neutrality. As a historian Foreign Minister Koht was in many ways predisposed to let his expectations and assessments be conditioned by precedents. The British preventive attack on Copenhagen in 1807 constituted one such precedent to which he was very alert. This explains in part why he was much more attuned to the possibility of British aggression against his country than German aggression. Britain's failure to anticipate the German attack on Norway is also partially explained by its history. As an island power accustomed to taking the initiative in opening new fronts against the enemy, it tended to perceive the Germans not as independent actors but rather as reactors to Allied initiatives. Consequently Britain was not ready to view ambiguous evidence as indicating that Germany was preparing such a coup (Holst, 1966, pp. 35, 41).

These two examples involving long periods of peace bring us to the contrasting case—the impact of recent war. That war's effect on perceptual dispositions is especially important because of two distinct factors. First, many analysts and policy makers have had firsthand experience of war and have been affected by it. Many citizens too have participated in a war that has influenced their perceptual dispositions. In this way war contributes to the creation of "national images" of allies and adversaries, of participants' strengths and military capabilities, of the way they act and fight a war, and of the way the war is started. War is a dramatic and dominating event, and the analyst's attention is drawn to its most salient aspects. Because of its dramatic and even traumatic nature a recent war will distort the perception of a new threat. Winners of the last war may neglect the weaknesses of their conceptions, while losers may overemphasize them and be oversensitive to potential threats (Betts, 1977, p. 164).

For example, in 1956 Israel opened its attack on Egypt by dropping paratroopers deep into enemy territory thirty miles east of the Suez Canal, followed by a dash by a mobile column across southern Sinai. Subsequently the Egyptians thoroughly studied this Israeli war plan, expecting the next war to be carried out along similar lines. Israel's actions in 1967—especially the opening attack on Egyptian airfields and the concentration of the Israeli land effort in north-central Sinai— was thus completely unexpected, which caused Egypt's swift military collapse. The Egyptians seem to have ignored two factors, absent in 1967, that had caused Israel to act as it did in 1956: the paratroopers' operation and related moves were designed to give an excuse to the British and French to intervene in order to "protect" the Suez Canal; and the deployment of Egyptian forces in Sinai in 1956 was relatively thin compared to that of 1967.

The Egyptians were also influenced in 1967 by inapplicable lessons from another recent war—their intervention in Yemen between 1963 and 1967. As President Nasser's mouthpiece, Mohamed Hassanein Heikal, wrote later, the Egyptian military leadership overestimated its army's capabilities following its military operations in Yemen; it ignored the fact that "the military leadership that emerged in Yemen was one for limited operations, while the leadership required for the war against Israel was one of knowledge and capability of operating a division or a group of divisions and armies, on a large scale" (Al-Ahram, Cairo, June 21, 1968). General Salah al-Hadidi, former Director of Egyptian Military Intelligence, elaborated on this point later (Hadidi, 1972):

> The war in Yemen was conducted without giving the troops a clear picture of the battle. Their image of the war was one of punishment operations against tribes equipped with primitive arms . . . Air weapons, as weapons of supreme value, were neglected . . . The operations in Yemen were marked by extreme lethargy, both on our part and on the part of the tribes . . . Antiaircraft units were not used, and the troops were not dispersed in a way that would reduce their vulnerability . . . the success of the war in Yemen, where the Egyptians were operating at a distance of 2,000 miles from their home bases, taking control of most of the country, and winning almost all the battles— led to overconfidence in the troops and at headquarters at various levels, yet there was no proper understanding of the source of this overconfidence. Because of this arrogance, the Egyptian General Staff did not correctly estimate the possible political and military reactions of Israel.

A more striking example may be the wrong lessons Israel learned from its last war. Before the 1973 war the Israelis felt that their army was so superior to the Arabs' that for the Arabs to launch an attack would be sheer madness. This was not only an intelligence assessment; it was shared by the political and military leadership, both the coalition and opposition parties, and in fact almost everyone (Talmon, 1973). This assessment was based on the Six-Day War, the

War of Attrition between 1967 and 1970, and to a lesser extent the 1956 war, in which Israeli superiority was overwhelming. Yet several of the lessons that nourished this assessment were wrong. The Israeli victory in 1967 had been achieved very quickly, in part as a result of an early air strike and a surprise attack that caused the physical and mental collapse of the Egyptian military structure. Undoubtedly Israel would have gained the victory even without the surprise effect, probably within a few more days, but the swiftness of the Egyptian collapse led to an overestimation of the gap between the two armies. Nor was Israel's estimation of its military superiority undermined by the War of Attrition, in which the Egyptians failed to achieve their aims and were therefore forced to agree to a cease-fire. In its consideration of future strategy along the Sinai front, Israeli thinking was greatly influenced by the War of Attrition (Herzog, 1975, p. 276). Furthermore, in both the 1956 and 1967 wars Israel managed to surprise Egypt. It can be assumed that this factor, in addition to the successes and reputation of Israeli intelligence, created the feeling that Israel itself could not be surprised. Then too Israel fought the 1973 war with the weapons of the previous war. The effect of massive use of antitank and antiaircraft missiles by the Arab armies was not sufficiently recognized beforehand, for these missiles had not been employed on such a scale during the War of Attrition and in fact had never before been tested in major war conditions by any army.

Of course there are also cases where the lessons of the past should have been learned but were obscured by other factors and ignored. Thus the French refused to believe that the German blitzkrieg in Poland could be repeated in France. Although the French Deuxième Bureau was impressed by the rapidity with which German units could be brought into action, the Bureau claimed that certain strategic considerations were peculiar to the Polish operation (absence of frontier fortifications, a less than fully mobilized enemy, extreme superiority of German forces) and would not necessarily pertain elsewhere. Any operation against France would, the Bureau felt, be of a different character, even though there were in fact certain parts of the Western Front where similar tactics could be employed (Strong, 1970, p. 55). The problem is that there is no rule telling when and how the lessons of the last war should be learned.

Finally, the fact that historical analogies are both an important source of conceptions and a central element of the analytical process creates a kind of vicious circle. Because of the problematical and biased nature of learning from history, there is a good chance that

distorted or outdated conceptions will form a basis for present conceptions, which in turn will form a basis for future conceptions.
Such images tend to persist without being questioned, especially
when analytical reasoning combines with historical analogy. This
explains in part why the conceptions that Singapore and Hawaii
were impregnable fortresses and that the Ardennes were impassable
prevailed until they were refuted by surprise attacks.

Evaluating Incoming Information

Evaluating incoming information is a routine but vital part of the
intelligence research process. Usually an intelligence analyst reads
hundreds of items of information daily. Most are insignificant or
irrelevant to the problems occupying him; some he reserves for
possible later reanalysis. Only a few of them—up to several dozen—
are immediately evaluated. This procedure consists of two main
elements: evaluating the accuracy of the information and interpreting the information and analyzing its significance.

The accuracy of the information can be evaluated according to
several criteria. For one, the analyst attempts to verify the information according to the extent to which it is supported or refuted
by other information. The problem is that many pieces of information cannot be totally confirmed or rejected in this way. As a
result the analyst must turn again to his own conception of the
enemy's behavior and judge the accuracy of the information according to the extent to which it appears conceivable or sensible.
Not only is such a criterion subjective and inaccurate but it can also
be misleading.

After evaluating the accuracy of the information, the analyst attempts to interpret it and understand its significance. This process
can be described by the schema theory. The analyst starts by checking whether there already exists an explanation of the case indicated
by the information. If there is, then the new information is checked
to see if it adequately fits any of the specifications based on that
explanation. If it does, the new information is interpreted with the
help of the existing schema. If there is more than one explanation,
the analyst selects the one with the largest number of logically
independent reasons that reinforce the explanation. If the analyst
has no explanation that sufficiently supports the case, he scans his
memory for similar past events that might provide an explanation
for the new case. This search goes on until the analyst chooses the

past event most like the current situation (Axelrod, 1973; Shapiro and Bonham, 1973).

I have already explained the ways in which incoming information is treated. Here I shall discuss one vital aspect of the verification of incoming information—analysis of the source of the information. Evaluating information depends to a large extent on the analyst's attitude toward its source. The same information will be judged differently if it is provided through broadcast information, a human source, or signals intelligence. The range of the diversity of sources is very large; each has its own unique characteristics, its access to information, its quality and reliability, its strengths and biases, and its vulnerability to manipulation and deception.

Intelligence analysts usually consider separately the reliability of the source and the inherent credibility of the message; their final assessment rests on the evaluation of both factors. Yet there is a strong relationship between the two. There is considerable experimental evidence that the response to new information is related to the perceived credibility of the source, and that people pay more attention to information provided by trusted sources. When a source has high credibility, people generally accept the information and do not evaluate it critically. Conversely, if the source is considered untrustworthy or uninformed, the information may be ignored altogether or may be regarded as biased or incomplete. Consequently the greater the credibility of the source, the more willing people are to change their opinions in accordance with its contents. There is also a relationship between the quality and quantity of the information and the reliability of the source: the credibility of the source is more important when the content of the information seems to be questionable. The more limited the information, the greater is the emphasis placed on the credibility of the source.[4]

The problem of evaluating the reliability of the source is complicated. In most of our cases of surprise attack analysts refused to believe excellent sources, thereby rejecting information that would have warned them of imminent attack. Several factors influence the attitude of the analyst toward the source. The analyst tries to evaluate both the competence of the source and his access to accurate information, judged in the light of past experience. When a source has been wrong on one issue, the analyst's judgment of the source and his new information tends to be negative. But the criterion of prior accuracy is insufficient. Even an excellent source may have provided inaccurate or incorrect information in the past—which has nothing to do with the quality of his present information. And even poor or accidental sources may bring firsthand information. Analysts still reject information on the basis of its suspected source, however, and not on its merit.

Thus the best agent of the most effective Soviet espionage network during the Second World War provided a report by mid-June 1941 stating that "a general German attack on Russia would take place at dawn on June 22," and gave details of the army groupings and the primary objectives. That agent had previously been suspected in Moscow of being an Abwehr agent, owing to his insistence on the ambiguity of his own position and his consistent refusal to name his subsources. Only after the actual invasion did Stalin gain full confidence in his messages (Whaley, 1973, pp. 100-101).

The credibility of the source is also judged to a large extent on the basis of its presumed access to high-quality information and its ability to transfer it undistorted. Inevitably this means that the source's credibility depends also on the analyst's perception of its objectivity and motivations. The extent to which the source has a personal attitude toward or interest in the subject will affect its image of reliability. When the source is perceived to benefit from a change of policy resulting from its information, it may be discredited and its warning ignored. Also, conflict between the source and the analyst influences the latter's attitude toward the source.

Thus U.S. decision makers were skeptical of the report by the Indian ambassador to China, K. M. Panikkar, stating that the Chinese had threatened to enter the Korean War if U.N. forces crossed the thirty-eighth parallel partly because the ambassador was known to oppose American policy. In President Harry Truman's words, "Mr. Panikkar had in the past played the game of the Chinese Communists fairly regularly, so that his statement could not be taken as that of an impartial observer" (Truman, 1956, p. 362). Sometimes the discredited source suffers from the image of a whole group or nation. South Korean leaders frequently warned against the danger of a North Korean attack; yet their warnings were ignored because it was assumed that they were making a case for obtaining heavier military equipment to counter the North Korean acquisition of Soviet tanks. Moreover, in MacArthur's headquarters there was a tendency "to place minimum credence in Oriental agents and a feeling that South Koreans especially had a tendency to cry 'wolf' when there was no beast in the offing" (Ridgway, 1967, p. 14).

The credibility of a source, and thus the influence of later messages, is also diminished if an initial message is too contradictory to the analyst's beliefs. Thus before the Israeli attack in October 1956 the Egyptians received information about French-Israeli collaboration. "A Frenchman went to our embassy in Paris," recollects Heikal, "and was paid £1,000 for some information about the French-Israeli collusion, but when he returned a few days later and asked for £5,000 for more information about Israeli meetings and joint military planning, his tale was not believed and on orders from Cairo he was turned away as a crook" (Heikal, 1973, pp. 105–107).

Similarly the most important warnings of the impending German invasion of the Netherlands were provided by the Dutch military attaché in Berlin, Major Gijsbertus Sas. Sas's main subsource was his old friend Colonel Hans Oster, who happened to be the deputy chief of German counterintelligence. Yet Sas's superiors in The Hague did not trust Oster as a source. The more detailed the information Sas relayed, the more Oster's reliability was disputed. "Sas was almost recalled from his post when he persisted in vouching for his informant, particularly after reporting that this informant was also planning the assassination of Hitler—and had told him, a foreign attaché, about it. No one could imagine that such a Prussian officer in fact existed" (Mason, 1963, p. 557; see also Pearson and Doerga, 1978, p. 32).

Human sources are often aware that if their reports too greatly contradict their consumers' beliefs, they will not be accepted. This awareness may in turn lead them to distort their reports. Thus Leopold Trepper, the head of the Soviet "Red Orchestra" espionage network that operated in Germany during the Second World War, recollected years later: "The Director of Soviet Military Intelligence told me: We have more than enough agents in Germany. Yet, before they send their reports, they read the Soviet press thoroughly, and they would not dispatch anything which contradicts official policy. They do not inform us of anything which indicates that Hitler is preparing for an all-out war" (Ma'ariv, Tel-Aviv, February 14, 1975; see also Trepper, 1975, p. 73).

For some kinds of sources the analyst also has to ask himself whether the reports are part of the enemy's deception plan. The Dutch military leadership suspected a German trap in the Oster leaks (Mason, 1963, p. 564). And after the 1967 war the Egyptians partially attributed their being caught by surprise to misleading information transmitted to Egypt by its communist allies. Heikal claims that "the Israelis assumed, and rightly, that Egypt would trust the reports coming from the Soviet bloc and would doubt the validity of reports coming from the West, and therefore provided the Communists with false information" (Ben-Porat, 1973, p. 68). Even if Heikal is wrong about the Israeli deception, this example illustrates the problem the analyst faces in evaluating reports received even from friends.

The existence of an excellent source presents the opposite problem—namely overconfidence in its capabilities. Sometimes a few extraordinary sources are so reliable that the analyst assumes that if the opponent ever decides to go to war, these sources will know, and tell, about it. Consequently the analyst, certain that he will receive his warning in advance, is not alert to the possibility of war. Meanwhile, if the enemy is successful in concealing his war decision, the sources will not provide the expected warning. Thus before Pearl Harbor the Magic intercepts "provided only a steady undercurrent of background suspense" on the forthcoming attack; yet the knowledge of the existence of this excellent source provided a comfortable feeling that the Military Intelligence Division had its finger on the Japanese pulse and that it would thus learn of all of Japan's intentions (Wohlstetter, 1962, p. 300).

Another disadvantage of a good source is the tendency to place too great a reliance on that one particular source, especially—as happened before Pearl Harbor—when information from the source is handled separately from that of all other sources. The dependence on a single source keeps increasing as other less reliable sources are increasingly neglected. Thus before the Cuban missile crisis the capability of U-2 pictures to provide relatively firm evidence of military activity in Cuba made analysts less inclined to rely on agents' and refugees' reports for conclusions regarding Soviet activities and intentions. Washington had been receiving a flow of reports about nuclear installations in Cuba through refugee channels; yet the intelligence community treated this information with suspicion not only because it had been misled by Cuban refugees before but also because no one could be sure whether these sources could tell a surface-to-air from a surface-to-surface missile (Schlesinger, 1965, p. 800; George and Smoke, 1974, p. 474).

Choosing among Alternative Hypotheses

Selecting the preferred hypothesis is the aim of the intelligence analysis process. There is always more than one way to explain the enemy's intentions and behavior: the enemy may be planning to go to war now or in the distant future; he may be trying blackmail through a show of force; or he may just be strengthening his defense. Choosing among competing hypotheses provides the basis for operational decisions—whether to do nothing or to issue an intelligence warning or even take countermeasures.

Ideally the selection of a hypothesis should follow a long and systematic analysis: generating a full set of hypotheses and evaluating each of them; examining all relevant information; and choosing the hypothesis that best fits the evidence. Yet often this is not the case. In intelligence, because of pressures of time and by consumers, and because of various constraints and distortions, analysts tend to choose the first hypothesis that seems close enough rather than systematically examining all alternative hypotheses in order to determine which is best. Thus "the analyst identifies what appears to be the most likely hypothesis, that is, the tentative estimate, explanation, or description of the situation that appears most accurate . . . The careful analyst will then make a quick review of other possible hypotheses and of evidence not accounted for by the preferred judgment to ensure that he . . . has not overlooked some important consideration" (Heuer, 1980b, pp. 23a–24).

This approach of selecting a hypothesis involves several difficulties and distortions. As Heuer suggests, analysts generally concentrate on confirming a hypothesis rather than disconfirming hypotheses. Analysts do not naturally seek disconfirming evidence, and when such evidence is received, it tends to be discounted (Heuer, 1980b, pp. 26–27). Moreover, because of the tendency to assimilate information into preexisting conceptions, the development of alternative hypotheses is inhibited once a satisfactory interpretation or hypothesis is established. Thus a perception of a low probability of war may lead to a minimal effort to search for alternative explanations. The strengthening of Chinese forces in Tibet in 1962 was attributed by the Indians to China's effort to keep order and suppress the rebellion there. Nehru's basic belief that China would not attack India inhibited a search for alternative explanations even though the strength of the Chinese forces in Tibet was seen to exceed the requirements of policing tasks (Vertzberger, 1978a, p. 137).

The problem is complicated since in intelligence analysis there is no agreed-upon way to test and verify hypotheses. There are, however, some general rules for determining the *likelihood* of a hypothesis. The credibility of a hypothesis increases (1) when a consequence of the hypothesis is verified; (2) as the different means used to test the hypothesis support it; (3) as the observable bits of evidence that support the hypothesis are seen to bear some relationship to each other; (4) as the number of instances in which the hypothesis was supported increases; (5) when an incompatible or rival conjecture is refuted; (6) when it is consistent with another hypothesis that is highly credible; and (7) when it is simpler than other hypotheses supported by the same observables (Clauser and Weir, 1975, pp. 176–178). Yet these rules do not establish with certainty that a particular hypothesis is true. In intelligence analysis there is often no final proof of the truth of hypotheses. Sometimes even in retrospect there is no agreement as to which hypothesis proved true, and there is even less agreement in advance. The main criterion for establishing the validity of a hypothesis is whether it provides a plausible interpretation of incoming information without being clearly refuted by it.

Yet both the information and the enemy's behavior are usually too ambiguous to make this possible. In addition, since a large set of partially confirmed conceptions and guesses figures in interpreting information, it is possible to interpret it in many ways. As Jervis suggests, many psychological experiments indicate that people do not understand the inference process and the impact that their beliefs have on their interpretation of information. They often think that the facts have only one possible meaning, and they perceive information to be less ambiguous than it really is. Therefore they are overconfident of their hypotheses and prematurely exclude alternative hypotheses. As a result they often regard evidence that conforms to their hypotheses as disconfirming competing hypotheses. They tend to overlook the fact that evidence they regard as supporting their hypothesis may also be consistent with several alternative hypotheses. They cannot understand how other people can claim that the same event supports a different hypothesis. Hence they become increasingly intolerant of others' positions (Jervis, 1976, pp. 173, 182; Jervis, 1977, pp. 174–175).

In fact, given the ambiguity and deceptive potential that characterize information about a coming attack, there really is no way to determine objectively which hypothesis is the correct one. As Jervis (1976, pp. 176–179) remarks, when the information is so incomplete, the known facts are often best accounted for by an incorrect explanation, and the correct hypothesis is not supported by the main body of the evidence. For this reason those who were ultimately shown to be right may have been less reasonable, less open to new information, or less willing to modify their images than those who were proven wrong.

Unfortunately analysts have to face this problem of selecting a hypothesis or interpretation in almost every aspect of their analytical judgment. As Wohlstetter wrote about Pearl Harbor, "For every signal that came into the information net in 1941 there were usually several plausible alternative explanations, and it is not surprising that our observers and analysts were inclined to select the explanations that fitted the popular hypotheses" (Wohlstetter, 1962, p. 393). But is a better way of selecting interpretations available to these analysts? How are they to judge which interpretation is the most plausible?

To illustrate the dilemma let us refer once more to the cases of Pearl Harbor and the German invasion of Norway. In 1941 the Americans rejected rumors about a plan of attack on Pearl Harbor. Although the assessment proved wrong, this does not mean that that assumption was not logical. In fact the American judgment was consistent with Japanese judgment at this time, since the plan of attack of Admiral Isoroku Yamamoto, the Commander in Chief of Japan's Combined Fleet, was in direct contradiction to Japanese naval tactical doctrine (Wohlstetter, 1962, p. 386). In Norway Foreign Minister Koht was convinced that Germany would prefer a neutral Norway. The assumption, at least until the emergence of the possibility of Allied intervention in Norway, was not unreasonable. In the German armed forces, opinions were divided as to the advisability of the invasion; some considered it a wasteful and dangerous diversion from Hitler's main objective of a successful blitzkrieg in the West (Holst, 1966, pp. 38–41).

The case of "Barbarossa" illustrates even better the problem faced by analysts. In April 1941 the presence of massive German troop concentrations facing the Russian front was beyond doubt. Yet at the time these concentrations suggested at least four different hypotheses. (Whaley, 1973, pp. 223–225, 241).[5] Thus it was argued by some that Hitler intended to attack Russia regardless of Soviet military or political countermoves. In retrospect this was the case; but at the time this hypothesis was accepted only by those leaders who had a deep understanding of Hitler's basic intentions toward Russia and his peculiar style of action, and who could shake off the assumption that Hitler would not fight on two fronts. This was how Churchill suddenly grasped the meaning of German movements.

Alternatively some held that Hitler intended to attack only if

Russia refused to comply with his forthcoming ultimatum. This was Stalin's hypothesis. A third interpretation held that Hitler did not intend war but would use a military demonstration as a bluff to obtain further Russian concessions. This was British Foreign Secretary Anthony Eden's initial interpretation. Similarly the British Joint Intelligence Committee assumed as late as May 23 that Hitler was aiming at a new agreement with Russia that would provide Germany with the economic assistance required for a long war against the United Kingdom; the threat of force was intended to bring about this agreement (Churchill, 1950, p. 355).

Last, it was suggested that Hitler did not intend to attack Russia, at least not before England was defeated, but merely sought a defensive reinforcement of his eastern frontier in case Stalin decided to attack. This hypothesis was part of Hitler's deception plan to lull the Russians and was accepted by some of the British intelligence agencies until early June.

The problem analysts faced in this case was an extremely difficult one, since it had to take into account the ambiguous information and the possibility of an effort at deception by the enemy. All four hypotheses were plausible; most of the information could support any of them, while the remaining data could have been twisted to fit the chosen interpretation. In fact Stalin's ultimatum hypothesis may have best fitted the information then available to the Soviets, since it took into account or explained more of the relevant data—both genuine and false signals—than any of the other interpretations, including the correct one. In all fairness to Stalin one must mention that he shared this hypothesis with at least eighteen non-Russian observers, including British and American ministers and foreign ambassadors in Moscow (Whaley, 1973, pp. 241–242).

Why are analysts not willing to study information from different angles and in the context of unpopular as well as popular hypotheses? Sometimes they do. A good case in point is Churchill before "Barbarossa." But this process is quite rare and time-consuming. In the majority of cases the "most difficult mental act of all is to rearrange a familiar bundle of data, to look at it differently and escape from the prevailing doctrine." We have already noted that an analyst, having once formed an hypothesis, assimilates incoming information into this image rather than reorganizing all the information to support a new one. The nature of the intelligence information does not encourage him to reexamine the evidence from a different point of view. Mixed information, "which gives equal support to each of two opposing views, does not reduce confidence for holders of either view but instead reinforces confidence for holders of both views." Therefore, "it is common to find actors believing that strong evidence, if not proof, for their views is supplied by data that, they fail to note, also supports alternative propositions".[6] As De Rivera explains: "We take our perception of the world for granted . . . If someone else points out that our perceptions may be wrong we may intellectually admit the possibility, but we continue to act as though our perceptions were true . . . It is precisely in this feeling of certainty that the danger lies" (1968, p. 21).

Sometimes—especially in the early stages, when information is scarce—analysts and planners may avoid making the painful choice among hypotheses by describing the various hypotheses and letting the policy makers choose the most likely or appropriate one. Typically they will construct a spectrum of alternative scenarios leading from the present situation to the target event.

Constructing scenarios for an event has an advantage: it makes that event more readily imaginable and facilitates the understanding of the circumstances that may lead to it. Yet as Tversky and Kahneman (1973, pp. 229–230) argue:

> In evaluating the probability of complex events only the simplest and most available scenarios are likely to be considered. In particular, people will tend to produce scenarios in which many factors do not vary at all, only the most obvious variations take place, and interacting changes are rare . . . The tendency to consider only relatively simple scenarios may have particularly salient effects in situations of conflict. There, one's own moods and plans are more available to one than those of the opponent. It is not easy to adopt the opponent's view of the chessboard or of the battlefield . . . Consequently, the player may tend to regard his opponent's strategy as relatively constant and independent of his own moves. These considerations suggest that a player is susceptible to the *fallacy of initiative*—a tendency to attribute less initiative and less imagination to the opponent than to himself.

More important, even constructing a precise scenario of the attack does not provide any guarantee against surprise if it cannot overcome a firm belief that the opponent cannot or will not go to war. Thus the French held maneuvers in 1938 that exactly paralleled the actual German attack. Yet General Gamelin explained away that result with the supposition that in the real event adequate reserves would be available to plug the hole in the Ardennes. This supposition turned out to be erroneous after the Allies moved the reserve to the far left wing into Belgium (Betts, 1982, p. 30).

The case of Pearl Harbor is even more striking. In late 1937 Colonel Edward Markham, a White House adviser, was instructed to prepare a survey of Pearl Harbor's defenses. In the conclusion of his report Markham wrote: "War with Japan will be precipitated without notice. One of the most obvious and vital lessons of history is that Japan will pick her own time for conflict . . . If and when hostilities develop between the United States and Japan, there can be little doubt that the Hawaiian islands will be the initial scene of action" (Rich, 1981, p. 47). On March 31, 1941, the Commander of the Naval Base Defense Air Force and the Commander of the Hawaiian Air Force prepared an estimate in the event of a sudden hostile action against Hawaii. The outline of possible enemy action as set forth in the estimate was a startling harbinger of what actually occurred: "It appears that *the most likely and dangerous form of attack on Oahu would be an air attack.* It is believed that at present such an attack would most likely be launched from one or more carriers which would probably approach inside of 300 miles . . . Any single submarine attack might indicate the presence of a considerable undiscovered surface force *probably* composed of fast ships accompanied by a carrier."

As if that were not enough, even the exact timing of the attack was predicted. On April 1, 1941, the Chief of Naval Operations sent a dispatch to the commandants of all naval districts saying, "Past experience shows the Axis powers often begin activities in a particular field on Saturdays and Sundays or on national holidays of the country concerned." Naval intelligence personnel were therefore advised to "take steps on such days to see that proper watches and precautions are in effect." And on August 20, 1941, the Commander of the Hawaiian Air Force wrote to the commanding general of the Army Air Force, "The early morning attack is, therefore, the plan of action open to the enemy" (U.S. Congress, 1946a, pp. 84–85, 89–90). The attack, of course, took place at dawn on Sunday, December 7.

External Obstacles to Perception

Judgmental biases, the persistence of conceptions, the way information is interpreted to fit them, and distortions in the analytical process seem to be the main causes of misperception of war signals. Yet in most cases other obstacles have been involved as well. These derive not from the analyst's set of beliefs or logical processes but from external factors that increase the noise, thus making it difficult to extract the signals. The obstacles we shall consider are deception, preoccupation with other issues, and accidental factors.

Deception and Surprise

The issue of the enemy's role in causing strategic surprise, mainly by deception, calls for a comprehensive study in itself; in this context, however, it must be dealt with briefly. In most cases of strategic surprise the enemy's own activities, and particularly planned deception, account for some part of the surprise effect. In the case of "Barbarossa" there were at least sixty-seven known German documents concerning deception planning (Whaley, 1973, pp. 247–266). Similar evidence exists in the cases of Pearl Harbor and the Yom Kippur attack.

Strategic deception is aimed at manipulating and distorting the perception of reality held by the opponent's policy makers and analysts in order to project a desired image and achieve strategic advantages. According to Daniel and Herbig, any deception has three goals: "The immediate aim is to condition a target's beliefs; the intermediate aim is to influence the target's actions; and the ultimate aim is for the deceiver to benefit from the target's actions" (1982, p. 5).

Generally the enemy tries to deceive his victim in two complementary ways. First he seeks to reduce the number of true signals and keep them quiet—that is, to conceal and disguise evidence about the forthcoming attack. Thus the Japanese security system was an important and successful block to perception; it was able to limit knowledge about the attack only to those closely associated with details of the planning. In the Japanese Cabinet only the Prime Minister and the Navy Minister knew of the plan before the task force left its final point of departure. Moreover, the Japanese Navy's detailed war plan was issued in seven hundred copies, giving full details of the attack on the Philippines, Malaya, and so on, but pointedly deleting the Pearl Harbor missions of the submarine scout advance force and the attack and destroy task force, stating only that they would be included among units that "will operate against the American Fleet." This most sensitive part of the order was communicated verbally, and then only to a very limited number of senior officers (Whaley, 1969, p. 249).

In fact, the attacker's success in concealing his preparations for war can never be complete. There is no known case in which the victim had no warning indicators at all. (The only possible exception since 1939 is probably the dropping of the A-bomb on Hiroshima.) Thus an improved collection effort by the potential victim may reduce the risks of this kind of deception.

Hence a major effort is needed on the part of the attacker to increase noise in order to deceive the victim and divert his attention from the warning signals. There are two ways to distort the meaning of the signals. The first is to increase the ambiguity of the true signals or to produce signals that suggest a nonthreatening explanation, such as large-scale routine maneuvers or overall defensive posture; in both these cases it is very difficult to discriminate between true and false signals until it is almost too late.

Thus orders for the German deception plan for "Barbarossa" stated, "The troop movement for Barbarossa is to be seen as the greatest deception operation in the history of war, intended as a cover-up for the final preparations for the invasion of England . . . the troops deployed in the east are to be kept as long as possible under the impression that this was simply conceived as a deception, that is, as defensive rear cover for the forthcoming blow against England" (Whaley, 1973, p. 248). At the same time, the "Barbarossa" preparations were presented as a defensive measure against Russia, either in response to Russia's reinforcement of its frontier or as a precaution during Germany's advance into the Balkans (Hinsley, 1979, p. 463).

A second approach aims at leading the victim to place his confidence in a specific wrong direction by increasing the number of false signals and reducing their ambiguity. Thus before the 1956 Sinai war Israel successfully created a strong impression, by leaking rumors and threats, that it was going to move militarily against Jordan rather than Egypt. The attacker may also alter those aspects of his behavior that he believes to be closely observed in order to project an incorrect image. Thus to mask their intentions the North Koreans momentarily adopted a more conciliatory posture before their attack on South Korea, halting their border raids and issuing "peace proposals" that called for a single national election (Leckie, 1962, pp. 11, 40–41).

An attacker may plan an attack that in terms of time, place, and method is expected by his victim while seeking to achieve surprise by changing, through deception, the victim's expectations. Or the attacker may choose to reinforce his victim's beliefs while planning an attack at a different time and place and using a different method. As Heuer suggests, because of people's tendencies to perceive what they expect to perceive and to assimilate incoming information to existing conceptions, "it is far easier to lead a target astray by reinforcing the target's existing beliefs, thus causing the target to ignore the contrary evidence of one's true intent, than to persuade a target to change his . . . mind" (Heuer, 1981a, pp. 298–299). Of course this requires familiarity with the victim's conceptions and a correct appreciation of his perception of normalcy. Thus in 1973 the Egyptians were aware of Israel's belief that the Arab armies were militarily inferior and that the Arab leaders were reluctant to go to war. Consequently the Egyptian deception plan aimed at strengthening these assumptions (Yasri, 1974, pt. 9).

The enemy's use of deception offers the analyst an easy and acceptable explanation since almost any evidence can be rationalized to fit the deception hypothesis (Heuer, 1981a, p. 314). But it is very difficult for analysts to identify signals as the result of a deliberate deception plan. For one thing, there is usually no reliable information reporting the existence of a deception plan. Only a few people in the enemy camp are familiar with the existence of such a plan. Unlike military preparations for war, the implementation of a deception operation does not require the participation of many people; and most of the participants are not aware that they are engaged in deception.

It is almost impossible for the analyst to prove the existence of a strategic deception, in part because it concerns intangible matters such as intentions or motives. The analyst tries to impose reason and order on the incoming signals. Yet adopting the deception explanation too often will undermine the credibility of the analyst, because he will not be able to test and prove this hypothesis; all he can do is introduce another source of uncertainty into his estimate (Feer, 1980, p. 145; Epstein, 1980, p. 128).

Heuer notes also that alertness to the possibility of deception can influence the degree of the analyst's receptivity to new information and may prompt a more careful review of the evidence. Sometimes, though, increased alertness may be of no value, as it leads the analyst to be more skeptical of all the evidence. "If deception is not present, increased alertness may predispose an analyst to perceive it erroneously. If deception is present, and if the deceiver's goal is to exploit and reinforce one's preconceptions, heightened alertness may lead the analyst to dismiss the wrong evidence" (Heuer, 1981a, p. 320).

Although deception may contribute to surprise, it is nevertheless usually not a primary cause of surprise. In some of our surprise attack cases deception had no effect at all, or its effect was merely tactical (Hinsley, 1979, p. 440; Levran, 1980, p. 19; Laqueur, 1985, pp. 286–291). In a few cases—such as "Barbarossa"—deception played an important role in strengthening existing erroneous beliefs, but in none of the cases did deception create erroneous conceptions.

Preoccupation with Other Issues

In many cases of strategic surprise an attack occurs when the intelligence community or the decision makers are preoccupied with other issues. This reduces their ability to read the war signals in two significant ways.

First, the focus on another issue serves to distract or lessen the attention that should be given to the possibility of war. Thus during the last week before Pearl Harbor the U.S. government was absorbed with the Atlantic and European battle areas. President Roosevelt himself was so deeply interested in the European situation that he left Far Eastern matters almost entirely to Secretary of State Hull. Compared to Germany's war machine the threat of Japanese attack seemed remote and manageable. Far East information itself was only a small part of a huge body of data that concerned primarily European affairs. Interest in Europe rather than the Far East also characterized public opinion, as evidenced in the press and polls (Wohlstetter, 1962, pp. 230, 278).

Similarly before the 1956 war Nasser was preoccupied with the outcome of the nationalization of the Suez Canal and could pay little attention to the possibility of an Israeli attack. During the week before the 1973 war Israeli leaders were preoccupied with an attack by Palestinian guerrillas on a train carrying Russian Jewish immigrants into Austria. The Israeli Prime Minister left for Europe to deal with the issue and came back to Israel only three days before the war.

Second, whenever the preoccupying issue is the possibility of another war, background noise is increased and may consequently result in a misreading of the signals of the actual impending attack. Thus before April 9, 1940, both the Allies and Germany showed unmistakable interest in Norway's orientation in the war. The warning signals concerning Allied intentions to intervene in Norway had been fairly unambiguous and frequent, consistently pointed in one direction, and accorded with the prevailing expectations of Norwegian leaders. In contrast the messages concerning German preparations seemed less reliable. They did not condition expectations over a prolonged period, and most important they coincided in time with the acceleration of the warning indicators concerning Allied intentions. Consequently the Norwegians assumed that the main danger lay in an Allied attempt to provoke Norway into entering the war on their side, an effort that might cause Germany to retaliate against Norway. The German threat was consequently considered coincidental to the Allied threat, and the Norwegians were quite unresponsive to signals indicating that the Germans were getting ready for preemption (Holst, 1966, pp. 37–39).

Accidental Factors

Finally, as Wohlstetter notes, "In intelligence work the role of chance, accident and bad luck is always with us" (1965, p. 705). A whole series of accidental shortcomings and mistakes played a role in the case of Pearl Harbor. Before the attack it was bad luck that the United States had cut all traffic on the Northwest Passage to Russia, thereby rendering visual observation of the Pearl Harbor task force impossible. It was bad luck that there was a radio blackout in Hawaii on the morning of December 7. And it was bad luck that the pursuit officer at the interception control board in Pearl Harbor at the moment of the attack was an inexperienced lieutenant who later testified: "I did not know what my duties were. I just was told to be there and told to maintain that work" (Wohlstetter, 1962, p. 12).

Moreover, on the morning of December 7 it was learned from a message decoded by Magic that the two Japanese diplomats negotiating with the American administration in Washington had been directed to submit an ultimatum to the United States at exactly 1 P.M. Eastern Standard Time. Intelligence analysts recognized that the specified time in Washington was sunrise in Hawaii and surmised that a dawn attack might be launched. Hence the chiefs of the Army and Navy decided to send out a last-minute warning to Hawaii and other U.S. bases, ordering them to be on the alert for a massive attack. If the warning had been radioed promptly, it would have given Hawaii two hours' advance warning; but Army Chief of Staff General George Marshall chose not to use his scrambler telephone to inform Hawaii. Unfortunately the War Department radio was unable to contact Army headquarters in Hawaii because the office was not open that Sunday morning. Two other direct radio communications to Hawaii were available and were used by both the Navy and the FBI. But the message-center signal officer did not know that the message was urgent because General Marshall in his haste had neglected to mark it as such. So the message was routinely sent by Western Union. It arrived in Honolulu at 7:33 A.M. and was still in the hands of the messenger, who was delivering it by mo- torbike to Army headquarters, when the bombs started to explode (Janis, 1972, p. 233; Rich, 1981, p. 50).

Finally, one of the most unfortunate circumstances attending the handling of the Magic intercepts was the fact that several significant Japanese messages were not translated until after the attack. One of them, dated December 2 but not translated until December 30, was sent from Tokyo to Honolulu: "In view of the present situation, the presence in port of warships, airplane carriers, and cruisers is of utmost importance . . . Wire me in each case whether or not there are any observation balloons above Pearl Harbor . . . Also advise me whether or not the warships are provided with antimine nets." An- other message from the Japanese Consul General in Honolulu, dated December 6 and translated December 8, spoke about the balloon defense in the vicinity of Pearl Harbor: *"I imagine that in all prob- ability there is considerable opportunity left to take advantage for a surprise attack against these places"* (U.S. Congress 1946a, pp. 229–230). Similar accidental factors can be found in other cases; on the whole, though, it is clear that the weight of these factors is relatively small. Surprise is not accidental.

Changing a View

Choosing among competing hypotheses is the last stage of the an- alytical process, but it is not a final one. The analytical process never stops; conceptions and views may develop and change. The discus- sion in Chapter 4 of the persistence of beliefs and the way infor- mation is fitted into hypotheses brings us to the conclusion that, for the analyst to change his views—in our case with regard to the probability of imminent war—though not impossible is a very slow process and one in which time may prove decisive. Images are vul- nerable to specific events or to new and striking information, but they may not change until it is too late. On October 5, 1973, a day before the Egyptian-Syrian attack, Israeli intelligence began to consider more seriously the possibility that war was imminent. The reasons for this change in attitude were the arrival of new and irrefutable reports and perhaps the suspicious and inexplicable fact that the families of Soviet advisers in Egypt and Syria were being airlifted out. Yet this change in attitude remained embryonic until too late. Had the Arab attack come three or four days later, it is possible that it would not have been a surprise.

The difficulty of changing views is partly attributable to the way early warning indicators evolve. Since it rarely takes a single striking signal to assure the analyst that war is imminent, "we must wait for a number of signals to converge in the formulation of a single hypothesis about the intentions and actions of an opponent. This is a necessary but slow process" (Wohlstetter, 1965, p. 695).

The main problem has to do with the persistence of the analyst's conceptions and the way he perceives and treats incoming information. I have suggested that erroneous conceptions are not often changed through mere exposure to new evidence. Usually the gradual addition of small amounts of contradictory information is not likely to produce a significant conceptual change since the information will be fitted into existing conceptions or dismissed by one of the mechanisms discussed in Chapter 4. At a certain stage, however, even these mechanisms may fail to deal with information that challenges the prevailing conception. At that stage the analyst may recognize an incongruity between the conception and some new evidence. When this occurs, a process of gradual changes must be initiated. Thus new evidence that appears consistently contrary to the analyst's conceptions may produce change, albeit at a slower rate than would result from an unbiased view of the evidence (Ross, 1977, p. 374).

One general principle underlies this process of change. Analysts and policy makers attempt to change as few of their beliefs and conceptions as possible. Those revisions that are made to accommodate new evidence are often local in scope and minimal in character. If analysts can explain most occurrences to their own satisfaction with minor changes in their existing conceptions, they will rarely feel the need for drastic revision of these conceptions. Moreover, if information is so contradictory that it cannot be ignored, they will first revise peripheral beliefs—that is, "those beliefs that are least important, that are supported by the least information, and that are tied to fewest other beliefs" (Jervis, 1976, p. 291).[7] Analysts will try above all to preserve those conceptions that are central to their entire belief system, for changing peripheral beliefs does not set off as large a chain reaction of additional changes required to reestablish consistency as does changing basic beliefs.

Yet when these minimal changes are still unable to account for the discrepant information, more far-reaching changes are required. If even widespread changes in peripheral beliefs are not sufficient, then the central beliefs themselves must change, setting off a series of further changes. In this case the decision to reject a conception is simultaneously a decision to accept another, and the judgment leading to that decision involves comparing both conceptions with the evidence and with each other. Once the analyst realizes "that the idea he has accepted contradicts many other things he believes, the same dynamics that protected the old concept will spread the implications of the new one by altering subsidiary beliefs" (Jervis, 1976, pp. 304–305, 291; see also Kuhn, 1970, p. 77).

Rejection of the old conception and emergence of the new one is a painful process, and no one can tell in advance when the shift may take place. In science, as Kuhn describes it, "sometimes the shape of the new paradigm is foreshadowed in the structure that extraordinary research has given to the anomaly . . . More often no such structure is consciously seen in advance. Instead, the new paradigm, or a sufficient hint to permit later articulation, emerges all at once, sometimes in the middle of the night, in the mind of a man deeply immersed in crisis" (1970, pp. 89–90).

A similar process may take place in the course of intelligence analysis. The change in the American view during the Cuban missile crisis is a typical example. In 1962 General Joseph Carroll, Director of the Defense Intelligence Agency, became suspicious of Soviet activities in Cuba on the basis of several pieces of data from different sources. He "had had thousands of reports like this. What gradually formed in his mind was a hypothesis based on the integration of three or four pieces of evidence . . . Gradually over a period of time . . . sometime between the 18th of September and the 14th of October, there was formulated in his mind a hypothesis specifically that there was the possibility of a Soviet ballistic missile installation in a particular area" (Wohlstetter, 1965, pp. 695–696).

When the analyst's conception concerns the threat of war, the process of change is usually gradual and often incomplete. In his attempt to maintain the core of his conception in the face of discrepant evidence, the analyst may modify some of its components.

First, when the existing conception becomes insufficient to answer the questions raised, he may begin to broach the probability of war. Thus late at night on October 4, 1973, the Israeli evaluation began to change under the impact of accumulating evidence, and "the red lights lit up one after the other." During the night Defense Minister Dayan's perception of the probability of war was strengthened, especially when he received news of the exit of Soviet advisers' families from Egypt and Syria. To a smaller extent the Director of Israeli Military Intelligence also brought up the probability of war. He was quoted later as having said on the morning of October 5: "I think that Israel is not going to war. But the situation today is fraught with more question marks than yesterday" (Brecher, 1980, pp. 76, 183, 192).

When war has been considered only a long-range possibility, strong contradictory evidence may force the analysts to shorten that range. Thus in 1928 the British Committee of Imperial Defense recommended that it should be assumed for the purpose of framing estimates that there would be no major war for ten years and that this assumption should be reviewed annually. After the Japanese intervention in Manchuria this assumption was abandoned in 1932, when it became clear that Britain might find itself at war with Japan not in ten years but in ten days. Yet this assumption had already had a far-reaching effect on Britain's ability to rearm, since many of the great industrial firms had resorted to the production of goods for civilian consumption (Kirby, 1957, pp. 8, 11, 452). Ultimately this change in view was in any case insufficient to prevent a surprise attack in Singapore.

It is common knowledge that in the face of disturbing evidence analysts may change their minds concerning small-scale military actions while still not foreseeing all-out war. Thus on September 30, 1973, an American intelligence memorandum concluded that "the political climate in the Arab States argues against a major Syrian military move against Israel at this time. The possibility of a more limited Syrian strike . . . cannot, of course, be excluded." And on October 4 another memorandum concluded; "We continue to believe that an outbreak of major Arab-Israeli hostilities remains unlikely for the immediate future, although the risk of localized fighting has increased slightly" (U.S. Congress, 1975, p. 641).

Two examples illustrate the process of conceptual change. An examination of the American intelligence estimates formulated during the critical weeks before the major Chinese offensive into Korea on November 25, 1950, reveals a gradual change of view with regard to Chinese intentions. This change, in response to deeply disturbing evidence, was only partial and came too late to prevent the surprise. In early September General Charles Willoughby, MacArthur's intelligence officer, played down the possibility of Chinese intervention; the Chinese, he argued, were sensible and would keep out of the Korean affair. On October 12, after China began concentrating large forces in Manchuria, the CIA produced a somewhat less reassuring estimate of Chinese intentions. It granted that the Chinese had the capability for effective intervention but held that such intervention would not necessarily be decisive. It saw no convincing indication that the Chinese intended to resort to a full-scale entry into the war and concluded that Chinese intervention was not probable in 1950. On October 20 the CIA slightly revised its estimate and, abandoning the earlier hypothesis that the Chinese threat of intervention was a bluff, suggested that the Chinese were interested in nothing more than setting up a buffer zone near the Yalu.

Since October 25 dozens of Chinese soldiers had been captured by U.S. forces, but they were believed to be reinforcements for North Korean troops. The U.N. report covering the period of October 16–31 in mentioning the capture of Chinese prisoners said there was no positive evidence that Chinese units as such had entered Korea. On November 3 the Far East Command estimated that 16,500 Chinese troops were in contact with U.N. forces and that total Chinese forces might possibly number 34,000. On the same day the Joint Chiefs of Staff dispatched a message to MacArthur expressing their concern over the "overt intervention in Korea by Chinese Communists units." MacArthur replied the next day, stating that while this was a "distinct possibility . . . there are many fundamental logical reasons against it and significant evidence has not yet come to hand to warrant its immediate acceptance." General Willoughby said at that time that the great number of Chinese divisions identified in North Korea might have been only elements of divisions, not full divisions. Yet on November 6 a CIA estimate concluded vaguely that with their entry into Korea the Chinese were risking not only some of their forces but also their prestige in Asia. It had to be taken into account, the CIA held, that the Chinese knew what was at stake—in other words that they were ready for a general war. MacArthur himself sent a report on November 7 saying: "Unquestionably . . . *organized units* of CCF (Chinese Communist Forces) have been and are being used against U.N. Forces . . . Such forces will be used and increased at will" (Appleman, 1961, pp. 762, 764). Two days later he expressed a more optimistic view, writing that the Chinese would not intervene in full force and, in the event that they did so, his air force would destroy them.

By mid-November American estimates had gradually advanced another step. American leaders were now less certain that the Chinese objective was limited to creating a buffer zone near the Yalu. A National Security Council meeting of November 9 considered the possibility that the Chinese intention was to impose a war of attrition on U.S. forces in South Korea; the possibility that China would opt for a more ambitious attempt to drive U.N. forces completely out of the peninsula seemed less likely. On November 24, on the eve of the full Chinese offensive, the CIA produced its most sober estimate. It stated that the Chinese would at the very least increase their operations in Korea and that they would seek to immobilize U.N. forces, subject them to attrition, and maintain the semblance of a North Korean state. The estimate, which came too late to serve as a warning, "stopped short of attributing to the Chinese the intention of trying to drive U.N. forces out of Korea" (George and Smoke, 1974, pp. 211–212).[8]

The British estimate of German intentions prior to "Barbarossa" underwent an even more striking change. In fact it presents one of the few cases of a complete and timely change of opinion. Until March 1941 Churchill accepted the British intelligence assessment that war between Germany and Russia was very unlikely. British intelligence was aware of the extensive German troop movements to the Balkans; but a number of factors, such as continued German air attacks on Britain and the evidence of war supplies being sent from Russia to Germany, combined to make everyone believe that Hitler and Stalin would reach an agreement. On March 26 intelligence intercepted from Enigma, the German cipher machine, indicated that three of the five panzer divisions moving toward Greece and Yugoslavia had been rerouted to Poland just after Prince Paul of Yugoslavia had agreed to adhere to the Tripartite Pact concluded between Germany, Italy, and Japan, and were then sent quickly back to the Balkans again when Yugoslavia revolted against the agreement. "To me it illuminated the whole Eastern scene like a lightning flash," said Churchill. "The sudden movement to Cracow of so much armour needed in the Balkan sphere could only mean Hitler's intention to invade Russia in May . . . The fact that the Belgrade revolution had required their return to Rumania involved perhaps a delay from May to June." Churchill immediately arranged for a warning to be sent to Stalin (Churchill, 1950, p. 357; see also Hinsley, 1979, pp. 451–452).

In fact this illuminating report was not all that unambiguous. It confirmed that German tanks were needed in Poland—but for what purpose? Why not assume, as Stalin did, that German demands would precede an attack? Or, as Eden felt, that Hitler was bluffing? Of course one has to remember that Churchill was not bound, as Stalin was, by the belief that Hitler would not invade Russia before defeating England. As early as June 1940 Churchill wrote to Prime Minister Jan Smuts of South Africa: "If Hitler fails to beat us here, he will probably recoil eastward" (1949, pp. 227–228). In any case it took Churchill a couple of months to change his view.

The British intelligence agencies were even more hesitant than Churchill. On March 30 some of the agencies concluded that the Enigma evidence pointed to the possibility of some large-scale operation against Russia, "either for intimidation or for actual attack." Yet later Military Intelligence (MI) showed signs of wavering, and on April 16 it claimed that it was impossible to tell whether the rumors about a German invasion of Russia had any solid basis. MI's position was undecided until May 23 when, on the basis of the Engima evidence, it ceased to hesitate. Although it admitted that German preparations might be intended only to intimidate Russia, it concluded that they pointed to a decision to "satisfy German military requirements by occupying western USSR." Still MI remained undecided as to whether Germany's object was to attack Russia or to frighten it into submission to German demands. "Fundamentally this was because it could not bring itself to accept that an attack would make sense" (Hinsley, 1979, pp. 451, 457, 466, 469).

By the beginning of June it was agreed by most British intelligence agencies that Germany might be planning a surprise invasion of Russia. A special estimate issued on May 31 surveyed the Enigma intelligence to that date:

> It becomes harder than ever to doubt that the object of these large movements of the German army and air force is Russia ... There is everywhere the same steady eastward trend. Either the purpose is blackmail or it is war. No doubt Hitler would prefer a bloodless surrender. But the quiet move, for instance, of a prisoner-of-war cage to Tarnow looks more like business than bluff. It would no doubt be rash for Germany to

become involved in a long struggle on two fronts. But the answer may well be that the Germans do not expect the struggle with Russia to be long.

Finally on June 7 British intelligence concluded that there was little doubt that Germany was planning a "very large-scale operation against Russia" (Hinsley, 1979, p. 474).

Three reasons seem to account for this rare change of assessment. First, the basis for the change was a combination of highly reliable indicators and numerous inexplicable developments that moved the British gradually to question their former hypothesis. A second factor was the analysts' own prejudices. Earlier I suggested that Stalin had rejected the idea of an imminent German invasion because he was committed to his treaty with Germany. Churchill's judgment was free of such a commitment. Indeed he hoped for a German attack against Russia and looked for evidence that might indicate it. Third, what had prevented the British until March–April 1941 from understanding that Hitler was going to attack Russia was the rival conception that Hitler was planning to invade the British Isles and would not risk war on two fronts. This theory underwent a substantial change by April, which facilitated the change of the hypothesis with regard to "Barbarossa."

Thus after October 1940 British intelligence began slowly and cautiously to surmise that Hitler might have postponed his plan to invade Britain. Despite the conflict of evidence and the absence of indicators that the invasion had been abandoned, by October British intelligence had changed the formula used in its reports from "invasion could come at any time" to "situation unchanged: no indication that a decision to invade has been taken." On October 10 the Joint Intelligence Committee concluded that while the danger of invasion would remain as long as Germany had numerical superiority in the air, a number of new factors—the enemy's failure to win the air battle, the shortening days, the worsening weather, and the growing strength of the British defenses—were now combining to make invasion a "hazardous" undertaking. "The assessments were based on operational considerations, rather than on intelligence indications, and the operational authorities were not so confident" (Hinsley, 1979, pp. 189–190).

On January 10, 1941, Hitler again postponed the invasion, for the last time; but British intelligence continued to believe that invasion was still Germany's main objective. On that date the Combined

Intelligence Committee still thought that the invasion would come as soon as the Germans had achieved air superiority. "Since photographic reconnaissance and Sigint showed the Germans to be still engaged in invasion exercises, these were understandable conclusions, and this was all the more the case because there were occasional reports of Germany's intentions from other sources that could not easily be ignored." Only on April 27 did the Joint Intelligence Committee concede that the danger had declined (Hinsley, 1979, pp. 261–264).

Keeping these examples in mind, one can easily see the great difficulties involved in reversing a hypothesis, especially when the time between the decision to go to war and its actual outbreak may be no longer than several days, as in the case of the Six-Day War. There is no magic formula that can tell an analyst when to revise his hypotheses and in what direction; surprise can result from a change of opinion in the wrong direction. As we have seen, during the spring and summer of 1973 Defense Minister Dayan's evaluation changed from a perception of high probability of war—his instructions to the General Staff on May 21 were, "Gentlemen, please prepare for war . . . in the second half of this summer"—to a perception of only a remote threat—on July 30 he stated, "The next ten years will see . . . no major war" (Brecher, 1980, pp. 62–63).

PART THREE

The Environment

6

The Analyst and the Small Group

The intelligence analyst is never a lone hand. His conceptions are inextricably interwoven with those of other people around him. His participation in a larger organization must influence his hypotheses, his way of thinking, and his conclusions. The environment within which the analyst operates, though it may have some positive impact on his judgment, is inevitably a major source of misperceptions.

In this chapter we will look at the small group within which the analyst works. Decision makers usually operate within a group made up of other decision makers, advisers, and experts. Intelligence analysts are a part of a somewhat larger group of analysts—colleagues, superiors, and subordinates—whose job it is to produce a collective assessment or warning. A strong interdependency and a close and stable relationship exist among the members of these small groups; each member depends on the others for his assumptions and conceptions in a variety of ways (Cohen, 1964, pp. 100–101). This dynamic has a considerable impact on the manner in which the enemy's behavior and the potential for war are perceived.

Working in a small group may have a positive influence on the accuracy of the analyst's judgments. The group may broaden his perspective, allow him to take into account new and formerly unfamiliar points of view and reconsider questionable hypotheses and assessments. Members of the group contribute vital knowledge, expertise, and experience to the analytical process. The group affords the individual the opportunity of looking at the same evidence from diverse viewpoints, acquiring additional evidence essential to his assessments, and testing the validity of his assumptions. Discussions within a small group may expose the weak points of arguments presented by individual members; an analyst's erroneous judgment may even be corrected. In general it can be said that the deliberations within the small group are a vital part of the analytical and decision-making processes.

Yet membership in a group also has some inevitable and serious drawbacks. Let us consider how group dynamics may contribute to the failure to anticipate a surprise attack.

The Other Opinion

In most of our cases of surprise attack, despite the final collective assessment that war was unlikely, some dissenting opinions had in fact been voiced. Before the Chinese invasion of northern India, for instance, senior Indian officers had warned Delhi that a continuation of its "forward policy" of establishing posts and showing presence in territories claimed by China would risk a military confrontation detrimental to India (Vertzberger, 1978a, p. 123). And on the eve of the Six-Day War there were a few Egyptian officers who claimed that war was likely, but "their voice was not heard" (*Al-Ahram*, Cairo, June 21, 1968). What happened to these voices?

Some of these dissenters may have fought for their opinions, only to see them suppressed or ignored. A month before the attack on Pearl Harbor the American ambassador to Tokyo, Joseph Grew, sent a strong warning to Washington predicting that if negotiations between Japan and the United States failed, the Japanese might make "an all-out, do-or-die attempt, actually risking national Hara-kiri, to make Japan impervious to economic embargoes abroad rather than yield to foreign pressure." Such an attack, he warned, might come "with dangerous and dramatic suddenness" (Janis, 1972, p. 98). Six days before the Yom Kippur War an Israeli lieutenant in Southern Command Intelligence submitted to the intelligence officer of the command a document that assessed the Egyptian deployment as an indication of preparations to go to war. Two days later he submitted an additional document indicating that the Egyptian exercise might be a cover-up for preparations for war. His superior did not distribute the evaluation, and it was omitted from the command intelligence report (Herzog, 1975, p. 46).

Sometimes dissenters do not seriously try to challenge the existing view, although they may carry their doubts with them until the attack. After the Yom Kippur War several members of the Israeli

Cabinet and senior officials of the Ministry of Foreign Affairs claimed that on the eve of the Arab attack they felt uneasy about the intelligence assessment and had a sense that war might break out (Nakdimon, 1982, pp. 53–54, 89–90). Prior to the Chinese attack on India many Indian Army officers suspected China's intentions, yet most of the senior officers hesitated to fight for their opinions. The field commanders realized that there was no chance to change the strategy dictated by the civilian policy makers without an internal confrontation; unprepared for such a confrontation, they did not make their reservations clear to the General Staff (Vertzberger, 1978b, p. 480).

The suppression of contradictory views can be partly explained by the position of their proponents. Dissenters are often low-ranking officers and officials who are less committed than their superiors to the predominant conception, and this is precisely the reason why their views can be easily ignored or rejected. Thus in 1941, in the lower, operational echelons of the U.S. Army and Navy, some officers seemed to sense the gathering crisis and even see the immediate danger to Hawaii. There is evidence indicating that at least some junior officers in the fleet believed the ships at Pearl Harbor to be far from immune; they openly discussed the danger among themselves and took active steps on their own initiative to prepare their ships for a possible air attack. Other officers tried to take steps to meet the danger but were discouraged by their superiors. On December 4 Commander Arthur McCollum, Chief of the Far Eastern Section of Naval Intelligence, was sufficiently alarmed by conditions to prepare a dispatch to fully alert the fleets in the Pacific. He sought permission to send this dispatch at a meeting attended by four senior admirals but was discouraged from doing so on the grounds that the warnings already sent to Hawaii were sufficient (U.S. Congress, 1946b, p. 46; Janis, 1972, pp. 93–95).

Sometimes opinions are rejected or ignored on the grounds that the dissenters are nonexperts, outsiders, or not responsible for issuing warnings, or that they "oppose everything" and therefore should not be taken seriously. Experts within an organization tend to reject nonexperts' warnings and opinions; the experts' argument is that they are in the best position to evaluate information and developments. John McCone, Director of Central Intelligence at the time of the Cuban missile crisis, was considered one such dissenter. McCone had argued as early as the spring of 1962 that the Soviets might install medium-range missiles in Cuba. From the French Riviera, where he had gone for a three-week honeymoon, McCone bombarded his deputy with telegrams emphasizing his speculations, but the deputy did not distribute them outside the CIA. In McCone's absence the Board of National Estimates met in Washington on September 19. It considered the McCone hypothesis but concluded that the establishment of a Soviet missile base in Cuba was improbable. Apparently from the standpoint of the CIA McCone was considered a nonexpert because of his lack of political or intelligence experience and expertise in Soviet affairs. In addition his warnings apparently were not taken seriously "for he often played the devil's advocate in arguing with his own estimators" (Hilsman, 1964, p. 173; see also Schlesinger, 1965, p. 799; Abel, 1968, pp. 7–12).

Yet to attribute the rejection of deviating opinions to the status of their advocates is to understate the problem. In several cases of surprise attack some of the dissenters have been high-ranking officers and officials or important experts. Prior to Pearl Harbor Admiral Richmond Turner, the Chief of War Plans in the Navy Department, was the only officer in Washington in the higher echelons who held a strong belief that Hawaii would be attacked (U.S. Congress, 1946a, p. 234). Before the Chinese invasion of Korea George Kennan, a leading expert on Soviet affairs in the State Department, repeatedly made realistic predictions concerning China's probable reactions to the crossing of the Thirty-eighth Parallel. Kennan's views had some impact on the thinking of the department's policy planning staff. Yet Secretary Acheson, who was aware of these opposing views, apparently did not invite their holders to brief President Truman's advisory group or to discuss their views in depth (Janis, 1972, p. 62). In May 1962 the Director of the Indian Intelligence Bureau warned that there was a possibility of a Chinese military attack in the fall (Mullik, 1971, p. 330). And in late September 1973 the Head of the Israeli Mossad intelligence service and the Deputy Chief of Staff claimed separately that the probability of war was relatively high. The latter tried, by his own account, to persuade the Director of Military Intelligence, General Zeira, to change his assessment of the likelihood of war, but Zeira refused, arguing that with regard to the enemy he was the better expert (Bartov, 1978, pp. 247, 298; Nakdimon, 1982, pp. 79–80).

It would seem, therefore, that to understand how dissent is discouraged, rejected, and ignored, we should look at the psychological pressures and group processes that act on analysts.

Groupthink

The central study analyzing the influence of group processes on the thinking of group members is Irving Janis's *Victims of Groupthink* (1972). Although this study refers mainly to decision-making processes and high-level advisory groups, many of its observations are relevant to the analytical process within small groups of intelligence analysts or policy makers.

Janis defines *groupthink* as "a mode of thinking that people engage in when they are deeply involved in a cohesive in-group, when the members' strivings for unanimity override their motivation to realistically appraise alternative courses of action." The main hypothesis regarding groupthink is summarized as: "The more amiability and esprit de corps among the members of a policy-making in-group, the greater is the danger that independent critical thinking will be replaced by groupthink." Janis further explains: "Over and beyond all the familiar sources of human error is a powerful source of defective judgment that arises in cohesive groups—the concurrence-seeking tendency, which fosters overoptimism, lack of vigilance, and sloganistic thinking about the weakness and immorality of outgroups" (1972, pp. 9, 13).

According to Janis (1972, pp. 197–198; 1971, pp. 80–81), groupthink is characterized by eight major symptoms, four of which are relevant for our case:

An illusion of invulnerability . . . which creates excessive optimism and encourages taking extreme risks;

Collective efforts to rationalize in order to discount warnings which might lead the members to reconsider their assumptions . . .

Stereotyped views of enemy leaders . . . as too weak and stupid to counter whatever risky attempts are made to defeat their purposes;

Direct pressure on any member who expresses strong arguments against any of the group's stereotypes, illusions, or commitments . . .

Janis's groupthink theory has some obvious deficiencies. In particular it seems possible to account for many of the characteristics he attributes to groupthink by other factors. Many of the judgmental biases described in the second part of this study, especially with regard to information processing, can well explain failures in analysis and decision making. Such failures can also be explained with reference to difficulties in processing information owing to organizational obstacles and communications problems (Fischhoff and Beyth-Marom, 1976).

Ben-Zvi (1977) mentions additional deficiencies of the groupthink theory. For instance, Janis minimizes the influence of the national leadership on the deliberations and conclusions of the group in cases in which the national leader does not participate in its discussions. In this sense the theory concentrates on the pressures created by the group itself and ignores pressures and influences from above. Similarly the theory ignores those national and ideological conceptions and images that influence perception in international relations. The theory also neglects organizational and bureaucratic processes that affect the way a decision is implemented.

Although the groupthink theory cannot by itself fully explain failures in assessments and decision making, it clarifies an important aspect of these failures that complements other sources of failures such as judgmental biases and organizational obstacles. Even if the cohesiveness of the group is not necessarily a central factor in creating groupthink, as Janis claims, the phenomenon of groupthink and most of its symptoms play an important role in the formation of erroneous estimates.

Here we turn to the influence of group processes on misjudgment, in particular with regard to the enemy's expected behavior. The most familiar group pressures in this context are those that directly or indirectly induce individual members to conform. These pressures explain to a large extent why dissenting voices are seldom heard. Yet at the same time group processes influence the entire way of thinking of a group's members and may distort the perception of an impending threat.

Pressures for Conformity

Differences of opinion as to the perception of threat are quite common among analysts, and their disagreements have a twofold result. An analyst who disagrees with the majority of his superiors and colleagues may fight for the adoption of his interpretation of the information to the extent that the ensuing debate prevents him from sympathetically examining opposing interpretations. Yet since the intelligence agency has to submit its collective assessment, the individual analysts eventually have to compromise and reach some agreement. There are powerful forces within the group that help them reach that agreement.

Numerous studies note the influence that the group brings to bear on the individual. Cartwright and Zander (1960) suggest that two general kinds of forces work toward producing conformity: those that arise from conflicts within the individual as he observes that his views are different from those of others, and those induced by the members of the group who seek directly to influence the individual's opinions.

There are various explanations for an individual's willingness to change his views and accept those of others, even though no direct pressures are exerted on him. One explanation is that the individual hopes to reduce the unpleasantness generated by cognitive dissonance when his views differ from those of the group. Another maintains that pressure to conform arises from the individual's need to be accepted by the group and to be considered correct in his judgment. Indeed the individual may feel that in order to maintain his status and even his membership in a group, he must change his view to meet its standards. In this sense the individual hopes to gain the social rewards of being close to the other members of the group and to avoid the social punishments attendant on deviating from it (Deutsch and Gerard, 1960; Verba, 1961, pp. 22–24; Klineberg, 1965, p. 92). Janis describes this tendency with regard to decision-making groups: "A member of an executive in-group may feel constrained to tone down his criticisms, to present only those arguments that will be readily tolerated by the others, and to remain silent about objections that the others might regard as being beyond the pale . . . Such constraints arise at least partly because each member comes to rely upon the group to provide him with emotional support for coping with the stresses of decision-making" (1971, pp. 75–76).

The second force that induces an individual to conform is the behavior of others. Members of a group often exert pressures on one another quite consciously in order either to help the group maintain its existence and accomplish its goals or to develop validity for their opinions. A group may exert strong pressures on its members to agree with the leader or the majority even when an individual feels that the majority opinion is wrong. Group pressures may be overt and sometimes even formalized, but they may also be subtle and difficult to pinpoint (Cartwright and Zander, 1960, pp. 168–169; George, 1980, p. 93).

Organizations often display what De Rivera calls a "climate of opinion" (1968, pp. 70–73). A feeling of what is or is not "realistic" sets the boundary of opinion and makes it a strong restrictive barrier. Thus if an analyst claims that war is imminent when the majority of the other analysts, colleagues and superiors alike, consider this assessment unrealistic, he may not be taken seriously. If the analyst wants to be taken seriously he must accept the reality in which others are operating, must begin to think in their terms, build arguments that are directed to their beliefs although they are different from what he really thinks, or else he must abstain. This is especially true of analysts who carry out the uncertain job of making assessments and predictions: they feel the need to present a good image of themselves so that their opinions will be heard and respected. It is not surprising, therefore, that Hilsman (1956, p. 99) found that in the American intelligence community intelligence officers seemed to share the attitudes of the operators and administrators.

The prevailing climate of opinion in Washington and in the Far East Command in Tokyo in 1950 was hostile to warnings of North Korean aggression. This hostility was founded on a belief that subversion was the main communist threat in the Far East and that the enemy would shrink from direct military action. The military as well as the political environment was unreceptive to intelligence pointing to China's capacity to intervene (DeWeerd, 1962, p. 452).

The willingness of a member of a group to accept the other members' views depends on several conditions. One is the quality of the incoming information. The more ambiguous the information, the stronger the tendency of the individual to accept his colleagues' view. Another condition is the division of opinion within the group. The larger the majority supporting a view within the group, the more willing is the dissenter to change his mind. He will also be more willing to accept the dominant view when the more important and authoritative members of the group, and especially its leader, support that view. Then there is the personality of the dissenters. People who are concerned about their relations with others or who are fearful of disapproval and rejection are likely to conform to others' opinions. The attractiveness of the group for the individual and the degree to which he is in communication with others in the group form another condition for conformity. Individuals with strong affiliative needs, who give priority to preserving friendly relationships, may tend to yield to the view of the majority (Cartwright and Zander, 1960, pp. 173–175; Festinger, Schachter, and Back, 1960, p. 253; Vertzberger, 1978b, pp. 141–142).

Here the cohesiveness of the group plays an important role. Small groups tend to be more cohesive than larger ones. Cohesiveness improves group performance since it provides an atmosphere in which the clash of competing views can be minimized and consensus can be reached without excessive interpersonal friction and rivalry. Yet cohesion implies conformity; the more cohesive the group, the more effectively it can influence its members. In particular, in situations in which a great deal is at stake, members of the group may regard maintaining the cohesion of the group as the overriding goal (Festinger, Schachter, and Back, 1960, p. 259; George, 1980, pp. 87, 89).

Janis (1972, p. 5) describes how members of a cohesive in-group suppress deviant opinions:

> Whenever a member says something that sounds out of line with the group's norms, the other members at first increase their communication with the deviant. Attempts to influence the nonconformist member to revise or tone down his dissident ideas continue as long as most members of the group feel hopeful about talking him into changing his mind. But if they fail after repeated attempts, the amount of communication they direct toward the deviant decreases markedly. The members begin to exclude him, often quite subtly at first and later more obviously.

Finally, conformity is fostered by the consensus approach to intelligence production. The production process is by nature consensus-oriented, be it at the organizational or interorganizational level or at the less structured analyst-to-analyst level. Such consensus is necessary and desirable for two main reasons. The formation of the complicated intelligence assessment requires coordination among various intelligence analysts and divisions, each with different expertise, approaches, and opinions. Coordinating these analysts and divisions and achieving an agreed-upon assessment consistent with their beliefs and attitudes necessitate a difficult bargaining process leading to compromise. Moreover, intelligence consumers and policy makers usually require one all-encompassing assessment in answer to their questions; this demand provides another impetus for intelligence consensus.

As the Church Committee put it, the coordination process may produce a " 'reinforcing consensus' whereby divergent views of individual analysts can become 'submerged in a sea of conventional collective wisdom,' and doubts or disagreements can simply disappear in the face of mutually reinforcing agreements." The outcome is another contribution to the problem, discussed in Chapter 1, of the language of intelligence and intelligence warning. In the words of the committee:

> Finished intelligence frequently lacks clarity, especially clarity of judgment . . . it is often presented in waffly or "delphic" forms, without attribution of views. Opposing views are not always clearly articulated. Judgments on difficult subjects are sometimes hedged, or represent the outcome of compromise, and are couched in fuzzy, imprecise terms. Yet intelligence consumers increasingly maintain that they want a more clearly spelled out distinction between different interpretations, with judgments as to relative probabilities. (U.S. Congress, 1976, p. 272)

The problem is not only that of unclear and sometimes misleading wording and the consequent disappearance of disagreements. Perhaps more important is that the need to reach a consensus creates an obstacle for the individual analyst, who may cease to question basic assumptions agreed on by the group. This obstacle is described by the Subcommittee on Evaluation, which investigated the performance of U.S. intelligence prior to the collapse of the Shah's regime in Iran:

> The mechanics of NIE [National Intelligence Estimate] production tend to discourage a sound intellectual process. After limited discussion of the terms of reference, various sections of the NIE are drafted by different elements of the intelligence community. From the moment when these contributions are linked together in a first draft, basic reasoning and assumptions tend not to be questioned . . . The NIE process, which should have provided a way for analysts to challenge each other's models, instead mired key personnel in a frustrating search for superficial consensus. (U.S. Congress, 1979, p. 5)

The Leader and the Expert

Pressure for conformity can be created not only by the opinion of the majority but also by the opinions of two important members of the group: the leader, whether the head of intelligence, the commander in chief, or the head of state; and the expert, whether an intelligence expert, an experienced diplomat, or a reputable senior military commander. If they are wrong, there is a good chance that the corrective measures of the group will not be sufficient and the final assessment will be erroneous.

Group pressures toward conformity are sometimes strengthened by leadership practices that make it difficult for dissidents to suggest alternatives and to raise critical issues.

> During the group's deliberations, the leader does not deliberately try to get the group to tell him what he wants to hear but is quite sincere in asking for honest opinions. The group members . . . are not afraid to speak their minds. Nevertheless, subtle constraints, which the leader may reinforce inadvertently, prevent a member from fully exercising his critical powers and from openly expressing doubts when most others in the group appear to have reached a consensus. (Janis, 1972, p. 3)

Janis describes the impact of such pressures as manifested in the case of Pearl Harbor:

> During the week before the attack it would have been doubly difficult for any of Kimmel's advisers to voice misgivings to other members of the group. It was not simply a matter of taking the risk of being scorned for deviating from the seemingly universal consensus by questioning the cherished invulnerability myth. An even greater risk would be the disdain the dissident might encounter from his colleagues for questioning the wisdom of the group's prior decisions. For a member of the Navy group to become alarmed by the last-minute warning signals and to wonder aloud whether a partial alert was sufficient would be tantamount to asserting that the group all along had been making wrong judgments. (1972, p. 92)

The role of the leader is especially important when assessment takes place within a decision-making group that is headed by a prominent, strong leader. Extreme examples are found, quite naturally, in totalitarian regimes. Stalin viewed with grave suspicion the warnings from the British and the Americans about the forthcoming German attack. He presumably understood that the very survival of Britain depended on the German Army's becoming engaged elsewhere and that Russia was the only power left in Europe that could supply this diversion. Stalin's tendency to view all these warnings as capitalist provocations created a climate of opinion that heavily influenced Soviet intelligence's treatment of all information pertaining to German intentions. This was described in 1966 by G. A. Deborin of the Institute of Marxism-Leninism of the Soviet Communist party:

> Golikov [then the head of the GRU, Soviet Military Intelligence] did not so much inform the government as to lie to it. His reports were in many cases completely untrue. They were always in two parts: in the first part he reported information which he classified as *"from reliable sources"*; here, for example, he included everything that supported the forecast of Germany's invading Great Britain. In the second part of his communications he reported information *"from doubtful sources"*: for example, information from the spy Richard Sorge about the date on which Germany would attack the USSR. One must expand the criticism of the personality cult and say that certain people composed their reports in such a way as to please Stalin, at the expense of the truth. (Whaley, 1973, p. 195)

Yet strong leaders in nontotalitarian regimes can create a similar climate of opinion. Thus Norwegian Foreign Minister Koht was looked on as a virtually exclusive authority on matters pertaining to foreign relations.

> His colleagues and assistants in the Foreign Office were only seldom given ideas to work with and authority to formulate and advance opinions and suggestions. When issues of foreign affairs were debated during cabinet meetings the discussions were largely limited to the response to immediate and specific issues and did not provide any opportunity for different perspectives to be brought to bear on the intermediate and long-term trend of events or on hypothetical contingencies. (Holst, 1966, pp. 36-37)

And prior to the Chinese invasion of India in 1962 decisions were made within a small group headed by Prime Minister Nehru. The members of the group, lacking an independent power base, derived their power from him. The group's cohesion, its internal consensus, and Nehru's personal authority made it very difficult to express deviant assessments. The Director of the Intelligence Bureau, for example, received information concerning Chinese military preparations; yet he preferred to provide Nehru with assessments that supported the leader's beliefs, either because he did not want to lose his personal access to Nehru by being the source of pessimistic evaluation or because of genuine admiration for the prime minister (Hoffman, 1972, p. 971; Vertzberger, 1978b, pp. 401, 497–498).

The role of the leader is also important within intelligence analysts' evaluation groups. This is particularly true in military intelligence organizations, which are often composed of analysts holding different ranks and positions. A study of decision-making committees composed of military men of different ranks found that low-ranking members might withhold important facts, suggestions, or negative reactions and might agree to a decision whose merit they did not recognize (George, 1980, p. 88). But even in groups where no leader has been appointed or chosen, a dominant member may have an undue impact on the group's conclusions. "He may achieve this through active participation, putting his ideas across with a great deal of vigor. Or he may have a very persuasive personality. Finally, he may get his way simply through wearing down the opposition with persistent argument" (Martino, 1972, p. 20).

When this is the case, the danger is not only that different hypotheses are not considered or that subordinates suppress their opinions in order to keep their jobs; when a leader exercises such authority his colleagues, feeling that he must understand what is going to happen, will actually relax their alertness to the possibility of war. Before the Tet offensive of January 1968, for example, two DIA analysts wrote a paper accurately outlining the likely enemy course of action. The paper was never passed on, the implicit question being: "How could you possibly know more than General Westmoreland?" (McGarvey, 1973, pp. 323–324).

The tendency toward conformity is sometimes influenced by yet another factor: the expert. When the individual faces a contradiction between his own perception and other opinions, he may weigh the evidence supporting the different opinions; but if other members of the group are for some reason considered experts, he will be more likely to accept their beliefs (Cartwright and Zander, 1960, p. 173).

The expert derives his power and influence within the group from several possible sources; the most important is the quality of the information available to the expert and the judgments he makes based on it. Psychological experiments show that the more valid the expert's information, the more influential he is in causing others to adopt his proposed solutions. Moreover, the confidence people have in an expert may also depend on the type of judgment he makes. In some instances the expert's judgment may be based on information that is not readily available to the layman. In other cases the expert's judgment may be based not on special information but rather on his ability to interpret information already available. Confidence in an expert may be greater when his judgments are based on the special collection of data than when they are based on the interpretation of available information. In addition confidence in an expert may also be greater when his judgments are pleasing to the recipient of the information or when he has a history of success (Di Vesta, Meyer, and Mills, 1964; Kelley and Thibaut, 1969, p. 22).

Intelligence analysts are also heavily dependent on colleagues and assistants in preparing their assessments. Because of the enormous amount of incoming data, the desk officer has to rely considerably on his assistants' analyses without having the time to check their assumptions and the way they treated the information. He must also rely on colleagues' assessments regarding specialized subjects— for example technical or purely military ones—that are not within his expertise yet affect his assessment. This applies even more so to decision makers who consume intelligence assessments.

As we have seen, the power of the expert creates a high degree of uniformity and consensus within the organization, which makes it difficult for those who do not agree to voice their opinion. But experts have weaknesses; seldom do they know everything. There is no reason to believe that the thinking process of experts is significantly different from that of lay people. "When forced to go beyond the limits of the available data or convert their incomplete knowledge into judgments usable by risk assessors, they may fall back on intuitive processes, just like everyone else" (Fischhoff, Slovic, and Lichtenstein, 1980, pp. 26–27). Thus when decision makers depend on experts, a mistake in evaluation at the lower levels may be passed upward undetected, ultimately resulting in a major failure.

Golda Meir, the Israeli prime minister in 1973, describes the outcome of such dependency on experts on the eve of the Yom Kippur War: "How could it be that I was still so terrified of war breaking out when the present chief-of-staff, two former chiefs-of-staff (Dayan and Chaim Bar-Lev, who was my minister of commerce and industry) and the head of intelligence were far from sure that it would? After all, they weren't just ordinary soldiers. They were all highly experienced generals, men who had fought and led other men in spectacularly victorious battles" (1975, p. 357). Such a feeling of dependency may exist not only between persons but between organizations as well. Thus Quandt explains the failure of American intelligence to anticipate the Yom Kippur War as a result of its dependency on Israeli evaluations: "Perhaps as important as these conceptual errors was a sense that Israel had the greatest incentive and the best capabilities for determining whether war was likely or not. After all, Israel, not the United States, would be the target of any Arab military threat; Israeli intelligence had an excellent reputation, drawing on sources unavailable to the United States; therefore, if the Israelis were not overly worried, why should Americans be?" (1977, p. 169).

Group Risk Taking

In addition to exercising pressures for conformity, groups tend to be more willing than individuals to accept risky evaluations. Most studies support this assumption, although the evidence is not conclusive; indeed some studies have found that with certain types of tasks, the presence of others makes individuals more cautious (Kelley and Thibaut, 1969, p. 3; George, 1980, p. 97). With regard to evaluating an enemy threat, however, the assumption that groups on balance tend to be less cautious than individuals appears to be justified.

That assumption was defined by Wallach and Kogan: "If members of a group engage in a discussion and reach a consensus regarding the degree of risk to accept in the decisions which they make, their conclusion is to pursue a course of action more risky than that represented by the average of the prior decisions of each individual considered separately" (1965, p. 1). There are several explanations for this tendency. It is assumed that the process of group discussion is the factor producing a shift in the willingness to accept risks. The information provided about other members' opinions makes individuals move toward a position of greater risk. The presentation of information may tell the individual that other people are willing to take a higher degree of risk than he would have anticipated. As a result the individual becomes willing to accept greater risk taking (Wallach and Kogan, 1965, p. 4; Kelley and Thibaut, 1969, pp. 79–80).

Perhaps more important is the fact that in the process of group discussion the responsibility for accepting risky evaluations and decisions is shared by all the group members, though not equally.

When an analyst or decision maker presents a strategic assessment, he takes upon himself a considerable risk, especially if his opinion seems to differ radically from others'; if the assessment proves wrong, he may lose credibility—or worse, his job. During the group discussion, however, the members may come to feel that they share the responsibility for any negative consequences for risky evaluation and that blame for failure will not be imputed to any single member. The fact that other members of the group at least generally agree with his assessment makes the individual more willing to stick his neck out. Moreover, "while group discussion to consensus yields a risky shift when each of the group members is responsible only to himself, the same sort of discussion to consensus results in an even stronger shift toward enhanced risk taking when each group member has been made responsible for the others as well as for himself" (Wallach and Kogan, 1965, p. 2).

A third explanation of the risky shift can be found in what Janis calls "the illusion of invulnerability." When members of a cohesive group share a sense of belonging to a powerful, protective group, they "tend to examine each risk in black and white terms. If it does not seem overwhelmingly dangerous, they are inclined simply to forget about it" (1972, pp. 36–37).

Finally, Kelley and Thibaut (1969, pp. 81–82) suggest that those who initially present more risky evaluations may exert a stronger influence within the group than those who take conservative stands because risk takers are endowed with generalized skills of persuasiveness. Some properties associated with taking risky positions may be particularly influential. The language used by the proponent of such a position and the heightened intensity with which he states his argument may give him a disproportionate weight in open discussion (Wallach and Kogan, 1965, p. 3).

Most of these elements play a role in the group process of evaluating an enemy's intentions and likely behavior; but there are sometimes offsetting factors too. Cautious analysts and policy makers may dominate group discussions and lead the group to a conservative assessment. Among some top analysts or policy makers there is a tendency to take the middle road and avoid extreme theories or policies. (This is one of the reasons why analysts may reject "wild" theories of lower-rank analysts as irresponsible, thereby suppressing contradictory views). In particular, following a spectacular failure of estimates, analysts and policy makers may tend to be overcautious.

On balance, however, analysts and decision makers in group environments tend to drop some of their caution, feel less vulnerable, ignore warning signals, and endorse riskier assessments. Again, Golda Meir's description of the climate of opinion on the eve of the 1973 war is telling: "On Friday, 5 October, we received a report that worried me. The families of the Russian advisers in Syria were packing up and leaving in a hurry . . . That one little detail had taken root in my mind, and I couldn't shake myself free of it. But since no one around me seemed very perturbed about it, I tried not to become obsessive" (1975, p. 356).

7

Organizational Obstacles

Intelligence analysts work within an organizational framework, usually in a military or civilian intelligence agency. The military intelligence agency is in turn part of a larger military organization. The underlying assumption of my study is that misjudgment by the individual analyst is the cornerstone of estimate failures. At the same time, there can be little doubt that intelligence agencies, like all organizations, are subject to various general inefficiencies and obstacles as well as afflictions peculiar to intelligence agencies, all of which contribute to those failures.

Structural blocks to perception stem from various factors. Organizations may have a vested interest in the status quo and thus tend to discourage abrupt changes of beliefs. Communication patterns within a large organization are often inefficient. Bureaucratization, hierarchy, specialization, centralization, routine, and secrecy may distort or hinder information processing and impede analysis and proper judgment. Organizational problems may also be caused by intraservice and interservice rivalries.

The Military as an Organization

The preeminent feature of organizational activity, as defined by Allison, is "its programmed character: the extent to which behavior in any particular case is an enactment of preestablished routines." Reliable performance of the organization's task by its subunits requires standard operating procedures, which constitute routines for dealing with normal situations. These procedures are designed to be simple, unambiguous, and resistant to change. "Routines allow large numbers of ordinary individuals to deal with numerous instances, day after day, without much thought. But this regularized capacity for adequate performance is purchased at the price of standardization" (1971, pp. 81, 89–91). The alternatives defined by the organization are severely limited in both number and character. Moreover, major organizational modes of operation are straight; that is, behavior at any one time is only marginally different from behavior at any other time.

Established routines are sometimes an important factor in the failure to predict surprise attack. Organizational routines resist change and channel new problems into existing programs. Although surprise attack is not rare in the history of war, an army—including an intelligence community—generally does not expect to be surprised. Consequently it may tend to treat a growing threat as merely routine and to respond to it with limited and inadequate programs. Hence the activity of the victim's army up to the moment of attack is often identical with its behavior the day before. Moreover, the number of options designated by the army in case of war is limited (Allison, 1971, pp. 89–90).

In peacetime a soldier's routine demands that he report anything unusual or suspicious. In wartime or under emergency conditions he is expected to do much more, especially if he is a senior officer: to take initiatives, to find out what is happening, to give orders to his subordinates, to alert his superiors and colleagues, and to transmit an atmosphere of emergency. Yet standard operating procedures might prevent accurate perception of the signals that indicate an attack. On the morning of December 7, 1941, almost everyone in Pearl Harbor behaved as usual. An hour before the Japanese attack, when an American destroyer patrolling the harbor spotted the conning tower of a submarine, dropped depth charges on it, and then intercepted a sampan, which surrendered, the chief of staff of the naval district did not see any imminent danger. "We were vaguely alarmed, but could see no specific threat involved . . . We felt that by referring the matter to the Commander-in-Chief that we had done all that we possibly could even if the attack were real." In other words the second in command of the district felt that he had fulfilled his duty by placing the matter in the hands of a higher authority (Wohlstetter, 1962, pp. 16–17).

Most armies have long-range plans to deal with possible enemy attack, but few prepare contingency plans in case of surprise attack. Furthermore, long-range planning tends to become institutionalized and then disregarded (Allison, 1971, p. 92). For years prior to December 1941 American war plans and maneuvers in the Hawaiian area took full account of the possiblity of a Japanese attack by air. "As far back as 1936 war games and drills in the Hawaiian Islands had been planned on the basis of a surprise attack on Pearl Harbor . . . defined as a surprise air raid by Japan." But the actual organizational routines proceeded without reference to that planning. "There had never been any attempt to cover the full 360 degrees around the islands by long-distance reconnaissance." Moreover, despite two alerts in July and October 1941, "before December 7 Short [the Army commander in Hawaii] held no drill or alert in which the boxes of ammunition were opened" (Wohlstetter, 1962, pp. 68, 13, 104; see also U.S. Congress, 1946b, p. 29). In other cases no such contingency plans were even prepared. For example, the former Director of Egyptian Military Intelligence indicated that the plan for the defense of the Sinai Peninsula in 1967 was based on the assumption that any Israeli attack would be "routine" (*Al-Khawadith*, Beirut, September 1, 1972). And in 1935, when Marshal Mikhail Tukhachevsky, the Soviet First Deputy Commissar of Defense, urged that Red Army war games assume a scenario of a German surprise attack, his suggestion was resisted by the Chief of the General Staff (Erickson, 1975, pp. 1–3).

Even new specific assignments may not significantly alter organizational priorities and procedures (Allison, 1971, p. 91). Traditionally Army Intelligence (G-2) in Hawaii was primarily in the business of detecting subversive activity. But in May 1940 General Marshall requested than an evaluation branch be established within G-2 for the "maintenance of current estimates of predicted activity in . . . the Far East." This request entailed an increase in the number of officers on the G-2 staff from twenty-two to nearly eighty men by December 1941. Yet at the time of the attack military intelligence was still "specifically concerned, particularly concerned, and practically solely concerned" with antisubversive precautions and operations (Wohlstetter, 1962, pp. 279, 75, 290).

Incompatible imperatives assigned to an organization present additional problems, since while meeting one objective the organization may neglect another (Allison, 1971, p. 92). The aerial arm of the U.S. Navy stationed in Hawaii had two imperatives: to train pilots for an attack on the Japanese mandated islands and to carry out distant reconnaissance of enemy activities. Given the available aircraft, it was impossible to satisfy both imperatives, so the Navy concentrated on the first. In order to conserve resources for the primary mission, aircraft were returned to base on weekends for maintenance. Had a limited number of aircraft been attending to the second imperative on Sunday, December 7, the base would have had an hour's warning. But attention to that objective had been neglected in favor of concentrating on preparations for an offensive attack (Wohlstetter, 1962, pp. 12–13; Allison, 1971, pp. 92–93).

Rivalry, Coordination, and Communication

Another set of problems derives from the size and complexity of intelligence agencies, which are often part of an even larger organization—the military. Large intelligence communities usually comprise several distinct intelligence agencies. Centralized intelligence began to materialize only after the Second World War. The first effort in that direction came with the founding of the CIA in 1947; but even the CIA has encountered vigorous competition from the more recently founded DIA. The Soviets and the British followed with similar experiments in 1947 and 1964 respectively but have not developed centralized intelligence to this day. Needless to say, the organization of intelligence during the Second World War was even more chaotic.

One problem created by size is that a large organization requires and encourages specialization in order to increase efficiency in the production of information. Yet specialization creates much irrelevant or misleading information. Different estimates from different units produce ambiguity and ambivalence, while estimates that agree may conceal deviating opinions and tend to obscure issues. In addition, experts are often too distant from policy, while policy makers may be too dependent on experts' estimates. Complex organizations also require a hierarchical structure in order to ease internal control and motivate hard work. Yet hierarchy blocks upward communication, facilitates misrepresentation of information, and permits low-level personnel to be ignored by the higher levels (Wilensky, 1967, p. 175; Stech, 1979, pp. 132, 356). Moreover, as Hareven explains, "the nature of the hierarchical dialogue depends to a considerable extent on the personalities of the officials . . . when officials at successive levels lack judgment, their mutual influence is liable to produce disturbance rather than control and balance." Hareven suggests that in 1973 the Director of Israeli Military Intelligence, General Zeira, frustrated the intelligence hierarchy by imposing his views and not allowing dissenters to appeal to their superiors (1978, pp. 5, 15). Last, bureaucratic politics at various levels—within the intelligence organization, among intelligence agencies, and between the intelligence community and policy makers—affects the analytical process.

Specialization, hierarchy, and bureaucratic politics often distort information processing. Subordinates, who have to decide what information to pass on to their superiors, may withhold a disproportionate amount of discrepant information. Subunits tend to exaggerate the importance of some events and minimize that of others. The content of data may be changed in transmission. Ambiguity about responsibilities and standard operating procedures pertaining to the handling of information may lead to ignorance and neglect of critical evidence. Different units within the organization may hold conflicting assumptions regarding the significance of incoming information and consequent warning. Interpersonal difficulties may result in inadequate or distorted transmission of information. Scarcity of time and resources prevents proper handling of information and may lead to the selective and incomplete dissemination of information to its consumers (Downs, 1967, p. 189; Jervis, 1976, p. 143; Stech, 1979, pp. 169, 173).

Thus British intelligence failed to anticipate the German invasion of Norway because it had been "too loosely organised to ensure that all the available evidence was properly weighed on an inter-departmental basis." In the Admiralty the geographical section dealing with Germany was responsible for interpreting Special Intelligence Service (SIS) and diplomatic reports bearing on German intentions in Scandinavia; but the center responsible for operational intelligence did not receive all the SIS and diplomatic information. To make matters worse, relations between the two sections were not good. In Military Intelligence a similar situation prevailed. MI2, responsible for interpreting reports received from Scandinavia about German intentions there, did not receive reports of preparations in Germany. These were studied by MI3, which did not see the information from Scandinavia. Also, relations between these two sections were poor (Hinsley, 1979, pp. 168, 119).

The difficulties of information handling should also be considered in the context of the larger problems of coordination and communication within or between complex departments or organizations. People tend to forget that members of another department or organization do not share their own information, missions, and concerns. They often ignore the possibility that because of different background factors the same message will be read differently elsewhere, and that what is obvious in one place is understood differently in another. Warnings can be misunderstood (see Chapter 1), with the result that implementation of measures designed to meet the threat of war is inadequate. For example, as a result of the November 27, 1941, war warning, General Short, the Army commander in Hawaii, decided to implement alert number 1, the lowest of three possible levels of alert: "Defense against sabotage and uprisings. No threat from without." In explaining the considerations that led to his decision he stated that he was relying on the Navy to provide him with adequate warning of the approach of a hostile force, particularly through distant reconnaissance, which was a Navy responsibility. Admiral Kimmel then testified that he did not realize that the Army had been alerted to prevent sabotage only; he thought that the Army was on an all-out alert and in fact did not know that the Army had any other kind of alert. He also assumed that Army radar would be in full operation (U.S. Congress, 1946a, pp. 120, 125, 151). To close the circle, "Most top officials in Washington had only the haziest idea of what information was sent as a matter of course to the theaters, and since intentions were excellent, everybody assumed . . . that all essential or critical items of information were being sent out quickly" (Wohlstetter, 1962, p. 168).

Similarly, during the last days prior to the Arab attack of October 1973 the Israeli Minister of Defense and the Chief of Staff relied on the existing intelligence assessment in part because they believed that Military Intelligence had used the special early-warning measures at its disposal. Only after the war broke out did they learn that the Director of Military Intelligence had made a personal decision not to activate these measures. The latter, for his part, comforted himself with the knowledge that the standing army was considered by the General Staff to be capable of withstanding an initial assault. Prime Minister Meir relied on both assumptions: "I was convinced that the army was ready for any contingency—even for full-scale war. Also my mind was put at rest about the question of a sufficiently early warning" (Meir, 1975, p. 354; see also Bartov, 1978, p. 304; Herzog, 1975, p. 51).

Erroneous assumptions regarding the knowledge and behavior of others lead to two further mistakes. When people believe that others share their information and concerns, they do not bother to inform them of new developments. As the Roberts Commission, established following the Pearl Harbor attack, stated: "On and after November 27, 1941, the commanding general, Hawaiian Department, and the commander in chief of the Pacific Fleet, independently took such action as each deemed appropriate to the existing situation. Neither informed the other specifically of the action he was taking, and neither inquired of the other whether or not any action had been taken, nor did they consult as to the appropriateness of the actions taken by them respectively" (Sherwood, 1950, p. 425). Indeed part of the explanation for such a shortcoming has to do with interservice rivalry and the concern not to offend the sensibilities of others. Kimmel explained his failure to acquaint himself with what the Army was doing by saying: "When you have a responsible officer in charge of the Army and responsible commanders in the Navy, *it does not sit very well to be constantly checking up on them*" (U.S. Congress, 1946a, p. 153).

Meanwhile, when people assume that others share their information and concerns, they do not attempt to verify their assumptions or to ensure the implementation of orders. Thus the November 27 war warning ordered General Short "to undertake such reconnaissance and other measures as you deem necessary" and to "report measures taken." Short reported: "Re your 472. Department alerted to prevent sabotage. Liaison with Navy." Short's message was not clearly responsive to the order. Yet during the nine days before the attack, not one responsible officer in the War Department called on Short to alert the Hawaiian Department as consistent with instructions. "It does not affirmatively appear that anyone upon receipt of General Short's reply 'burdened' himself sufficiently to call for message No. 472 in order to determine to what the report was responsive." The congressional investigation committee concluded: "It was the responsibility of General Marshall to see that General Short was properly alerted. General Short, after being ordered to report his state of readiness to General Marshall, was entitled to assume that this state of readiness was satisfactory to the Chief of Staff unless he heard to the contrary . . . Because of [General Marshall's] silence, General Short was led to believe that the Chief of Staff approved his alert against sabotage" (U.S. Congress, 1946a, pp. 256, 266-L, 266-M).

A second set of problems has to do with rivalry between organizations. Such problems are more frequent, of course, where there are several competing agencies, but they also exist among various bodies of the same organization. Conflict of interest within the community may prevent the taking of any action that is not absolutely necessary. The information center and the radar sets in Pearl Harbor were not being operated on a regular twenty-four hour basis on December 7 owing to bickering over the question of control between the Air Force and the Signal Corps. For the same reason no liaison officers were present or even assigned. Consequently there was no possibility of correct and rapid indentification and interception of aircraft (Wohlstetter, 1962, p. 9).

Because of competition, "issues that arise in areas where boundaries are ambiguous and changing, or issues that constitute new territories are dominated by colonizing activity" (Allison, 1971, p. 93). As a result areas of responsibility between competing organizations are inadequately defined and consequently neglected. The failure of the alert system on three occasions prior to the Pearl Harbor attack had not been sufficiently alarming to generate a proposal of central coordination of intelligence and communication. Naval Intelligence regarded its own sources as superior and lacked the incentive for merging with an inferior, while Army intelligence had little interest in combining intelligence operations. On the basis of quite separate sources and types of information, each of the Army and Navy units at Pearl Harbor had a different estimate of likely contingencies for the end of 1941. As the congressional investigation committee explained: "The failure to integrate and coordinate Army-Navy efforts in Hawaii appears to have been attributable to a feeling on the part of each commander that he would intrude upon the prerogatives of the other and thereby invite similar intrusion if he inquired as to what the sister service was doing" (U.S. Congress, 1946a, p. 245; see also Wohlstetter, 1962, pp. 166–167, 35–36).

Lack of clear-cut allocation of responsibility often results in a "none of my business" attitude. The question one asks is often "What should I do within the confines of my formal responsibility?" rather than "What is to be done?" On December 6, 1941, Naval Communications intercepted the first thirteen parts of a crucial memo from the Japanese government to its ambassador in Washington. The memo was read by the president and nine senior officials and officers. Owing to the practice of decision making by war cabinets, councils, committees, and individuals, "official responsibility of each man was so blurred that each man became indifferent to his own individual responsibility." Admiral Turner, the Chief of War Plans, for example, later claimed that the officer who showed him the memo "informed me that Admiral Wilkinson and Admiral Ingersoll and Secretary Knox had all seen it before it had been shown to me. I considered the dispatch very important, but as long as those officers had seen it, I did not believe it was my function to take any action." And Admiral Ingersoll, Assistant Chief of Naval Operations, later explained: "When I read the 13 parts there was nothing on which the Navy Department as such could that night take action." No one did take action that night; all waited for the next day. Because of the confusion in Washington, "the high principle of *individual responsibility* was apparently lost to sight." The result was that none of the readers of the crucial dispatch was sufficiently concerned to do anything about it (U.S. Congress, 1946b, pp. 34, 46; 1946a, p. 218).

Similarly when the Chief of the Army Military Intelligence Division (MID) received a series of Japanese espionage messages, which included the significant report that the Japanese had divided Pearl Harbor into five sectors, his first reaction was that as naval messages these were of no concern to MID. He refrained from using the material for fear of coming into conflict with the Navy's use of it (Wohlstetter, 1962, pp. 301–302).

In a period of heightened danger one might expect the center to try to coordinate the activities of the diverse organizations, but this does not necessarily occur. Washington did not know what was going on in Pearl Harbor and assumed that the "system of mutual cooperation was working within its limitations and that local commanders were fully discharging their responsibilities" (U.S. Congress, 1946a, p. 245). And no single person or agency in Washington possessed all the available information at any one time. Each department and agency processed the signals it had collected, provided its own interpretation, and occasionally shared it with others. If the department considered the information important, it tried to push it up to the highest levels. Only rarely was material from one source weighed against material from another, nor were sources weighed and evaluated for their comparative accuracy over a period of time (Kirkpatrick, 1969, pp. 150–151).

The rivalry between organizations was even more intense at the upper echelons. "Proper demarcation of responsibility between these two divisions of the Navy Department [War Plans and Naval Intelligence] did not exist. War Plans appears to have insisted that since it had the duty of issuing operational orders it must arrogate the prerogative of evaluating intelligence; Naval Intelligence, on the other hand, seems to have regarded the matter of evaluation as properly its function." On the eve of the attack on Pearl Harbor, the Office of Naval Intelligence was aware of the dangers of an American-Japanese confrontation; but the office lacked the bargaining power or the status it needed to compete effectively with the Office of Naval Operations and thus was not consulted in the formulation of the warnings issued to the Pacific theater in late November. Another result of the rivalry in Washington was a total absence of meetings of the Joint Army-Navy Intelligence Committee during the two months before the attack: "There were still discussions and difficulties going on between the War and Navy Departments as to just what the functions of that committee would be, where it would sit, what rooms it would have, what secretary it would be allowed, et cetra" (U.S. Congress, 1946a, p. 254; 1946b, p. 45; see also Wohlstetter, 1962, pp. 312–319, 322–323).

Internal mechanisms do, however, exist within the intelligence community and the military for reaching a consensus among competing agencies and services. Such "agreed intelligence" reflects the least common denominator of the various agencies' assessment, and members of the intelligence community are the first to admit the damage caused by such procedures. As the Church Committee claimed: "Some members of the intelligence and foreign policy communities today argue that the consensus approach to intelligence production has improperly come to substitute for competing centers of analysis which could deliver more and different interpretations on the critical questions on which only partial data is available" (U.S. Congress, 1976, p. 272).[1] The former Director of the DIA advanced a similar argument: "I have seen . . . countless inter-agency sessions on estimates in which perceptive insights and relevant data have been shunted aside, sent back for reconfirmation, or watered down because they would not fit with some agency's position, or because they stood to block inter-agency consensus on a particular point" (Graham, 1979, p. 25).

The need to reach a consensus can sometimes present a genuine stumbling block. On December 1, 1941, the Office of Naval Intelligence attempted to produce a document pointing out the possiblity of Japanese operations in the Kra Peninsula (bottleneck of Malaya) and against the Philippines, Guam, Wake Island, and Hawaii. The document was not disseminated because the head of the Navy War Plans Division, officially charged with preparing estimates, demanded changes that were unacceptable to Naval Intelligence. Consequently the estimate was still in interservice liaison at the time of the attack on Pearl Harbor (Brinkley and Hull, 1979, p. 36).

Intrinsic Problems in the Intelligence Organization

In addition to the inefficiencies and difficulties common to many organizations, some problems and constraints are specific to the intelligence community.

The "Cry Wolf" Phenomenon

Among the most subtle obstacles to accurate interpretation of vital signals is the "cry wolf" phenomenon. One of its manifestations is the ambiguous warning, discussed in Chapter 1: the warning against an attack from any possible direction. The more common and more damaging case, however, is the previous false alarm. This preceded most, if not all, of our instances of surprise attack. Before the Pearl Harbor attack, for example, there had been three periods of extreme tension in American-Japanese relations—in June 1940 and again in July and October 1941—that resulted in alerts in Hawaii. Before the Yom Kippur War there were three periods of escalation in which Israeli intelligence noted Egyptian mobilization and preparations for war—at the end of 1971, in December 1972, and in May 1973 (Herzog, 1975, pp. 43–44).

There are two main reasons why intelligence agencies cry wolf too often. In the first instance the intelligence warning that the enemy intends to go to war is correct, but the enemy changes his mind. Between November 12, 1939, and May 10, 1940, Hitler postponed his attack on the Western Front twenty-nine times, often at the last minute (Mason, 1963, p. 557). In the second instance sometimes it is the success of intelligence itself in exposing the enemy's intentions that leads him to postpone his plans; the warning will nevertheless be perceived as a false alarm. In fact it is usually impossible to tell at the time if an alarm is truly false or if the enemy has changed his mind, whether because of being found out or for other reasons. Thus it is very difficult to judge the accuracy of an assessment and to correct it if necessary (Brody, 1983, p. 47).

In addition psychologists have found that the rewards for interpreting a signal correctly and the costs of failure in detection or of false reports have a striking effect on how well a person decodes a signal (De Rivera, 1968, p. 56). From the viewpoint of intelligence, to issue a war warning is risky because of the costs involved in acting on false alarms. Hence the decision to issue a warning is also a function of the extent to which the intelligence agency is willing to take such risks. But since intelligence agencies consider their first and most important mission that of providing advance warning, they place a high cost on the failure to report a signal. Usually they believe that it is more dangerous to underestimate than to overestimate threats. When the issue is war, they feel that it is preferable to sound an alarm, though it may prove false, than to take the chance of being caught unprepared. Since nobody wants to be blamed for an intelligence failure, too many false alarms are given.

False alarms have a considerable impact. High costs can be incurred when faulty analysis is responsible for reporting a signal when there is none. Despite the priority given to advance warning, intelligence agencies are sometimes overcautious about giving false warnings, which would decrease their credibility. Hence intelligence agencies tend to report vague estimates and suppress warnings. In explaining why additional warnings were not sent to Hawaii, some have suggested that there was a desire to avoid crying wolf too often lest the commanders become impervious to messages designed to alert them (U.S. Congress, 1946a, p. 256).

The effect of previous false alarms is harmful to the entire process of information analysis. Decision makers tend to ignore warnings if their intelligence agency has previously cried wolf. In the Senate hearings after the North Korean attack, Secretary of Defense Johnson testified that intelligence reports had cried wolf so often before June 1950 that nothing in the reports of that time "put us on notice that anything was going to happen in Korea" (DeWeerd, 1962, p. 440). One official later explained in a letter: "Our intelligence agencies were frightened by the Roberts Commission which investigated Pearl Harbor and have gotten into the habit of warning about everything all the time. The result is useless to policy makers because a large percentage of their warnings turn out to mean nothing. During the week of the attack nothing was called to the attention of the policy makers pointing a finger toward Korea" (Paige, 1968, p. 98n.).

Not only an agency but also a source of information that previously cried wolf may lose its credibility. Thus prior to the German invasion, the Norwegian foreign minister did not trust his embassy in Berlin after two previous false alarms; his immediate reaction on receiving similar signals in April 1940 was to consider them unsubstantiated rumors. The Dutch thought no better of their own embassy in Berlin. Beginning in November 1939 the Dutch received numerous direct warnings from their military attaché in Berlin of an imminent German attack. These warnings led to three major alarms, when tension increased as the possibility of a German attack was seriously considered by at least some officials in The Hague. Yet each time Hitler changed his mind about the attack; the cumulative effect of these aborted decisions was to undermine the credibility of the attaché (Holst, 1966, p. 40; Pearson and Doerga, 1978, p. 27).

In general too a source will be more reluctant to report information if he has previously provided a false warning. Thus the Norwegian embassy in Berlin deliberately sent vague warnings about German intentions to invade Norway because it had been criticized for reporting unreliable rumors in the past. Similarly when the Dutch military attaché in Berlin received reliable information on May 3, 1940, that an invasion of the Low Countries was planned for the following week, he did not pass the message on to The Hague because during the preceding months he had sent many similar warnings, which had been received with disbelief (Holst, 1966, p. 40; Hinsley, 1979, p. 135).

Furthermore, recurrent warnings that turn out to be false alarms induce a kind of fatigue and decrease sensitivity. Initial warnings are taken seriously; but as time passes and alerts prove to be false, sensitivity decreases. At the time of the first alert in Pearl Harbor in June 1940 a daring and difficult enemy raid on Hawaii was believed to be probable, whereas a year later it was considered to be an extremely costly and unlikely gamble for the Japanese. By the end of 1941 the Pacific Fleet in Hawaii was tired of checking out Japanese submarine reports in the vicinity of Pearl Harbor; in the week preceding the attack it had checked seven, all of which proved to be false (Wohlstetter, 1965, p. 649).

Yet if past failure to predict a coming attack contributes to misperception of signals, past successes will have the same effect. Personal involvement gives an event greater impact, especially if the analyst's views were validated. Experiments have shown that the probability that individuals will maintain a hypothesis despite disconfirmation depends on their past success with the hypothesis (Betts, 1982, p. 123). If an intelligence agency had previously received signals of a coming attack but has correctly estimated them to be false, it will tend to regard similar future signals as the critical indicators.

In such cases the agency pays insufficient attention to the *reasons* why the past estimate was correct, and variations in the situation may not be noticed. Decision makers thus tend to rely on successful intelligence agencies without seriously questioning the validity of their estimates.

Navy Intelligence in Hawaii was not particularly disturbed by the loss of radio contact with the Japanese carriers after November 16, 1941. Frequently throughout 1941 and earlier, radio intelligence traffic had failed to locate carriers and other warships. In all these cases Navy Intelligence had correctly assessed that the ships were heading for home waters, where they used direct low-power radio contact with shore stations. Since these assessments had always been justified by events, intelligence did not consider the loss of signals in December 1941 an indication of war (Wohlstetter, 1962, p. 42).

The Worst-Case Analysis

The "cry wolf" phenomenon is associated with a more basic tendency within intelligence communities when evidence is ambiguous—to emphasize the worst scenario that might develop. "When a situation is not clear-cut, and various interpretations are possible, it is indeed the duty and tradition of intelligence to point out the worst possibility" (Greene, 1965, p. 132). The reason for that tendency is similar to that for "cry wolf." Brown, Kahr, and Peterson have suggested, following discussions with intelligence analysts and their supervisors, that "there may be less of a penalty for crying 'wolf' than for failing to predict an unpleasant outcome. The analyst perceives a smaller penalty, or negative value, associated with the error of overestimating the probability than with the error of underestimating it" (1974, p. 432). Kissinger describes the same phenomenon in the CIA: "Its analysts were only too aware that no one has ever been penalized for not having foreseen an opportunity, but that many careers have been blighted for not predicting a risk. Therefore the intelligence community has always been tempted to forecast dire consequences for any conceivable course of action, an attitude that encourages paralysis rather than adventurism" (1979, p. 37).

On the face of it, worst-case analysis should provide a solution to the problem of surprise attack, for intelligence agencies always assume the worst possibility, they will always take into account an enemy attack. In practice this is not the case. Intelligence agencies do not always point out the worst possibility. Existing beliefs, overconfidence, and lack of alertness might overcome the tendency to assume the worst. Moreover, the worst-case approach is not sufficient to guarantee security. Decision makers tend to discount a consistent emphasis on the greatest possible danger. Such an approach can reduce their options, while their own experience tells them that less dangerous developments are more likely to take place. Assuming the worst means incurring extraordinary expenses and may provoke enemy countermeasures or preemption. And as Betts argues: "Even if worst-case analysis is promulgated in principle, it will be compromised in practice. Routinization corrodes sensitivity. Every day that an expected threat does not materialize dulls receptivity to the reality of danger . . . Seeking to cover all contingencies, worst-case analysis loses focus and salience; by providing a theoretical guide for everything, it provides a practical guide for very little" (1978, p. 74).

The recurrence of surprise attacks is the best proof that worst-case possibilities are not considered seriously enough when most needed. To the extent that worst-case analysis is used, not only does it usually not prevent surprise, but the damage it causes to the credibility of intelligence agencies and sources actually contributes to the success of surprise attacks.

The Wait-and-See Attitude

Usually after major intelligence failures one can hardly understand in retrospect how intelligence agencies could have ignored and misperceived so many alarming signals. Part of the problem lies in the general attitude within the intelligence community toward threatening situations and warning indicators.

The intelligence community commonly operates in an atmosphere of doubt, full of question marks and queer, inexplicable occurrences. Intelligence analysts must always cope with conflicting evidence and information of questionable reliability. They are accustomed to lacking vital information and having no answers to disturbing questions. They are often faced with potentially threatening situations. Thus unusual behavior on the part of the enemy does not necessarily put the community on extreme alert. In an atmosphere of constant crisis, intelligence analysts are not excited by each warning indicator and often adopt a wait-and-see attitude toward alarming signals.

There are two reasons for adopting this attitude. For one, analysts—expecially in a military organization—get bonuses for taking responsibility and keeping cool, not for putting policy makers on the alert too often. They are educated to make a systematic, balanced, and cautious analysis before deciding that they must change their assessment. Experience has taught them that most potential threats fail to materialize, and new information is constantly coming in. Hence analysts and decision makers often prefer to wait for additional information before sounding the alarm. Since a considerable part of intelligence information is contradictory, the arrival of alarming information is not surprising and does not lead to immediate reconsideration of the existing assessment.

The wait-and-see attitude was adopted, for example, by Admiral Kimmel at Pearl Harbor:

> Between 7:30 and 7:40, I received information from the Staff Duty Officer of the *Ward*'s report [concerning the discovery of a submarine off Pearl Harbor], the dispatch of the ready-duty destroyer to assist the *Ward*, and the efforts then underway to obtain a verification of the *Ward*'s report. *I was awaiting such verification at the time of the attack.* In my judgment, the effort to obtain confirmation of the reported submarine attack off Pearl Harbor was a proper preliminary to more drastic action in view of the number of such contacts which had not been verified in the past. (U.S. Congress, 1946a, pp. 138–139, emphasis added)

Kimmel's statement touches on another aspect of the same problem—the contradiction between the natural tendency to wait for verification of evidence and the fact that time may be running out. As the former Director of Intelligence and Research in the State Department, Ray Cline, explained: "You almost never know when something is going to happen. You wait until the evidence comes in and by the time you are sure it is always very close to the event" (U.S. Congress, 1975, p. 656). There is also always a delay, especially in large organizations, as reports shuttle between the source and the evaluation center, between accuracy checks and final evaluation, and between the center and the final report to the decision makers. Communication procedures and the use of technical equipment consume considerable time, from minutes and hours to days or even weeks. In the meantime the opponent may make his move.

Following the 1973 airlifting of Soviet advisers' families out of Egypt and Syria, Israeli intelligence began to change its low-probability assessment regarding the outbreak of war. On the morning of October 5 Director of Military Intelligence Zeira informed the Prime Minister that he anticipated confirmation of Egyptian intent from a reliable source by nightfall. By evening highly reliable information received by Military Intelligence could indeed have been interpreted to indicate that war was imminent. General Zeira, while disturbed by that information, decided to wait for another confirmation, expected late in the evening. Only at 2:00 A.M. did the irrefutable information come in, and by then it was quite late. Another Director of Israeli Military Intelligence, General Shlomo Gazit, later suggested that with better communication procedures the information could have arrived twenty-four or even forty-eight hours earlier (Bartov, 1978, pp. 317, 323; Gazit, 1981, p. 11). Had this happened, it might have changed the entire picture.

Security of Sources and Restriction of Information

Another problem connected with assessing and reporting intelligence information arises from the fact that although the intelligence agency wants to report all relevant information to the decision makers, the need to protect the security of sources requires limited use of that information. Hence the intelligence community must develop some system of classification whereby each analyst and decision maker gets only the information he needs to have. In some cases the release of critical information is delayed or prohibited in order not to expose its source—as with the famous Zimmermann telegram in the First World War.[2]

The golden mean between intelligence research and operational needs on the one hand and source security on the other is sometimes difficult to find. Before the Pearl Harbor attack only nine top government officials besides the president were allowed regular access to the Magic intercepts. Neither the intercepted messages nor essential information derived from them was sent to Hawaii. The substance of some exceptional messages had been transmitted, but even this practice was stopped in July 1941, although Kimmel and Short were never notified of the change. As a rule two high-level couriers—a navy commander and an army colonel—would wait in an outer office while such messages were read and then returned to them for further dissemination. After the authorized recipients had seen the messages, the only copies retained were kept by the chiefs of the Far Eastern sections of Army and Navy Intelligence (U.S. Congress, 1946b, p. 37).

These severe restrictions on the handling of sensitive information created considerable problems. First, decision makers were denied access to important information. Kimmel did not know, for example, that before the attack on Pearl Harbor the Japanese consul general in Hawaii had been briefed in detail to note the presence of particular ships in particular areas and at particular times. Nor did Kimmel receive any notification that the Japanese were continuing negotiations after November 26 merely as a cover for their war plans, a change in the political situation known to the Navy Department. Then too those who saw the messages had them in hand only momentarily and had neither time nor opportunity to make a critical and systematic review of the material. Furthermore, the unequal distribution of sensitive information invited trouble. Those allowed to read it generally did not know which other officials had access to it. The Chief of Naval Operations assumed, for instance, that Kimmel was reading all the Magic intercepts, an assumption particularly critical to Washington's decisions about the phrasing of its warnings to the theater and its communication with other decision makers. Finally, those who did not see the Magic material but who had learned somehow of its existence were sure that it contained military as well as diplomatic information and believed that the contents were more complete and precise than they actually were. This mistaken assumption increased the theater commanders' confidence in Washington's sensitivity to imminent war (Kimmel, 1955, p. 56; Wohlstetter, 1962, pp. 186, 394).

Once the intelligence community accepts the principle of selective distribution of information among the services and theaters—and in fact there is no alternative—there still remains the problem of determining the optimal distribution to reduce harmful consequences. Before the Pearl Harbor attack the Washington agencies received many more signals than the theaters concerning Japanese activities and intentions. Yet no single agency or individual had access to the total mass of information. While it was not practical or advisable to send to the theaters all the information available in Washington, the agencies there were not necessarily good judges of what material would be most useful to the theaters. Thus, owing to both the ambiguous wording of messages and the selective forwarding of information from Washington, Hawaii was not sufficiently receptive to the danger signals. In general the result of selective distribution of information is the prevalence of a feeling in the intelligence community that somebody else probably knows what is going on and will take care of the situation. This reliance, so often unjustified, on other analysts may contribute to the persistence of biased assumptions and to the neglect of discrepant information.

A generation after Pearl Harbor information distribution had not improved. The same problem manifested itself within the American intelligence community prior to the Yom Kippur War. On the morning of the Arab attack the Watch Committee, which was responsible for crisis alerts, met to assess the likelihood of major hostilities and concluded that no major offensive was in the offing. It was later assumed that one of the reasons for this failure was that some participants were not cleared to see all intelligence information, so the subject could not be fully discussed. The draft CIA postmortem concluded: "If the information contained in the NSA [National Security Agency] messages had been available prior to the time of the outbreak of hostilities, we could have clearly predicted that (a foreign nation) knew in advance that renewed hostilities were imminent in the Middle East" (*Pike Papers*, 1976, p. 20).

The need to maintain the security of sources creates another problem: since a major part of intelligence information is classified, the intelligence community is largely a closed system. Intelligence analysts cannot share classified information with analysts and observers outside the community. Thus ideas and data based on classified material are not subject to rigorous, informed, independent criticism by outside groups such as the academic community and the press (Wilensky, 1972, p. 243).

Finally, analysts and policy makers read intelligence information selectively because of the organizational time constraints under which they work. These constraints are generated by the enormous amount of information that has to be read and by the work required to integrate different interests and opinions within an organization. This pressure is especially heavy when war is impending. Consequently analysts and decision makers do not have the time to read information thoroughly or weigh different points of view judiciously. As pressures on the analyst to reach a quick conclusion increase, the amount of information on which he bases his assessment decreases. Since intelligence analysts are always under pressure not to withhold judgment, they are obliged to reach a conclusion quickly even if they realize that they may be incorrect (Jervis, 1976,

p. 194). This may cause misperception even though relevant information is available.

The "Current Events" Approach

Intelligence agencies give precedence to the urgent and immediate rather than to fundamental analysis. Pressures of time and limited resources and manpower dictate concentration on current intelligence. In addition, information on fundamental issues and social trends tends to be considered overly academic by field personnel, since it is usually not fast-changing. Furthermore, collecting information on these intangible issues is difficult and unrewarding, and in many cases field personnel lack the background and qualifications to pursue it effectively (U.S. Congress, 1979, p. 3).

More important, the "current events" approach reflects the growing demand by policy makers for information of current concern. Intelligence consumers usually need answers to immediate problems. Only seldom do they look for fundamental, in-depth analysis, especially with regard to political developments. Since policy makers show less interest in fundamental analysis, and since the relationship of fundamental analysis to policy issues is not readily apparent, intelligence communities tend to devote fewer resources to that kind of research (U.S. Congress, 1979, p. 3; 1976, p. 272). Also, intelligence analysts themselves are usally drawn to current, rather than fundamental research. The "action" is in current events, and for current analysis they can receive a bonus.

The outcome is clear. Current intelligence "is an important warning vehicle" and "most effective in reporting events that stand out clearly," but "it does not lend itself to assessments of the long-term significance of events" (U.S. Congress, 1979, p. 4). Focusing on current events, for example, reduces an analyst's ability to understand the enemy's intentions, especially his conceptual framework, as well as the influence of internal factors on his possible decision to go to war. An understanding of these factors cannot be based only on current analysis. The Church Committee concluded:

> According to some observers, this syndrome has had an unfavorable impact on the quality of crisis warning and the recognition of longer term trends. The "current events" approach has fostered the problem of "incremental analysis," the tendency to focus myopically on the latest piece of information

without systematic consideration of an accumulated body of integrated evidence. Analysts in their haste to compile the day's traffic, tend to lose sight of underlying factors and relationships. (U.S. Congress, 1976, p. 273)

Military Men and Surprise Attack

The military is inevitably implicated in the failure to prevent surprise attack. In most cases those who are responsible for strategic warnings are military men. Many of the intelligence agencies are military organizations. Countermeasures to face the enemy's attack are always taken by the armed forces. Is there a connection between the failure to foresee surprise attacks and the fact that many of those involved are military men?

Some of the qualities attributed to military personnel may indeed contribute to their vulnerability to surprise attack. They are described as more authoritarian, aggressive, decisive, and conservative and less tolerant than civilians. "Military and civilian writers generally seem to agree that the military mind is disciplined, rigid, logical, scientific; it is not flexible, tolerant, intuitive, emotional. The continuous performance of the military function may well give rise to these qualities" (Huntington, 1957, pp. 59–60). Janowitz (1960, pp. 24, 242–243) claims that military men are predisposed toward a status quo outlook; for them past events become a powerful precedent for the future.[3]

Military men in addition are educated to take great risks, accept personal responsibility, and solve problems by themselves without bothering superiors or relying on others. Even when they have doubts, they hesitate to ask for clarification of instructions lest this be interpreted as weakness. As General Zeira, the Director of Israeli Military Intelligence in 1973, later testified, "I am not accustomed to bringing matters in my sphere of responsibility before my superior officers" (Hareven, 1978, p. 15). Similarly on November 27, 1941, Admiral Kimmel received the "war warning" message. Every naval officer who later testified on the subject, including Kimmel himself, stated that never before had he seen an official dispatch containing the words *war warning*. Kimmel nonetheless opted to implement the warning without seeking clarification from Washington. General Short was instructed to undertake reconnaissance, but he took for granted that Washington had made a mistake and ignored the order. The congressional investigation committee noted:

While there is an understandable disposition of a subordinate to avoid consulting his superior for advice except where absolutely necessary in order that he may demonstrate his self-reliance, the persistent failure without exception of Army and Navy officers . . . to seek amplifying and clarifying instructions from their superiors is strongly suggestive of just one thing: That the military and naval services failed to instill in their personnel the wholesome disposition to consult freely with their superiors. (U.S. Congress, 1946a, p. 258)

Moreover, military men work within a rigidly hierarchical organization. Hierarchy and discipline conflict with intellectual independence and objectivity. Military men are under pressure not to undermine the positions and policies of their superiors. Officers who do not share their superiors' beliefs are open to reprisal on their fitness reports. As Blachman notes: "The promotion system created exceptional pressures for conformity on career officers. Promotion depends heavily on the evaluation report of one's commanding officer; one unfavorable mention in the report could postpone promotion for many years and, perhaps, permanently blight a career" (1973, p. 332).

Furthermore, in assessing external threats military men tend to emphasize the enemy's capabilities rather than his intentions. They feel professionally capable of estimating the enemy's fighting strength, while estimating his intentions seems to be an uncertain undertaking open to error. Hence they tend to base their threat perception on the enemy's capabilities while attributing to him the worst intentions: "If a state has the power to injure one's own security, it is necessary to assume that it will do so" (Huntington, 1957, pp. 66–67). In terms of anticipating surprise attack military men usually adopt the worst-case analysis. Because military men focus on capabilities, it becomes easy for civilian decision makers to reject their warnings, feeling that they understand those enemy intentions that military estimators ignore or distort.[4] Furthermore, the entire threat perception of military men might be biased and unbalanced. As Kennan described the background of the North Korean intervention: "The unexpectedness of this attack . . . only stimulated the already existent preference of the military planners for drawing their conclusions only from the assessed *capabilities* of the adversary, dismissing his *intentions*, which could be safely assumed to be hostile. All this tended to heighten the militarization of thinking about the cold war generally, and to press us into attitudes where any discriminate estimate of Soviet intentions was unwelcome and unacceptable" (1967, p. 497).

These traits and tendencies of military men may indeed contribute on occasion to the failure to predict surprise attack. Yet in the final analysis it seems that the involvement of military men in the intelligence and warning process per se is not an important component of such failure. While some traits of military men make them more vulnerable to surprise, other traits may offset this weakness. "Military intelligence analysts have one major advantage over their civilian counterparts. They bring to the interpretation of military data a professional understanding of the actual operation of military forces. This brings to their judgments on the likely combat performance of enemy equipment an authority that no civilian can match" (Freedman, 1977, p. 21). Moreover, the military man always stresses the dangers to military security, recommends caution, and favors preparedness (Huntington, 1957, pp. 66, 69).

Indeed it has not been proven that civilian intelligence agencies are less vulnerable to surprise attack than their military counterparts. The CIA, the dominant intelligence agency in the United States, was wrong about the North Korean and Chinese interventions in Korea and about the 1973 war in Israel. In 1941, until the final stage prior to "Barbarossa," both military and civilian intelligence services in Britain found it difficult to discard the belief that Germany would present Russia with demands and an ultimatum. The Foreign Office, for instance, "was never wholly convinced that 'Germany intended to attack Russia and not merely to use diplomatic and military pressure to intimidate the Soviet government' " (Hinsley, 1979, p. 480). And in 1962 the dominant intelligence agency in India was the civilian Intelligence Bureau; growing reliance on its estimates was one of the causes of the failure to anticipate the Chinese attack.

8

Intelligence and Decision Makers

Thus far this study has not dealt specifically with the military or political decision maker as a consumer of intelligence. In referring to the "analyst" I have meant either the decision maker as analyst of incoming information or the intelligence analyst per se. Focusing most of our attention on the latter seems justified; after all, the bulk of analysis work is done by the intelligence analyst. Moreover, more often than not in the recent past the failure to predict the coming of war could at least officially be attributed to the intelligence community. In fact, in all cases of surprise attack since 1939—with the possible exceptions of the German invasion of France and the North Korean attack on South Korea—the intelligence communities had previously expressed their opinion that war was not imminent. Consequently decision makers have tended to blame the intelligence community for the failure to predict a forthcoming attack. For example, Churchill prior to the invasion of Belgium and Russia, and Nasser after the 1967 war, blamed the intelligence services for their failure to see what should have been obvious.

Still the problem is not simply that of a failure of the intelligence agencies. Indeed many objective observers tend to place responsibility for the failure equally on the intelligence community, the political leadership, and even society as a whole, as was the case in Israel after the 1973 war. In some cases blame has been directed mainly against military decision makers, for example following the Pearl Harbor attack and the Chinese invasion of Korea. And whom should history blame for the failure to predict "Barbarossa"—Stalin or his intelligence?

In order to crystalize the issue we must examine several aspects of the relationship between intelligence and decision makers. These involve the way decision makers regard intelligence production and intelligence assessments; the relationship between decision makers' commitment to their policy and approach and their willingness to accept a discrepant assessment; and the influence of decision makers on intelligence assessments.

Decision Makers and Intelligence Production

To a large extent decision makers are analysts. Like intelligence analysts, decision makers form assumptions and estimates with regard to the enemy's likely behavior; they also read incoming information (including intelligence assessments) and carry out several stages of the analytical process; then they form their own estimate concerning the threat of impending attack. Their analysis is also influenced by many of the constraints and biases that distort the estimates of intelligence analysts.

But decision makers are not only analysts. In our case they are either national policy makers, military commanders, or officials charged in some way with carrying out national security policy. For them evaluating the situation is only a stage in the process of making their decision and implementing it. The analytical process used by the decision maker, however, is somewhat different from that of the intelligence analyst. The decision maker lacks the knowledge base of the analyst: he reads only a small part of the intelligence information, and he has no time for detailed analysis and prolonged deliberation. Consequently the analytical process undertaken by decision makers is shorter and more simplified than that of the professional analyst, and images and conceptions may play a larger role in it. As Hughes observes: "Not that intelligent analysis will always differ from the preconceptions of a given policy-maker. But it often will. And almost always there will be a difference between the clear picture seen by a convinced policy-maker and the cloudy picture usually seen by intelligence" (1976, p. 19). Finally, the commitment of decision makers to their own policies and views might have an important impact on the way they perceive a threat and set about countering it.

This different viewpoint creates several difficulties in the relationship between decision makers and intelligence. It has been observed that decision makers often act as their own intelligence analysts, especially during crises. In so doing, though, they often prefer the latest "hard facts" to extensive, refined analyses.[1] Decision makers often believe that they have a wider perspective and richer practical experience than professional analysts and that they are better equipped to consider data in a larger context. Decision makers also often accuse the intelligence community of submitting inadequate and irrelevant judgments. As Smoke notes, policy makers "do not rely entirely upon reports and analyses flowing upward to them from bureaucracies and staffs. From personal and vicarious experience they often feel that the conclusions of 'analysis' do not capture everything that is important in a situation, and they temper those conclusions with their intuitive judgment" (1977, p. 271). And the Church Committee concluded: "While intelligence analysts have a very good record in the area of technical assessment . . . the record is weaker in qualitative judgments, trend forecasting, and political estimating . . . some policymakers feel that intelligence analysts have not been especially helpful to policymakers on the more subtle questions of political, economic, and military intentions of foreign groups and leaders" (U.S. Congress, 1976, p. 267).

As a result of their tendency to act as their own analysts, decision makers may draw erroneous conclusions from raw data. They lack both the professional knowledge and the time to consider and weigh all the evidence objectively. "Precisely because they are generalists, they also are less sensitive to the particularities, intricacies, and ambiguities of specific problems. Raw data mean nothing out of context, and whereas leaders may understand the context of the big picture, they are less likely to grasp the context of the little picture" (Betts, 1980a, p. 119). The Church Committee concluded:

> By circumventing the available analytical process, the consumers of intelligence may not only be depriving themselves of the skills of intelligence professionals; they may also be sacrificing necessary time and useful objectivity. In making his own intelligence judgment based on the large volume of often conflicting reports and undigested raw intelligence instead of on a well-considered finished piece of intelligence analysis, a high official may be seeking conclusions more favorable to his policy preferences than the situation may in fact warrant. (U.S. Congress, 1976, p. 267)

In some cases decision makers feel they cannot trust the accuracy of intelligence assessments or use them effectively. Sometimes they conclude that intelligence assessments contain poor information, reflect low intellectual quality, lack rigorous analytical methods (Szanton and Allison, 1976, p. 199), or use ambiguous and evasive language. Mistrust of intelligence agencies is common especially in totalitarian regimes, where intelligence services combine the functions of detecting external threats to national security as well as disclosing internal threats to the regime's stability and survival. Stalin did not trust his intelligence services, which at the time of "Barbarossa" still had not recovered from the Great Purge of 1937–38. Such mistrust can produce harmful results. For one, intelligence assessments may be taken less seriously. As Wohlstetter observed with regard to Pearl Harbor, a general prejudice against intellectuals and specialists—not confined to the military but widely held in America—and the resultant low prestige attached to intellectual work made it difficult for intelligence experts to be heard. On December 5, after weeks of being ignored as mere data collectors, subordinate officers in intelligence and research units tried to communicate their more urgent interpretation directly to the chiefs of Army and Navy War Plans. "But their efforts were unsuccessful because of the poor repute associated with Intelligence, inferior rank, and the province of the specialist, or long-hair" (Wohlstetter, 1962, p. 312; see also pp. 70, 102, 395).

Indeed intelligence assessments may be left unread altogether. Hilsman (1956, p. 40) found that most of the material produced by intelligence is never read by policy makers or even brought to their attention. While this is explained to a large extent by the time constraints under which decision makers work and by the irrelevance of some intelligence material, it can nevertheless prove detrimental during a crisis. The British, for example, assessed in 1941 that Japanese aircraft were old-fashioned and of poor quality. In May 1941 a Japanese Zero fighter was shot down in China, and British Intelligence in Malaya passed on to all the services data about its unexpectedly good performance. Yet since this intelligence organization was considered ineffective and was held in low esteem, nobody read these reports, no action was taken on them, and the people most directly concerned—the British air crews—were never informed (Leasor, 1968, pp. 160–162).

In extreme cases of mistrust, such as that of Stalin, decision makers may concentrate the entire assessment process in their own hands. This practice is not unique to totalitarian regimes. In Norway prior to the invasion there were considerable restrictions on joint evaluation and discussion of the international situation by individuals and organizations in the government. Foreign Minister Koht preferred to handle matters alone and was allowed great freedom in this respect. Particularly conspicuous was the failure to achieve integrated and coordinated decision making between the ministers of defense and foreign affairs. Thus at no time was Koht really made aware of the constraints that the military establishment was imposing on his decision-making options as the crisis developed. Intelligence messages were exchanged between the two ministries, but their content and implications were never jointly discussed (Holst, 1966, p. 36).

The opposite case—of relying too heavily on intelligence sources—brings no better results. I have suggested that decision makers often have limited capability to evaluate independently intelligence information and view critically the assessments of their intelligence services. Usually the information the decision maker receives is selected and interpreted in the light of the existing conceptions within the intelligence community. Even when decision makers do obtain raw information, they are not always in a position to evaluate fully its significance or the reliability of its sources. Roosevelt read the Magic excerpts, but it is questionable whether he could independently evaluate the significance of changes in communication or tone.

Moreover, civilian decision makers often have limited understanding and knowledge of military capabilities, whether of their own or the enemy's army. Before the North Korean attack the State Department had been told by the Pentagon that such an invasion was out of the question: the South Korean forces were so well armed and trained that they were clearly superior to North Korea's. The greatest task of the United States, the State Department was told, was to restrain South Korea from attacking the North. Kennan concludes the story: "Having no grounds to challenge this judgment, I accepted it . . . and we passed on to other things" (1967, p. 485). Kennan's story illustrates the point: once a mistaken assessment is made by the intelligence community with regard to the enemy, it tends to be accepted by the decision makers. This is true especially when the intelligence community has a good reputation, in which case the decision makers tend to rely on its assessment without checking it carefully. This happened in Israel too before October 1973.

The limitations on decision makers' independent assessment capability regarding the enemy have another outcome. Decision makers often are not sufficiently aware of the problems inherent in making intelligence estimates, of the ambiguous nature of indicators, and of the difficulties of understanding the enemy's intentions. Hence they often require that intelligence give them a yes-or-no answer as to whether or not something is going to occur. Yet a study found that analysts "resented having to give a yes or no answer. They believed that they were describing what most likely would occur and mentioned several times that they went to great lengths to give the reader an appreciation of the factors upon which the outcome depended." Analysts felt that in many situations by saying yes or no it was they rather than the decision makers who were making the decision (Kelly and Peterson, 1971, pp. 4-3, 4-4). If decision makers were more sensitive to the vulnerabilities of intelligence estimates, they might be less inclined to rely invariably on them; then too they might be less frustrated with the quality of intelligence estimates, hence less inclined to substitute their own assessments for intelligence production.

It is difficult to find the golden mean in this dilemma. Intelligence estimates that have the most impact on decision makers and are of most use to them are those presented in clear, unambiguous language (Betts, 1981b, p. 260). But, in view of the weaknesses of intelligence, such estimates are the most vulnerable to failure; and intelligence failures and the loss of credibility they generate may lead decision makers to ignore intelligence assessments and rely on their own analyses.

Commitment to a Policy

Decision makers, and especially national policy makers, are usually committed to their policy. To change the policy might be difficult, expensive, and sometimes risky. Specific intelligence estimates and warnings often contradict the wisdom of particular policies. They might indicate that the existing policy is wrong and is leading to war—as in the case of Pearl Harbor. The required countermeasures are usually expensive and may provoke undesired escalation; this was an important consideration on Stalin's part in 1941. If the warning proves false, decision makers might be criticized for having taken unnecessary countermeasures; this consideration was not absent from the minds of Israeli decision makers in 1973.

Unlike the intelligence analyst, the decision maker cannot ignore the costs of accepting warnings. If he thinks that the evidence is not strong enough to justify the cost of action that undermines existing policy, he will not take adequate countermeasures. As I suggested in Chapter 4, this means that the more committed decision makers are to their policy, the less willing they will be to accept warnings that contradict their commitment; and the stronger this commitment is, the stronger the evidence required to bring about acceptance of warnings (Poteat, 1976, pp. 15–17). Unfortunately, when a threat increases, decision makers' commitment to existing policy increases as well; hence their willingness to accept warnings may decrease. George and Smoke describe this dynamic well: "To take available warning seriously may require policy-makers to make new decisions of a difficult or unpalatable character. There is a subtle feedback from the policy-maker's anticipation of the response he might have to make to warning that affects his receptivity to warning . . . Decision-makers are often reluctant to reopen policy matters that were decided earlier only with great difficulty" (1974, p. 574). Thus Stalin's rejection of evidence concerning the imminence of the German invasion can be explained in part by his commitment to his treaty with Hitler. Since August 1939 Stalin had built his foreign and security policy on that treaty. In the face of an obvious German build-up in Poland, Stalin did his utmost to keep the treaty alive, even by appeasing the Germans and avoiding any actions he believed might provoke a German attack. Stalin may also have been unwilling to admit that he had lost his ability to manipulate Hitler. Committed to his policy, he ordered the Anti-Aircraft Command to avoid firing over Russian territory and rejected many British and American warnings as capitalist provocation.

Similarly Nehru's strong personal commitment to his China policy and to Indian-Chinese solidarity led him to underestimate the Chinese threat. He rejected and denigrated information suggesting that China might resort to war. He refused to change his assumptions even when confronted by China's warning and even when a few senior officers called his attention to signs of growing threat should his "forward policy" continue (Vertzberger, 1978a, p. 128).

The same logic leads decision makers to look for supportive information and estimates. Once committed to a policy, they tend to prefer optimistic reports and intelligence estimates that enable them to pursue that policy. Hilsman (1956, pp. 43, 122) shows that the intelligence considered most useful and most welcome by decision makers is that which provides support for courses of action already decided upon. Allen Dulles, former Director of the CIA, also found that policy makers tend to become wedded to the policy for which they are responsible. "They are likely to view with a jaundiced eye intelligence reports that might tend to challenge existing policy decisions or require a change in cherished estimates of the strength of the Soviets" (1963, pp. 52–53).

In some cases decision makers may demand explicitly or implicitly that intelligence estimates conform to their views and support their policies. A former director of the DIA recalled that "too often the user has not been content with an objective judgment from his intelligence officer—he has wanted the answer that 'supports the program' " (Graham, 1973, p. 16). And the Pike Papers noted with regard to the war in Vietnam:

> Pressure from policy-making officials to produce positive intelligence indicators reinforced erroneous assessments of allied progress and enemy capabilities . . . Considerable pressure was placed on the Intelligence Community to generate numbers, less out of tactical necessity than for political purposes.
>
> The Administration's need was for confirmation of the contention that there was light at the end of the tunnel . . . In this sense, the Intelligence Community could not help but find its powers to effect objective analysis substantially undermined. (1976, pp. 18-19)

How Decision Makers Affect the Intelligence Process

The intelligence process is necessarily influenced by the fact that it is designed to serve decision makers. On the one hand intelligence should be, and often is, separated from policy. The function of policy is supposed to be the active one of making decisions, free from the strictures of intelligence; intelligence, for its part, is charged with the unbiased role of collecting and evaluating information separate from policy considerations. The absorption of analysts into policy debates and their proximity to decision makers is thought to be capable of distorting intelligence analysis and disrupting its professionalism and objectivity. On the other hand intelligence is subordinated to policy and must relate itself to the needs of decision making; for in the absence of policy guidance intelligence work may be aimless and unhelpful to decision makers. Intelligence analysts also strive to maintain direct contact with decision makers. A former Director of Israeli Military Intelligence believes that the ability of decision makers to understand intelligence and use it effectively depends on continuous contact with intelligence (Gazit, 1981, p. 12). And a former Director of the CIA suggests that "the analyst must have a sense of the final product to which his material contributes. He should have a direct relationship with the individuals occupying the policymaking offices . . . to permit easy and informal communication of interests" (Colby, 1980, p. 168). Here again, though, because intelligence is subordinated to policy, it is liable to be used to justify and support a policy, and analysts are likely to be influenced by their proximity to decision makers.

To achieve and maintain such a delicate balance between separation and communication is a difficult job. In many cases it is never accomplished; then intelligence is no longer focused on the central issues, and decisions may not be based on the best available information; in addition the intelligence process is adversely influenced by policy needs. Past cases, such as the Pearl Harbor surprise, reveal that senior field commanders and intelligence analysts are often not familiar with their government's policy and plans because decision makers are reluctant to expose their conceptual framework to intelligence analysts—particularly on the highest level of policy making.

The detrimental effect is threefold. First, analysts are not always sensitive to the needs of decision makers and do not properly direct their production toward issues that are important to policy. Intelligence, "being unaware of the precise situation envisaged by the policy-maker . . . vainly attempts to gather 'all' the facts and provide for all possible contingencies. In doing so it produces voluminous amounts of information, much of which is irrelevant to the actual policy problems, and that which is relevant tends to get lost in the mass which is not" (Wasserman, 1960, p. 163).

Second, intelligence analysts find it difficult to assess and predict the enemy's intentions and willingness to take risks since these depend to a large extent on their own government's future moves. As I mentioned in Chapter 3, this factor was especially important in the case of Pearl Harbor. In some instances analysts may be missing crucial information concerning another state's intentions that high officials have obtained through political contacts. Thus Henry Kissinger was blamed for sabotaging intelligence analysis pertaining to the Arabs' intention to go to war in October 1973 by withholding crucial evidence from analysts. According to the Pike Papers, "Kissinger had been in close contact with both the Soviets and the Arabs throughout the pre-war period. He, presumably, was in a unique position to pick up indications of Arab dissatisfaction with diplomatic talks, and signs of an ever-increasing Soviet belief that war would soon break out . . . The Secretary passed no such warning to the intelligence community" (1976, p. 20).

Third, intelligence analysts are sometimes unaware of the costs and benefits of their own assessment, especially when the issue is as critical as predicting a coming war. This point is well illustrated by the British assessment of the forthcoming German invasion of Russia. Until late May 1941 the British Joint Intelligence Committee (JIC) rejected rumors of a German invasion plan. It was not until June 5 that the JIC decided that there was a real possibility of war. Churchill (1950, pp. 354–361) later claimed that he had never been content with the form of collective wisdom represented by the JIC and that as early as 1940 he had arranged to see a daily selection of the original raw intelligence reports before they were sifted and digested by the various intelligence agencies. In this way he was able to form his own opinion. In March 1940, following an Ultra interception, derived from the decryption of secret German communications, he changed his mind and came to the conclusion that a German attack was impending. This difference of opinion is explained in part by a difference in positions (Hilsman, 1956, pp. 173–174). Unlike decision makers, who make predictions in terms of their costs and benefits as a basis for action, the JIC was charged simply with estimating probable developments. Hence it hesitated to recommend a decision to warn Stalin of a German attack until it had absolutely conclusive evidence. It lacked both the necessary information about British policy that would provide the judgmental criteria for such a decision and the authority to analyze that policy. Churchill, who had both the information needed for a policy analysis and the right to make that analysis, was in a position to evaluate the consequences of acting on a prediction based on such partial evidence. Thus he could decide to take action on the grounds that assuming the prediction was right was either more desirable or less dangerous than assuming it was wrong, or even than waiting for additional evidence.

If one danger arises when intelligence is too remote from policy, another emerges when intelligence is not separate enough from policy and is excessively influenced by it. Decision makers may create a climate of opinion within the intelligence community by imprinting their own beliefs and assumptions on it. Their opinions tend to percolate down through the community and influence the processes of collecting, selecting, and interpreting information. Decision makers' opinions are usually communicated within the intelligence community through hierarchical channels, often through the link of the intelligence chiefs, who convey the views of their agencies to the decision makers and transmit the latters' opinions throughout their own organizations. Decision makers' views and beliefs are also communicated through many informal channels, thereby indirectly influencing the intelligence processes.

The outcome can be harmful to the entire process. Intelligence sources may distort or censor their reports and warnings so as to avoid challenging existing policy. Thus Stalin's refusal to accept warnings made officers on the border unwilling to report or emphasize indications of German offensive border deployment (Whaley, 1973, p. 203).

Indeed, the possible suppression of alarming indicators can actually be standard procedure within the organization. Until the autumn of 1959 Nehru tried to conceal the conflict with China from the public. As a result the Ministry of External Affairs refrained from processing any information concerning Chinese penetration into Indian territory. "Such information was immediately filed away because Nehru became furious whenever mention was made of the possibility that the conflict might intensify" (Vertzberger, 1978a, pp. 125–126). Similarly in early 1979 the U.S. intelligence community failed to provide advance warning of the collapse of the Shah's regime in Iran partly because it was felt within the community that senior decision makers did not want to hear reports of this nature. The House of Representatives Subcommittee on Evaluation, which later examined the issue, found no evidence of a deliberate attempt on the part of decision makers to suppress warnings; but the U.S. embassy and military team in Tehran, the State Department, and the intelligence community "quickly learned that no one in the White House really wanted any negative information about Iran's Shah, its stability, or the military build up" (Mansur, 1979, pp. 29, 33). The subcommittee concluded:

> U.S. policy toward the Shah also affected intelligence analysis and production—not directly, through the conscious suppression of unfavorable news, but indirectly. From an analyst's perspective, "until recently you couldn't *give* away intelligence on Iran" . . . Policymakers were not asking *whether* the Shah's

autocracy would survive indefinitely; policy was premised on that assumption. Lack of imagination concerning alternative U.S. policies limited both the search for an accurate understanding of Iran's internal situation, and the receptiveness of intelligence users to such analysis.   (U.S. Congress, 1979, p. 2)

Decision makers may influence the analytical process as well. Analysts may overemphasize information that supports existing policy and give less weight to information that contradicts it. The former Director of the DIA admitted that "many analysts came to the conclusion that it was not in their interests to reach conclusions which seemed to run counter to established national policy" (Graham, 1979, p. 32). This probably was the case in Israel before October 1973, when declarations by political leaders that war was not to be expected in the near future might have influenced analysts' perceptions. Occasionally analysts may even change their estimates under the impact of decision makers. Thus in January 1968 the Joint Chiefs of Staff insisted that the Tet offensive in Vietnam had been a total military defeat for the enemy. "DIA didn't agree with this interpretation, but it watered down every paper it wrote on this subject so that its position was impossible to determine" (McGarvey, 1973, p. 325).

Finally, those intelligence officers on high levels who serve as intelligence advisers to decision makers may become reluctant to pass on information that might be rejected by the decision makers. As I have mentioned, only selective information reached the Soviet leadership prior to "Barbarossa." Similarly Nehru's advisers took care to select the information that supported his policy, thereby strengthening his belief that reevaluation was unnecessary (Vertzberger, 1978a, pp. 133–134).

The result is feedback: the decision makers contribute to the creation of a climate of opinion that influences the intelligence process, while intelligence provides information that supports the decision makers' assessment. That pattern is found, for example, in the Pearl Harbor case. The available information was not properly evaluated because the entire policy, hence the intelligence system, was geared to an understanding of the situation that implicitly assumed that any Japanese attack would be directed against Southeast Asia or Russia. As the congressional investigating committee found: "Intelligence was concentrated on information considered significant by the policy-makers and thus failed to evaluate adequately the really significant information" (cited in Wasserman, 1960, p. 166).

Decision Makers and Surprise Attack

The role of decision makers is an important link in the chain of failures that lead to surprise attacks. Decision makers influence the content of intelligence assessments. They have to accept or reject intelligence assessments; sometimes they have to choose among competing assessments. Correct intelligence assessments cannot prevent surprise if they are rejected by decision makers. And it is the decision makers, not intelligence, who are responsible for taking appropriate and timely countermeasures to face an enemy offensive; if they fail to do so, owing to whatever considerations, constraints, and shortcomings, intelligence warnings will not prevent surprise attack.

Decision makers form assessments of their own concerning the enemy and his likely behavior. They may be able to correct erroneous intelligence assessments because they have at least two advantages over intelligence analysts: since they are not constantly involved in the process of assessing intelligence, they might detect inadequacies in earlier assumptions and formulations of the assessment; and they are aware of the overall picture concerning the intentions and capabilities of both sides—their own and those estimated to be the enemy's. But more often than not, decision makers' assessments do not differ from those of their intelligence agencies.

Decision makers may even make their own contribution to the failure to anticipate an impending attack. One of the puzzling aspects of surprise attack is the unwillingness of decision makers to consider seriously less reasonable or less probable but more damaging eventualities. Even when they believe that war is not imminent, why do decision makers not take measures to face the less probable possibility that war will break out?

Four possible explanations come to mind. First, since the decision maker is an information analyst himself, his beliefs, like those of the intelligence analyst, will tend to be rigid, and when he forms assumptions about the enemy's likely behavior, he too will tend to focus on one possibility, ignoring the alternatives. He may also ignore or twist discrepant information and may tend to be influenced by group dynamics and pressures for conformity.

Second, decision makers are dependent to a large extent on their intelligence agencies. They are familiar with a relatively small amount of information, most of which is selected for them by the intelligence agencies. Though decision makers are able to form their own estimate with regard to the enemy's intentions, they are usually dependent on the intelligence estimate regarding enemy capabilities. After all, the intelligence community carries the authority of the expert.

Third, decision makers are not only dependent to a large extent on intelligence assessments; they also tend to simplify those assessments. Hilsman found that decision makers, partly because of their action orientation and the pressure under which they work, are distrustful of any solution that seems complex and have no patience with a lengthy analysis of involved alternatives. They "tend to reject not only the complex solution, but also the subtle reasoning, richness in qualification, and even the general attitude of experiment and inquiry characteristic of a scholarly approach . . . They do not like long papers, not only because they have trouble finding time to read them, but also because they feel that most problems are not so subtle and complex as to require extended treatment. The one-page, one-side-only brief must suffice" (Hilsman, 1956, pp. 58–59). Thus the intelligence analyst may sometimes hesitate between alternatives, believing that although war is not imminent, neither is it a possibility to be excluded. But since he is required to submit a brief paper with a clear-cut conclusion—that war is or is not imminent—his hesitations about the less probable possibility may not be revealed to the decision makers.

Fourth, decision makers will pay a price, whether in domestic or in foreign affairs, for taking countermeasures prematurely. If they believe that the evidence provided by intelligence is not strong and convincing enough to justify that price, they will postpone taking countermeasures for as long as they can. Since the evidence does not usually become conclusive until the attack is virtually imminent, the victim will then be only partly prepared.

CONCLUSION

Is Surprise Attack Inevitable?

I have attempted to explain surprise attack from three points of view: the process of surprise attack, the individual analyst, and the environment in which the analyst thinks and works. In this final chapter I shall consider certain elements common to all three topics. Rather than summarize, I shall attempt, by approaching the problem from a new perspective, to explain why surprise attacks are indeed almost inevitable. In other words, I shall confront the failure to eliminate surprise attack.

The Complexity of the Problem

One of the main conclusions of this study is that the failure to prevent a surprise attack does not evolve overnight. Surprise attacks are not the result of any single factor, nor do they occur because of mistakes committed on any one level. The study of instances of strategic surprise since 1939 reveals a long chain of errors and difficulties accounting for the failure to predict the imminence of war. In each case an accumulation of many complex problems was involved.

Thus far I have described a wide range of problems, errors, and biases. Obviously they are not equally important. Some are central and critical, others secondary, in terms of contributing to the failure to prevent surprise attack. For example, the relevance of factors such as judgmental heuristics, small-group dynamics, or organizational processes may vary; in some cases they may improve the victim's ability to judge his opponent, but usually they compound the difficulty of anticipating a coming attack. In either case, though, their contribution is not critical.

All told, three factors seem to be especially significant. One is the quality of information and data available for judging and predicting enemy behavior. The usual lack of direct evidence pertaining to the enemy's intentions and the ambiguous nature of the available warning indicators are critical factors that make it very difficult to assess correctly both the intentions and the capabilities of the opponent.

A second critical factor is the persistence of conceptions even in the face of contradictory evidence. Again the ambiguous nature of intelligence material makes it possible for the analyst easily to assimilate incoming information to his beliefs without changing them, even when a change is required. When conceptions become established, and when analysts become overconfident of their conceptions, it takes the test of reality—an enemy attack—to disprove them.

The problem is further complicated by an inherent interdependency among many of the aspects of surprise attack described in this study. Various assumptions that underlie conceptions and estimates are strongly interdependent, so that one wrong hypothesis may create a chain reaction. Similarly, estimates of the enemy's capabilities and intentions are inseparable, just as estimates and collection of information are interdependent. The prevailing conception defines and to a large extent dictates the direction and boundaries of the information collection effort, and biased or selectively collected information in turn influences the analytical process.

The interdependency factor also discourages the search for alternative assumptions. A conception that war is not to be expected in the foreseeable future generates no more than a minimal effort to question its validity; this reluctance to reevaluate the evidence from an alternative viewpoint in turn strengthens the wrong conception. As a consequence of this vicious circle it becomes difficult to see the weakness of the structure of assumptions.

Nor can the analytical process be separated from the environment in which it takes place. Intelligence production influences decision making; but at the same time a combination of factors—the climate of opinion within the intelligence organization, bureaucratic constraints, and the preferences and beliefs of the policy makers—heavily influences the way in which conceptions are formed and information is read. The intelligence assessment affects the operational concept and vice versa. Thus a strong interdependency is created among those who put forward the assumptions and assessments: the analysts, superiors, subordinates, decision makers, and experts, as well as politicians and military men.

From this viewpoint it is doubtful whether one can ever really determine who is to be blamed for estimate failure. On the one hand analysts and decision makers are interdependent and share responsibility for failure; on the other, since surprise attack is common, indeed almost inevitable, it is questionable whether anybody should be blamed for the failure to prevent it.

This strong interdependency makes it very difficult, perhaps even impossible, to locate the weak links in the chain and prevent future surprise attacks. There are too many weak links, and they are interdependent. Even if, for example, the analytical process could somehow be improved, failure to prevent surprise attack could still derive from human error or policy-making considerations. This is all the more true since, as we shall now see, dramatic improvements cannot be expected.

Why Safeguards Usually Fail

The constant recurrence of intelligence failure has brought about numerous attempts by commissions of inquiry, students of intelligence, and the intelligence communities themselves to suggest safeguards and improvements aimed at preventing future failure. By and large intelligence production has improved since the Second World War: the quality of certain kinds of information has improved; dissemination of information is more rationalized; intelligence agencies are capable of providing better data and more sophisticated analysis; early warning systems are more sensitive; there is better coordination among intelligence agencies and departments; and perhaps there is also a better understanding of the ultimate limitations of the intelligence system.

Yet there still exists no guarantee against intelligence failures and surprises. Despite the improved quality of production intelligence agencies do not appear to be more successful now than in the past. Intelligence failures still occur time and again; more than thirty years after Pearl Harbor the best intelligence systems failed to anticipate the Yom Kippur War or the collapse of the Shah's regime in Iran.

In general scholars and experts alike are pessimistic about the possibility of preventing such surprises. Their expectations are low: at most they hope to reduce the phenomenon of surprise, not do away with it. "There is no way to eliminate misperception. The world is too complex and the available information too ambiguous for that," notes Jervis (1977, p. 184). A similar point is made by George and Smoke: "Procedural and other efforts to improve recognition and utilization of warning can hope to meet with some success, but it would be dangerous to assume that the fundamental difficulties . . . can be fully or reliably eliminated" (1974, p. 576). And Betts explains in more detail why one should not be too hopeful regarding such safeguards:

> Curing some pathologies with organizational reforms often creates new pathologies or resurrects old ones; perfecting intelligence production does not necessarily lead to perfecting intelligence consumption; making warning systems more sensitive reduces the risk of surprise, but increases the number of false alarms, which in turn reduces sensitivity; the principles of optimal analytic procedure are in many respects incompatible with the imperatives of the decision process; avoiding intelligence failure requires the elimination of strategic preconceptions, but leaders cannot operate purposefully without some preconceptions. (1978, p. 63)

Most of the safeguards recommended are aimed at either improving the analytical and warning processes or at removing organizational obstacles and group influences. In looking at these proposals we shall see that most of the safeguards are impractical, do not solve any real problem, or ignore the costs and new difficulties they introduce. By and large they can improve the intelligence process marginally, but they cannot significantly reduce failure.

Improving the Analytical Process

Recommendations for improving the analytical process usually aim to reduce the difficulties and errors caused by ambiguous information, biased information processing, and misperception. Three main categories of safeguards are often suggested: increasing awareness of the limitations and problems involved in the intelligence process; improving the formation of hypotheses; and using more sophisticated methods for information processing.

Increasing awareness of limitations. Many scholars suggest that analysts and decision makers alike must be more aware of the nature of judgmental biases and of the limitations of the intelligence process if they hope to reduce the incidence of surprise attack. This argument holds that if analysts and decision makers become aware of common perceptual errors, they may be able to avoid them, thereby reducing overconfidence in prevailing beliefs. If they recognize that they are influenced by their expectations and tend to fit incoming information into preexisting beliefs, they may become more sensitive to alternative explanations and consequently examine discrepant information more carefully. If they understand that their interpretations of events are usually inferences that make heavy use of theory, they may reconsider the logic of their prior theories and adjust their confidence accordingly. Moreover, "an appreciation of the superficial nature of most learning from history would lead decision∤makers to think more about the causes of previous outcomes and so to be in a better position to determine what past cases are relevant to [their] current situation" (Jervis, 1976, pp. 423–424, 409–410; see also Nisbett and Ross, 1980, p. 293; Jervis, 1986).

In the same vein scholars argue that analysts and decision makers should be more aware of one another's limitations and weaknesses. Stein (1982a, pp. 53–54) says that decision makers both military and political must recognize that intelligence analysts deal with ambiguous information subject to alternative interpretations. Hence decision makers should be more skeptical about the reliability of intelligence estimates; they should require the presentation of alternative explanations of the evidence. Moreover decision makers should be aware of the limits inherent in intelligence warning and should take into account that adequate and timely warning of attack cannot be relied on. "Rather than plan on 'certain' warnings, military officers must build the contingency of surprise into their defense planning." For a similar reason Betts suggests that "the most realistic strategy for improvement would be to have intelligence professionals anticipate the cognitive barriers to decision makers' utilization of their products" (1978, p. 84).

Indeed awareness of the problematic nature of estimates and warnings can be increased somewhat. Such an awareness might encourage analysts to elaborate alternative assumptions and be more cautious in their assessments. Yet while this would at least not be damaging, neither would it eliminate misperception or prevent surprise. Most intelligence analysts are well aware of the problematic quality of the information they use and generally recognize that their analytical process might be biased. Yet when they are working under the pressure of time and the demands of those responsible for making decisions, they feel that they have no better way of forming assessments. And decision makers learn before long, especially after several intelligence failures, just how far they can rely on their intelligence community; but since they have to assess a situation before making a decision, the alternative is to rely on their own estimates. Psychological studies show that even when one is fully aware of the erroneous nature of perception, the error remains compelling; awareness does not in itself produce an accurate perception of reality (Kahneman and Tversky, 1979, p. 314). This means that even if analysts know of common perceptual errors, the limitations of human perception are often likely to prevail.

Improving the formation of hypotheses. Several strategies have been recommended for improving the formation of hypotheses and the interpretation of evidence. Most of these strategies are aimed at encouraging the analyst and decision maker to use alternative ways of thinking. Thus many scholars suggest that analysts and decision makers should make all assumptions, beliefs, and values pertaining to the enemy as explicit as possible. Jervis explains the logic behind this strategy: "People often not only have a limited understanding of the workings of others' arguments, they also do not know the structure of their own belief systems—what values are most important, how some beliefs are derived from others, and what evidence would contradict their views" (1976, p. 410).

A second strategy stems from the first. "To make their important beliefs and assumptions explicit, decision-makers should not only try to discover the crucial elements that underlie their policy preferences but should also consider what evidence would tend to confirm, or, more importantly, disconfirm, their views" (Jervis, 1976, p. 413). Smoke elaborates:

> Here analysts begin from a single, hypothetical image of a possible future situation and reason backward to adduce what hypothetical conditions in the present might lead to the actual occurrence of that future situation. Then they search through available information to see if those conditions are being met, or seem about to be met. Sometimes they begin from a future situation which at first blush seems very unlikely, but on examining its preconditions they discover that these are closer to being met than they would have initially believed. (1977, p. 264)

Such a safeguard was developed by the CIA in light of the deteriorating situation in Iran in the fall of 1978. The National Intelligence Officer for each geographic region was directed to hold monthly meetings of analysts, aimed at deliberately addressing the less likely hypotheses and predictions. Under this procedure analysts are expected to confront and try to disprove seemingly unlikely hypotheses at a very early stage (U.S. Congress, 1979, p. 8).

Heuer suggests a similar strategy in which analysts deliberately look for information that disproves their theories and refrain from employing a satisfying strategy that permits immediate acceptance of the first hypothesis that seems consistent with the information. They should ask themselves what if anything could possibly make them change their minds. To this end Heuer suggests a third strategy:

> To guide his information search and analysis, the analyst should first seek to identify and examine alternative models or conceptual frameworks for interpreting the already available information. Because people have very limited capacity for simultaneously considering multiple hypotheses, the alternatives should be written down, and evidence compared against them in a systematic manner.
>
> This permits the analyst to focus on the degree to which the evidence is diagnostic in helping him select the best among competing models, rather than simply the degree to which it supports or undermines his own previous belief. This helps overcome the tendency to ignore the possibility that evidence consistent with one's own belief is equally consistent with other hypotheses. (1979, p. 8)

Such strategies may somewhat increase the perceived likelihood of alternative interpretations and scenarios and may sensitize analysts and decision makers to discrepant information. Yet for a number of reasons they still do not make analysts and decision makers less vulnerable to surprise. For one thing it is very difficult to change established analytical approaches significantly. This is especially true with regard to decision makers. As Betts notes, "Few busy activists who have achieved success by thinking the way that they do will change their way of thinking because some theorist tells them to" (1978, p. 83).

Then too the use of such strategies may become no more than an intellectual exercise that does not really affect persistent beliefs. "The danger is that, if these things are done, they will be done routinely and without keen alertness to the likely obsolescence of all preconceptions" (Knorr, 1979, p. 85). Finally, when the issue at stake is whether or not the enemy intends to go to war, the problem is usually not to decide what the alternative scenarios are or to say what evidence supports each scenario or even to imagine beforehand what surprising events might occur. The problem is to determine which scenario and interpretation are the correct ones, and for answering this question those strategies are not very helpful.

Improving information processing. In recent years several quantitative approaches and empirical methods have been developed for facilitating information processing. All offer specific rules of procedure, data presentation, and data interpretation, and many of them permit statistical manipulation. Some of the most significant methods introduced in the American intelligence community are Bayesian analysis, the Delphi Technique, and Cross-Impact Analysis.[1]

These methods have several important advantages. They are systematic and relatively objective; their accuracy can be checked by replication; they are highly structured in their rules of approach; they are comprehensive and can usually examine all the variables at the same time; and the estimator can assign levels of confidence to the predictions based on laws of statistical probability (Brinkley and Hull, 1979, pp. 238–241).

So far none of these methods has been introduced on a large scale in intelligence communities. Beyond the problems specific to each of them, several common limitations explain their modest success. First, since most analysts refer to them with suspicion, there are problems in their application. It is one thing to direct several teams of analysts to learn to use such techniques; it is quite another actually to use them on a broad daily basis. Obviously the considerable time consumed by their use significantly limits their applicability. Moreover, while it would be possible to train teams of analysts in the use of complex quantitative approaches, it is not feasible to do the same with decision makers.

Another limitation has to do with the quality of data available for input into the conceptual framework. In many cases the information that goes into such models is subject to a high degree of error. Some necessary data may not exist at all. In addition many of these methods require analysts to have access to specific computer hardware and software.

Furthermore, some analysts claim that these methods are not really objective, since original assumptions will still bias the results. Others claim that such models present a distorted image of how actors interrelate and that their conclusions do not really apply to policy makers' concerns (Brinkley and Hull, 1979, pp. 256–257).

Finally, such techniques may force analysts to organize their modes of thinking and make their assumptions more explicit, but they do not help analysts overcome the problems inherent in ambiguous intelligence information, to choose among competing hypotheses, or to predict a unique event such as an enemy attack. As Knorr and Morgenstern observe, "The crucial limitation on our ability to identify and attach weights to the variable conditions determining unique events does not permit the programming of computers for the kinds of prediction we are interested in" (1968, p. 15). Given the complex nature of predicting surprise attack, it is doubtful that technological devices and quantitative approaches can make a significant contribution to eliminating surprise in the foreseeable future.

Our conclusion regarding the use of such methods must be rather gloomy. Perhaps, however, one should be more patient before categorically rejecting their usefulness—one can, at least theoretically, identify some advantages. Moreover, some methods have not yet been empirically tested and implemented long and seriously enough to prove their futility.

Improving Organizational Procedures

In many cases intelligence failures lead to attempts to improve organizational procedures. This is probably due to the fact that organizational reforms are more tangible than changes in analytical processes. A lack of reliable information, inadequate coordination, or a breakdown in communications seems a more convincing reason for failure than biases in analytical process; hence these suggest more promising possibilities for correction. In some cases organizational changes improve the intelligence process. Frequently their implementation involves considerable cost. Moreover, while changing a way of thinking is very difficult, attempts to achieve it are at least not damaging. In contrast, changes in organizational procedures may be easier to implement, but, as Betts has observed, "most solutions proposed to obviate intelligence dysfunctions have two edges: in reducing one vulnerability, they increase another" (1978, p. 73).

Under the category of improving organizational procedures let us look at five safeguards: improving the collection of information; reducing group influence and establishing a devil's advocate; establishing the pluralism of intelligence agencies; improving the warning system; and improving the relationship between the intelligence community and decision makers.

Improving the collection of information. Lack of information and warning indicators is usually not the reason for failure of estimates; yet an attempt to improve the collection of information is one of the most common safeguards recommended following a major intelligence failure. There is also an organizational incentive for improving collection: analysts always demand more information, and achieving better information is the raison d'être of intelligence collection agencies.

The problem, however, is not how to collect more information or even more reliable information but rather how to acquire direct evidence concerning the enemy's intentions. This is a very difficult task. Gazit (1981, p. 15) suggests the building of two collection systems, one aimed at penetrating the most intimate circle of the enemy's decision makers and the other built on a broad base, designed to locate early warning indications of extraordinary military preparations within the enemy camp. Other suggestions are aimed at removing the organizational and bureaucratic restraints on coordination between analysts and collectors and bringing them into close contact (Stech, 1979, p. 378; Gazit, 1980, p. 56).

It is relatively easy to develop a system that will concentrate on the collection of warning indicators. In fact the major achievements of collection agencies during the last generation have been in this field. It is very difficult, however, to build a system that can penetrate the top level of the enemy's decision makers. Gazit does not elaborate on the way in which this difficult task ought to be carried out.

Moreover, one has to remember that improving the collection of information has at least three drawbacks. First, the greater the amount of information collected, the more confusing and contradictory the noise received. Second, the more information coming in, the more difficult it is to process the data. Third, the more sensitive the information, the stronger the demand to protect sources and limit dissemination. I have already discussed the damages caused by these three drawbacks.

Reducing group influence. In most cases of surprise attack some officials have disagreed with the prevailing conception and believed, or claimed, that war was imminent. The problem is to devise ways of protecting such dissenters from the negative influence of the group or organization to which they are attached, encouraging them to fight for their opinions, and getting these opinions accepted by the group. Several safeguards have been suggested in this context by scholars.

A common suggestion is to establish organizational shortcuts that would allow any intelligence official convinced that the accumulating signals indicate imminent war to present his argument to the top levels of his organization (Dror, 1980; Betts, 1981a, p. 148; Stein, 1982a, p. 46). Such a "right of appeal" is granted in several intelligence agencies, but apparently with only modest success, for it seems that few junior officers are willing to alienate their superiors by going over their heads too often. Also, while junior officers are willing to disclose their opinions among colleagues, they seem much less eager to do so with top-level officials, especially since their estimates may well prove erroneous.

Since junior officers and subordinates are heavily influenced by superiors and leaders anyway, other safeguards are designed to offset leadership practices that bias the group's deliberations. Janis (1972, pp. 209–211) suggests that leaders in an organization's hierarchy should avoid setting a group norm that will elicit conformity with the leader's views among his subordinates. Leaders "should be impartial instead of stating preferences and expectations at the outset" of deliberations. They may enable the members of the group to develop an atmosphere of open inquiry and to explore a wide range of alternative assumptions. The leader should encourage the members of the group to give high priority to their objections and doubts and should accept criticism of his own judgment and demonstrate that he can be influenced by those who disagree with him.

Quite often, however, leaders and superiors do not follow such prescriptions, for they contradict the natural tendency to demonstrate authority. Janis himself admits that his recommendations have some potential disadvantages, especially if the leader regards an emerging consensus among the group members as a threat to his authority:

> Prolonged debates within the group can sometimes be costly when a rapidly growing international crisis requires an immediate policy solution in order to avert catastrophe. Open criticism can also lead to damaged feelings when the members resolutely live up to their role as critical evaluators and take each other's proposals over the bumps. Feelings of rejection, depression, and anger might be evoked so often when this role assignment is put into practice that it could have a corrosive effect on morale and working relations within the group. (1972, p. 210)

Another safeguard aimed at encouraging dissident views is to examine the problem by employing independent teams and departments. Several recommendations have been made in this area. In each intelligence organization there are three or four hierarchical levels of various degrees of specialization that deal with similar aspects of the enemy's behavior. If each of these levels were simultaneously to receive the same information and were to regard itself as being responsible for giving a warning, the organization would not be dependent on any single level (Gazit, 1981, p. 16). Alternatively it has been suggested that organizations should employ several analysts holding fundamentally different views about the enemy. Such a procedure would make it harder to build an unsubstantiated consensus (Betts, 1980a, p. 126). In order to challenge prevailing views, outside experts or qualified analysts who deal with other countries or issues within the organization should be invited to participate in deliberations or to reexamine information (Janis, 1972, p. 214; Graham, 1979, p. 32).

Such duplications and redundancy indeed have more advantages than disadvantages. They may expose disagreements, present additional views, and reduce the influence of judgmental biases and group dynamics. Yet such procedures have at least two major disadvantages. Various hierarchical levels, outside experts, and analysts of different backgrounds and opinions tend after a while to be influenced by the climate of opinion within the organization. Pressures to conform may partly offset the independent status of outside experts (Graham, 1979, p. 32). Then too, since decision makers usually prefer concise, previously coordinated estimates, the differences among the diverse opinions sometimes tend to become blurred in the final analysis.

Finally, the best-known suggestion is probably that of institutionalizing the function of devil's advocate. The idea is to assign to someone, either on a regular basis or in periods of crisis, the job of looking for information and articulating interpretations that run counter to prevailing assumptions. The expectation is that by arguing unpopular positions, including those that he himself does not really favor, the devil's advocate will encourage consideration of alternative interpretations of evidence.

The institutionalization of a devil's advocate may indeed encourage the examination of evidence from a different viewpoint; but it entails several clear disadvantages and weaknesses, and it is doubtful whether it can really challenge the prevailing conception. When the devil's advocate does not himself believe in the alternative interpretation he suggests, it is difficult for him to present it convincingly and successfully. Nor is the devil's advocate likely to be taken seriously by other analysts and decision makers (Betts, 1978, p. 80), since his advocacy is usually seen as a mere intellectual exercise and, almost necessarily, he is often wrong.

Indeed the devil's advocate may even cause damage if he adopts his alternative interpretation as the correct one. Since the main job of the "devil" is to criticize and undermine prevailing opinions, other analysts and decision makers may develop defense mechanisms against him, with the result that prevailing assumptions may become even more persistent. In any case the institution of devil's advocate does not offer any means for determining which interpretation is the right one.

Finally, a devil's advocate may compound the damage caused by the persistence of beliefs. As George argues, "hearing negative opinions expressed *and* rebutted may provide top-level officials with the psychologically comforting feeling that they have considered all sides of the issue and that the policy chosen has weathered challenges from within the decision-making circle" (1974, p. 196). While this is true of real dissenters, the damage caused by the devil's advocate is even greater, since he is inherently in a weaker position than the other participants.

Ensuring a pluralistic intelligence system. Most intelligence communities have more than one intelligence agency. This pluralistic pattern has emerged because of organizational needs and historical development. It is particularly the product of a concept developed after the Second World War which held that a pluralistic intelligence system would reduce the vulnerability of intelligence communities and improve decision making. In particular, recommendations to encourage pluralism were suggested following major intelligence failures. This was, for example, one of the main recommendations made by the Agranat Commission following the Yom Kippur War.

Undoubtedly the existence of one centralized, dominant intelligence organization entails considerable dangers. When the entire analysis effort is in the hands of one organization, the number of alternative hypotheses considered is necessarily limited. The climate of opinion within this organization may lead to the elimination of all hypotheses except the prevailing one. This was the case with Israel on the eve of the October 1973 war. All the political and military information was concentrated in Military Intelligence, which was responsible for the national assessment as well as for strategic and tactical warning. There was no parallel analysis and assessment system within the wider intelligence community to review the same data. Consequently, when Israeli Military Intelligence came to the conclusion that war was not imminent, there was no one on the scene to seriously challenge the hypothesis.

The pluralism of intelligence agencies offers several clear advantages. It is supposed to bring about a number of independent analytical processes in the different agencies. The separation of these processes may encourage the formation of competitive conceptions and alternative interpretations of information, thereby preventing a monopoly of intelligence estimates. Competition among agencies may challenge prevailing conceptions and expose their vulnerabilities. Moreover, once decision makers are presented with a wider range of opinions and estimates, they should become more aware of the weaknesses and limited reliability of intelligence estimates and may perhaps be more cautious in making their decisions.

The pluralistic intelligence system has clear disadvantages as well. To begin with, in most cases there will be no major differences among the assessments of the various intelligence agencies. The analytical process in each will be influenced by the same biases and constraints, and to a large extent all analysts will be influenced by the same decision makers and policies. Since none of the agencies is isolated, analytical processes in each of them are likely to affect those in the others. The outcome will be in most cases redundancy and duplication rather than pluralism. When this occurs, hearing the same assessment three times instead of once may contribute to the perseverance of decision makers' opinions rather than to open-mindedness.

Moreover, regarding the issue of the imminence of war, warning indicators are necessarily of a military rather than a political nature. An accurate estimation of the enemy's capabilities also requires a basic knowledge of military affairs and an ability to understand military information. In the case of strategic estimates and warnings, civilian intelligence agencies lacking military expertise are dependent on military intelligence agencies.[2] Consequently many potential differences of opinion among agencies become blurred.

Then too decision makers, lacking the time to read a large amount of material, prefer previously coordinated analyses. When receiving different opinions they may press for compromise. As a former Director of the DIA noted, "Competitive analysis might well be resisted by policymakers for whom a single estimate on any given subject is welcome relief from the responsibility to make judgments" (Graham, 1979, p. 27). Even when intelligence agencies are not officially required to coordinate their assessments, it is likely that a degree of coordination and integration will be affected by the staffs of the decision makers. Because of this need to compromise, "it does not necessarily follow that a pluralistic intelligence system will articulate rather than conceal interagency differences" (Chan, 1979, p. 178).

Another problem with presenting different opinions and interpretations is that the system does not provide any clue to choosing the right one. This is especially true for decision makers, who are influenced by commitment to their policies and operational considerations. Hence, even when presented with different intelligence estimates, they may not necessarily choose the correct one; rather the decision maker will choose the estimate that accords most with his own preconceptions, expectations, and policies.

Finally, pluralism brings about rivalry and friction among agencies, competition for the limited reserves of skilled manpower, and duplication of effort. The Pike Papers indicated that "there is a clear need to challenge organizational proliferation, duplication of activity and product, and overlapping of management layers." The papers quote from the preliminary postmortem CIA report on the October 1973 war:

> The coordination procedures which are followed by the Community during normal times are frequently abandoned during times of crisis—because the press of time may simply not allow regular processes to continue . . . And, in a way, this did indeed happen immediately before and during the October War in the Middle East. Coordination of the *Central Intelligence Bulletin*, for example, was suspended for a time, and the wartime Situation Reports and Spot Reports prepared by CIA, DIA and INR were unilateral and often duplicative issuances. This, if not a major problem for the analysts themselves, was certainly one for the consumers. (1976, pp. 24–25)

In the final analysis it has not yet been proved that a pluralistic intelligence system is a better guarantee against surprise attack than a monolithic one.[3] During the North Korean and Chinese interventions in Korea in 1950 at least three major organizations were involved in intelligence assessment: the CIA, the State Department, and MacArthur's headquarters in Tokyo. In 1962 the Indian Intelligence Bureau competed with Military Intelligence. In 1973 the fact that the Head of the Israeli Mossad intelligence service had a different opinion from that of the Director of Military Intelligence did not save Israel from surprise attack. And despite the establishment in 1961 of the DIA, the considerable expansion of the American intelligence community did not substantially improve its performance in October 1973 over that of 1950.

Lowering the threshold of warning. One recommendation that frequently follows surprise attacks is not to take too many chances but rather to resort to worst-case assumptions. There are several variations. In principle one can imagine developing such high levels of basic preparedness that even a belated warning will suffice to prevent surprise (see, for example, Betts, 1981a, p. 155). Another recommendation is to ascribe an exaggerated weight to evidence of impending threat: if warning indicators begin to accumulate, intelligence organizations should issue a warning and countermeasures should be taken, even though the apparent weight of contrary indicators is still greater. Or one should react in the light of the feasibility of an enemy attack, not of the assessment of its likelihood; from the moment the physical conditions that seem to enable the enemy to attack are created, adequate countermeasures should be taken. One should not wait for strategic assumptions to change: "when tactical actualities are at variance with strategic possibilities, the former should be given increased weight in the decision-making processes" (Ben-Zvi, 1976, p. 395; see also Betts, 1978, p. 73; Gazit, 1981, p. 18). Finally, it is worthwhile "to survey the hypothetical outcomes excluded by strategic premises as improbable but not impossible, identify those that would be disastrous if they *were* to occur, and then pay the price to hedge against them" (Betts, 1978, p. 88).

Yet it is impractical to raise the level of basic military preparedness too extensively. Few nations can afford—politically as well as economically—to stand guard for a long period of time against a potential rather than an actual threat. Also this approach entails the "cry wolf" phenomenon, which can in turn reduce sensitivity to additional warnings.

Strengthening cooperation between analysts and decision makers. Finally, it is often suggested that senior analysts should be close enough to decision centers to be aware of policy needs and to be able to contribute intelligence data and estimates to the decision-making process (Dror, 1980, p. 17; Knorr, 1979, p. 87).

Obviously it is important, even crucial, for analysts to be aware of their own state's policies and intentions. As the Pearl Harbor attack and the Israeli attack on Egypt in 1967 proved, the attacker's plans often depend on the victim's moves and intentions. Implementing this safeguard, however, confronts at least two difficulties. First, it is not easy to arrange such cooperation between analysts and decision makers. The latter are likely to refuse to share their secrets with and expose their personal weaknesses to intelligence analysts. In addition, as analysts draw closer to decision makers they are exposed to their influence, and this may distort intelligence estimates.

War without Surprise?

This study concludes on a pessimistic note: at best it is very difficult to prevent surprise attack. It is possible to bring about improvements in intelligence work and in the decision-making process, and this may eventually help to prevent or delay surprise in some cases— but it is unlikely that analysts and decision makers will be careful enough or lucky enough to prevent surprise attack over a long period of time. As the two Korean invasions and the Six-Day War showed, even the shock of a previous surprise attack is not likely to bring about long-lasting caution concerning assumptions. If the enemy is willing to wait patiently in order to achieve surprise, chances are good that he will succeed.

At this point one might expect to encounter a study of intelligence *successes*, which might lead us to some positive conclusions as to how surprise attack might be prevented. Such an intensive study is apparently not yet available. Moreover, such a hypothetical study's conclusions would probably not improve our ability to anticipate attacks anyway. Successful intelligence estimates are, after all, not rare. In fact many intelligence estimates and predictions are quite accurate; sometimes intelligence agencies manage to prevent operational or even strategic surprise during a war. But successes in anticipating imminent war are quite rare, even though this is the supreme test of intelligence communities and decision makers.[4]

Hence one should distinguish between intelligence successes in general, which are common, and successes in preventing surprise attack, which are exceptional. Anticipating a coming war is probably the most complex and difficult problem that analysts have to cope with. There is no other problem of estimation in which so many factors are involved: the combined political, military, economic, social, and ideological considerations that go into predicting a unique event; the estimation of the enemy's intentions, capabilities, and willingness to take risks; cognitive and perceptual biases; group influence, organizational obstacles, and the impact of decision makers; time pressures; deception. This is why successes in other fields of estimate—in which only a few of these factors are involved—is not necessarily relevant to the case of surprise attack. Furthermore, a successful estimate, or even a series of successes, does not guarantee that a future surprise attack will be prevented. In some cases it can even be argued that past successful estimates bear the seeds of a major future failure. This is what happened to Israel in 1973.

A study of wars that began without an element of surprise would probably not be much more illuminating. If we could analyze past successes with the idea of preventing surprise attack by determining whether the central factors involved in intelligence failure were absent, we might perhaps improve our ability to anticipate such attacks. Unfortunately, however, since 1939 there have been only a few cases in which the outbreak of war was not a surprise. Here are some cases for which documentation exists:

The British Prime Minister and British intelligence were not surprised by "Barbarossa."

On May 15, 1948, the Arab armies invaded Israel one day after its establishment as a state. The Arab attack did not surprise the Israeli leadership (Kimche and Kimche, 1973, p. 149).

The war between India and Pakistan in 1965 began with a Pakistani attack on India on September 1. According to the Indian version, the Pakistani attack presented a tactical surprise but not a strategic one (Kaul, 1971, pp. 29, 31, 70).

Jordan's decision to open fire on June 5, 1967, which started the war in the West Bank, did not surprise the Israelis.

Prior to the Chinese invasion of Vietnam in February 1979 the American intelligence community had provided "sufficiently accurate, timely notice of impending Vietnamese and Chinese actions that policy makers could prepare options and take certain actions in anticipation of hostilities" (Latimer, 1979, p. 52).

While we can undoubtedly learn from these cases, either they are specific to these exceptional instances and cannot be generalized to the entire issue of surprise attack, or the same factors involved in the successful cases can be found in cases of intelligence failure as well, thus obviating their relevance in explaining how surprise can be prevented.

What, then, are the lessons that can be learned from these cases? For one, an intelligence community with access to highly reliable sources of information is better equipped to predict an imminent attack. This explains why the British intelligence services anticipated the German invasion of Russia. Yet while this is a necessary condition for preventing surprise attack, it is not a sufficient one. The American intelligence community in 1941 and the Israeli community in 1973 had excellent sources, but neither anticipated the coming war.

Then too there is a better chance of preventing surprise when the adversary explicitly threatens to attack. The Arabs did not conceal their intention to invade Israel in May 1948, and the Chinese had been threatening to teach Vietnam a lesson since 1978. Yet similar explicit threats were made by the Chinese before they invaded Korea in 1950 and India in 1962 and by Egypt's Sadat from 1971 on—and all were perceived as bluffs.

Military clashes taking place prior to the major offensive might also alert the victim to the danger of an imminent attack. The confrontations in Palestine starting in November 1947 presumably alerted the Israeli leadership to the possibility of all-out war. A similar effect may have been created by the clashes along the Indian-Pakistani border that began in March 1965. Yet the opposite effect can also be generated: the victim may believe that the adversary does not intend to proceed beyond limited border incidents. Thus in the border incidents prior to the North Korean attack in 1950, the Chinese invasion of India in 1962, the Chinese invasion of Vietnam in 1979, and the Iraqi invasion of Iran in 1980, none of these acts alerted the victims to the danger of a major offensive.

Furthermore, it is easier for an outside observer to predict a coming war than it is for the victim—possibly because the observer is less influenced by commitment to a policy, persistent conceptions, and crisis pressures. Thus while Stalin failed to anticipate a surprise attack in 1941, the British expected it; and while the Vietnamese were confident in 1979 that China would not attack, the Americans did anticipate the invasion. The opposite case can also be made: that the observer has no advantage over the victim since the latter must be more sensitive and alert to the gathering storm. The British failed to anticipate the German invasion of Norway in 1940, and the U.S. intelligence community did not expect the Soviet invasion of Czechoslovakia in 1968 or the Arab attack on Israel in 1973.

Finally, surprise can be avoided when the attention of the victim is focused on a specific date for possible attack. Thus in 1948 the Israelis focused on May 15, the day after the end of the British mandate over Palestine and the establishment of the State of Israel, as a likely moment for enemy attack. Similarly in 1967 Israel's attention was focused on Jordan on June 5, the day the Israelis planned to attack Egypt. Yet this lesson does not provide any practical guide to anticipating attacks. In most cases there is either no specific date on which attention can be focused or too many dates, which could provoke false alarms.

Although we can provide a general explanation as to why surprise attacks are not prevented, at this stage there appears to be no general explanation for those cases in which an attack was anticipated. Each case has to be explained on its own merits. This may mean that successful surprise attacks are the general rule while their prevention is the exception.

Despite this pessimistic conclusion, I do not intend to suggest that nothing can be done to prevent surprise attacks. It is true that they occur too often—yet they are not inevitable like natural disasters. Although each of the safeguards mentioned earlier cannot by itself prevent surprise attack, several of them taken together may reduce its danger. Two safeguards in particular should be emphasized.

First, an intelligence community should strive to inculcate deliberately throughout its agencies and units a spirit of openness, caution, skepticism, and imagination. The community should encourage dissident opinions, put a premium on unconventional analytical approaches, and protect cautious, skeptical junior analysts who raise questions and doubts with regard to the prevailing conception. In this framework agencies should establish an internal control mechanism whose main function is to review prevailing assumptions and conclusions and their relationship to incoming information. Such an office, manned by experienced analysts, should attract and protect deviant views within the community and accustom analysts to the idea that their assessments are constantly questioned and reviewed. The fostering of this open and flexible spirit requires a great deal of education, but once it is achieved, many of the risks involved in the analytical process can be reduced.

Second, I suggested earlier that lowering the threshold of warning might involve high costs and lead to reduced sensitivity to warnings. While this is true, it may be worthwhile to pay the occasional price of false alarms, since the alternative is the trauma of surprise attack. In practice this means that from the moment when warning indicators pass a certain quantitative level, an intelligence warning should be issued and countermeasures taken regardless of the prevailing conception regarding the enemy. In order to minimize the damage of the "cry wolf" syndrome, the level of countermeasures should be adapted flexibly to each level of indicators. This also means that decision makers should encourage the intelligence community to accept the risk of false alarms, and that politicians and the press should be educated not to criticize decision makers for taking extra countermeasures. In the final analysis the cost of false alarms is partly offset by two advantages: the warning system is better equipped to discriminate between signals and noise; and the enemy may become convinced that his chances of achieving surprise are slim and that his opponent is determined to defend himself.

History does not encourage potential victims of surprise attack. One can only hope to reduce the severity—to be only partly surprised, to issue clearer and more timely warnings, to gain a few days for better preparations—and to be more adequately prepared to minimize the damage once a surprise attack occurs.

Notes
Bibliography
Index

Notes

Introduction

1. Barton Whaley examined 228 battles in some twenty wars from 1914 through 1974. Of these cases only 66 were launched without any initial surprise, while 160 battles did involve some kind of surprise. See Whaley, 1975, p. 1.

1. The Essence of Surprise Attack

1. In the Israeli case this factor was partially offset, since Israel had a long history of hostile relations with its neighbors, and since the assessment that war was a distant possibility had begun to take shape during the year before the war.
2. For a more detailed discussion of surprising innovations, see Betts, 1980b, pp. 566–569. Betts distinguishes between technical and doctrinal surprises. My own remarks concerning innovations are based partly on his discussion.
3. For a discussion of additional criteria important for warning forecasts such as coherence, resolution, calibration, reliability, and policy relevance, see Chan, 1984.
4. For some general principles governing probability statements, see Belden, 1977, p. 194.
5. Major-General Ehud Barak explains that the warning span fluctuates constantly owing to its dependence on collection capability, on the enemy's preventive measures, and on the enemy's overall preparedness for war. See Barak, 1985, p. 3.

2. Information and Indicators

1. See the discussion of indices in Jervis, 1970, pp. 18–19, 27–28, 35–36. See also Ben-Zvi, 1976, p. 383; Axelrod, 1979, pp. 245–246.
2. My discussion of the diagnostic value of information is based on the more detailed analysis of that issue in Lanir, 1983, pp. 126–127, 146–148.

3. For a short list of indicators of Russian intentions prepared by the Germans in central Russia in 1942, see Kahn, 1978, p. 102. For another list of indicators of Soviet intentions with regard to NATO, see Betts, 1982, pp. 191–192.
4. Major-General Daniel Graham complains about another problem in this context: the stream of both photography and signals intelligence grew to such an extent that the number of analysts in the American intelligence community working on information from both open and clandestine sources was continually reduced so additional personnel could be assigned to handle the technical collection load. See Graham, 1979, p. 30.

3. Intentions and Capabilities

1. See for example Brodie, 1965, pp. 378–379; Greene, 1965, pp. 132–133; Shlaim, 1976, pp. 362–363; Garthoff, 1978, p. 24; Handel, 1984, pp. 239–241.
2. In a way this element resembles what Jervis defines as "utopian intentions," which are "what a state would do in the absence of external constraints." "Utopian intentions" differ from Jervis's "basic intentions," which include the state's considerations of the costs and risks implied by external constraints. See Jervis, 1976, pp. 49–50.
3. Before the Cuban missile crisis U.S. analysts did foresee some of the advantages that the Soviet Union could achieve by deploying missiles in Cuba, but they did not give these advantages the proper weight in their estimates. See George and Smoke, 1974, pp. 447–479; Hilsman, 1964, p. 172.
4. Analysts also tend to ignore what may happen to their army after a surprise attack. Before Pearl Harbor, even though surprise attack was the phrase in fashion and had been taken into account in war games and drills in the Hawaiian Islands, there had been no realistic appraisal of what such a surprise could conceivably do to the U.S. Fleet and to air and ground forces, and no calculation of probable damage to men and equipment. See Wohlstetter, 1962, p. 69.

4. Conceptions and Incoming Information

1. I use the term *analyst* to refer principally to the intelligence analyst, since it is he who is at the center of the evaluation process. "The analyst," however, may also be anyone involved in evaluating enemy behavior and incoming information at the decision-making level, for example the field officer, the commander in chief, or the head of state.
2. See also Deutsch and Meritt, 1965, pp. 132–134; Axelrod, 1976, p. 114; Snyder and Diesing, 1977, p. 286.
3. For a more detailed description of the cognitive map approach, see

Shapiro and Bonham, 1973, pp. 155–157; Axelrod, 1976, pp. 58, 72–73; Bonham, Shapiro, and Trumble, 1979, p. 17.

4. See for example De Rivera, 1968, p. 28; Geller and Pitz, 1968, p. 199; Jervis, 1976, pp. 176–177, 187; Slovic, Fischhoff, and Lichtenstein, 1979, p. 39; Nisbett and Ross, 1980, p. 10; Ross and Anderson, 1982, p. 150.

5. See also Jervis, 1976, pp. 187–190, 194; Slovic, Fischhoff, and Lichtenstein, 1980, p. 10; Ross, 1977, p. 370.

6. See also Carroll, 1978, p. 89; Tversky and Kahneman, 1980, p. 61.

7. The catastrophe in the Philippines and MacArthur's strange passivity during the hours before the Japanese attack have never been adequately explained. Few reliable sources survived, and the main actors, including MacArthur himself, contradicted and blamed each other. See Manchester, 1978, pp. 205–212; Spector, 1985, pp. 107–108.

8. For some theories regarding information processing relevant to intelligence estimation, see Axelrod, 1973; Steinbruner, 1974, pp. 67, 101–102; Tanter and Stein, 1976, pp. 14–18; Axelrod, 1977, pp. 227–228; Bonham, Shapiro, and Trumble, 1979, p. 4; Heuer, 1980a, pp. 17–20.

9. This section draws heavily from the works of Amos Tversky and Daniel Kahneman, as well as that of Richard Nisbett and Lee Ross. An intensive attempt to apply psychological theories to intelligence work has been made by Richards Heuer, and part of this section follows some of his conclusions. Some of the works of Tversky and Kahneman, as well as related writings, are collected in Kahneman, Slovic, and Tversky, 1982.

10. See, for example, Slovic, 1972, p. 10; Tversky and Kahneman, 1973, p. 207; Tversky and Kahneman, 1974, p. 1124; and 1976, p. 28; Nisbett and Ross, 1980, p. 7; Slovic, Fischhoff, and Lichtenstein, 1981.

11. See for example Koriat, Lichtenstein, and Fischhoff, 1980, pp. 108, 111; Nisbett and Ross, 1980, p. 119. See also Kahneman, 1974, p. 10; Slovic, Kunreuther, and White, 1974, p. 195; Slovic, Fischhoff, and Lichtenstein, 1976a, p. 17.

5. The Process of Analysis

1. Choucri, 1978, p. 4, distinguishes between *prediction* and *forecasting*. A prediction generally focuses on one event or outcome and dispenses with probabilistic interpretation. A forecast deals with contingencies and is made in terms of alternatives and within a certain probability range. See also Freeman and Job, 1979, pp. 115–118.

2. See for example Knorr, 1964b, pp. 16, 3; Knorr and Morgenstern, 1968, pp. 12–14; Chuyev and Mikhaylov, 1975, pp. 41, 50–51; Clauser and Weir, 1975, pp. 41, 295; Knorr, 1976, p. 112; Dror, 1978, p. 2; Freeman and Job, 1979, p. 130; Sarbin, 1982, pp. 154–157.

3. See for example Martino, 1972, p. 67; Shapiro and Bonham, 1973, pp.

168–169; Axelrod, 1973, p. 1265; Axelrod, 1976, pp. 116–118; Heuer, 1980b, pp. 15–16.

4. See for example Hovland and Weiss, 1951, p. 642; Hovland, Janis, and Kelley, 1953, p. 73; Finlay, Holsti, and Fagen, 1967, pp. 33, 43; Paige, 1968, pp. 292–293; Johnson and Scileppi, 1969, p. 31; Jervis, 1976, p. 123.

5. Whaley (1973, p. 223) suggests a fifth hypothesis—that Hitler was expecting a Soviet attack and decided to strike first.

6. Beveridge, 1957, p. 106; Nisbett and Ross, 1980, p. 171; Jervis, 1976, p. 181.

7. See also Finlay, Holsti, and Fagen, 1967, p. 36; Stein, 1977, p. 437; Bonham, Shapiro, and Trumble, 1979, pp. 11–12; Tversky and Kahneman, 1980, pp. 60–61.

8. See also Truman, 1956, pp. 372–381; U.S. Congress, 1951, p. 1833; Collins, 1969, p. 175.

7. Organizational Obstacles

1. For a detailed analysis of how the coordination process can cause forecasts to go wrong, see Berkowitz, 1985.

2. The Zimmermann telegram was sent on January 16, 1917, by the German Foreign Minister to the German Minister in Mexico City. It outlined the German plan for the resumption of unrestricted submarine warfare and stated the probability that this would bring the United States into war. The Chief of British Naval Intelligence had the decrypted telegram for almost three weeks before transmitting its contents to his own government and to the American administration, being reluctant to expose the fact that British intelligence had broken the German code.

3. A similar charge is made by Enthoven and Smith (1971, p. 114).

4. I am grateful to Richard Betts for this comment.

8. Intelligence and Decision Makers

1. Strong, 1970, pp. 155–156; Cline, 1974, p. 133; Betts, 1978, p. 68; Stech, 1979, p. 379; Garthoff, 1978, p. 29.

Conclusion: Is Surprise Attack Inevitable?

1. For more information on these methods, see for example Martino, 1972, pp. 20–21; CIA, 1975; Tanter and Stein, 1976, pp. 19–26; Tanter, 1977; Schweitzer, 1977; Shreckengost, 1977; Heuer, 1978b.

2. This is the case for example in the Israeli intelligence community. See Hareven, 1978, p. 17.

3. Indeed today there is an argument for a return to the concept of a central agency for research and analysis; see Goodman, 1984, pp. 176–178. See also Andriole, 1984, p. 19.
4. Of course one may claim that this rarity can be explained in some cases by the possibility that intelligence success in exposing the enemy's intentions deterred him from attacking and thus prevented war.

Bibliography

Abel, Elie. 1968. *The Missile Crisis.* New York: Bantam.

Acheson, Dean. 1969. *Present at the Creation.* New York: Norton.

Agranat Report, The. 1975. Tel-Aviv: Am Oved. Hebrew. English edition: *The Agranat Report.* Tel-Aviv: Government Press Office, April 2, 1974.

Agrell, Wilhelm. 1979. "Military Intelligence and the Information Explosion." Discussion paper no. 129, July. Research Policy Institute, University of Lund, Sweden.

Ainsztein, Reuben. 1966. "Stalin and June 22, 1941." *International Affairs,* 42 (October): 662–673.

Allison, Graham. 1971. *Essence of Decision.* Boston: Little, Brown.

Amos, John. 1982. "Deception and the 1973 Middle East War." In *Strategic Military Deception,* ed. Donald Daniel and Katherine Herbig. New York: Pergamon.

Andriole, Stephen. 1984. "Indications, Warnings, and Bureaucracies." *Military Intelligence,* 10 (July–September): 18–24.

Appleman, Roy. 1961. *U.S. Army in the Korean War: South to the Naktong, North to the Yalu.* Washington, D.C.: Department of the Army.

Ascher, William. 1978. *Forecasting: An Appraisal for Policy Makers and Planners.* Baltimore: Johns Hopkins University Press.

Axelrod, Robert. 1973. "Schema Theory: An Information Processing Model of Perception and Cognition." *The American Political Science Review,* 67 (December):1248–1266.

——— 1976. *The Structure of Decision.* Princeton: Princeton University Press.

——— 1977. "How a Schema Is Used to Interpret Information." In *Thought and Action in Foreign Policy,* ed. G. Matthew Bonham and Michael Shapiro. Basel: Birkhauser Verlag.

——— 1979. "The Rational Timing of Surprise." *World Politics,* 31 (January):228–246.

Barak, Major-General Ehud. 1985. "Sugiot Behaf'alat Hamodi'in 1985" (Problems of intelligence performance, 1985). *Ma'arakhot*, 298 (March–April):2–5. Hebrew.

Barber, Noel. 1968. *A Twilight Sinister: The Fall of Singapore*. Boston: Houghton Mifflin.

Bar-Lev, Lieutenant-General Haim. 1975. "Surprise and the Yom Kippur War." In *Military Aspects of the Israeli-Arab Conflict*, ed. Louis Williams. Tel-Aviv: Tel-Aviv University Publishing Projects.

Bartov, Hanoch. 1978. *Daddo—48 Shana Veod 20 Yom* (48 years and 20 more days), Vol. 1. Tel-Aviv: Ma'ariv. Hebrew.

Beaufre, André. 1965. *1940: The Fall of France*. London: Cassell.

Belden, Thomas. 1977. "Indications, Warning, and Crisis Operations." *International Studies Quarterly*, 21 (March):181–194.

Ben-Porat, Yeshayahu, et al. 1973. *Hamehdal* (The shortcoming). Tel-Aviv: Hotza'ah Meyuhedet. Hebrew.

Ben-Zvi, Abraham. 1976. "Hindsight and Foresight: A Conceptual Framework for the Analysis of Surprise Attacks." *World Politics*, 28 (April):381–395.

———— 1977. "Mihem Korbanot Hakhashivah Hakvutzatit?" (Who are the victims of groupthink?) *Medinah, Memshal, Vykhasim Beinleumyim* (State, government, and international relations), 7 (Spring):141–151. Hebrew.

———— 1979. "Surprise: Theoretical Aspects." In *International Violence: Terrorism, Surprise, and Control*, ed. Yair Evron. Jerusalem: The Hebrew University of Jerusalem.

Berkowitz, Bruce. 1985. "Intelligence in the Organizational Context: Coordination and Error in National Estimates." *Orbis*, Fall:571–596.

Betts, Richard. 1977. *Soldiers, Statesmen, and Cold War Crises*. Cambridge, Mass.: Harvard University Press.

———— 1978. "Analysis, War, and Decision: Why Intelligence Failures Are Inevitable." *World Politics*, 31 (October):61–89.

———— 1980a. "Intelligence for Policymaking." *The Washington Quarterly*, 3 (Summer):118–129.

———— 1980b. "Surprise despite Warning: Why Sudden Attacks Succeed." *Political Science Quarterly*, 95 (Winter):551–572.

———— 1981a. "Hedging against Surprise Attack." *Survival*, 23 (July–August):146–156.

———— 1981b. "American Strategic Intelligence: Politics, Priorities, and Direction." In *Intelligence Policy and National Security*, ed. Robert Pfaltzgraff, Uri Ra'anan, and Warren Milberg. London: Macmillan.

———— 1982. *Surprise Attack: Lessons for Defense Planning*. Washington, D.C.: The Brookings Institution.

Beveridge, W. I. B. 1957. *The Art of Scientific Investigation*, 3rd ed. New York: Norton. Cited in Robert Jervis. *Perception and Misperception in International Politics*, p. 188. Princeton: Princeton University Press, 1976.

Blachman, Morris. 1973. "The Stupidity of Intelligence." In *Readings in American Foreign Policy*, ed. Morton Halperin and Arnold Kanter. Boston: Little, Brown.

Bonen, Zeev. N.d. "Technological Surprise." Mimeo.

Bonham, G. Matthew, Michael Shapiro, and Thomas Trumble. 1979. "The October War: Changes in Cognitive Orientation toward the Middle East Conflict." *International Studies Quarterly*, 23 (March):3–44.

Brecher, Michael. 1980. *Decisions in Crisis: Israel, 1967 and 1973.* Berkeley: University of California Press.

Brinkley, David, and Andrew Hull. 1979. *Estimative Intelligence.* Washington, D.C.: Defense Intelligence School.

Brodie, Bernard. 1965. *Strategy in the Missile Age.* Princeton: Princeton University Press.

Brodin, Katarina. 1975. *Surprise Attack: Problems and Issues.* Ministry of Defense, Stockholm.

——— 1978. "Surprise Attack: The Case of Sweden." *The Journal of Strategic Studies*, 1 (May):98–110.

Brody, Richard. 1983. "The Limits of Warning." *The Washington Quarterly*, 6 (Summer):40–48.

Brown, Rex, Andrew Kahr, and Cameron Peterson. 1974. *Decision Analysis for the Manager.* New York: Holt, Rinehart, and Winston.

Carroll, John. 1978. "The Effect of Imagining an Event on Expectations for the Event: An Interpretation in Terms of the Availability Heuristic." *Journal of Experimental Social Psychology*, 14 (January):88–96.

Cartwright, Dorwin, and Alvin Zander. 1960. "Group Pressures and Group Standards: Introduction." In *Group Dynamics*, ed. Dorwin Cartwright and Alvin Zander, 2nd ed. Evanston, Ill.: Row, Peterson.

Central Intelligence Agency. 1975. *Handbook of Bayesian Analysis for Intelligence.* OPR-506. Washington, D.C., June.

Chan, Steve. 1979. "The Intelligence of Stupidity: Understanding Failures in Strategic Warning." *The American Political Science Review*, 73 (March):171–180.

——— 1984. "Warning Forecasts: Evaluation, Heuristics, and Policy Context." In *National Security Crisis Forecasting and Management*, ed. Gerald Hopple, Stephen Andriole, and Amos Freedy. Boulder, Colo.: Westview Press.

Choucri, Nazli. 1978. "Key Issues in International Relations." In *Forecasting International Relations*, ed. Nazli Choucri and Thomas Robinson. San Francisco: W. H. Freeman.

Churchill, Winston. 1949. *The Second World War.* Vol. 1, *Their Finest Hour.* Boston: Houghton Mifflin.

——— 1950. *The Second World War.* Vol. 3, *The Grand Alliance.* Boston: Houghton Mifflin.

Chuyev, Y. V., and Y. B. Mikhaylov. 1975. *Forecasting in Military Affairs: A Soviet View.* Moscow. Published under the auspices of the U.S. Air Force.

Clauser, Jerome, and Sandra Weir. 1975. *Intelligence Research Methodology.* Prepared for the Defense Intelligence School, Washington, D.C.

Cline, Ray. 1974. "Policy without Intelligence." *Foreign Policy,* 17 (Winter):121–135.

Cohen, Arthur. 1964. *Attitude Change and Social Influence.* New York: Basic Books.

Cohen, Raymond. 1979. *Threat Perception in International Relations.* Madison: University of Wisconsin Press.

Colby, William. 1980. "Recruitment, Training, and Incentives for Better Analysis." In *Intelligence Requirements for the 1980s: Analysis and Estimates,* ed. Roy Godson. New Brunswick, N.J.: Transaction Books.

—— 1981. "Deception and Surprise: Problems of Analysts and Analysis." In *Intelligence Policy and National Security,* ed. Robert Pfalzgraff, Uri Ra'anan, and Warren Milberg. London: Macmillan.

Collins, J. Lawton. 1969. *War in Peacetime.* Boston: Houghton Mifflin.

Critchley, Julian. 1978. *Warning and Response.* London: Leo Cooper.

Daniel, Donald, and Katherine Herbig. 1982. "Propositions on Military Deception." In *Strategic Military Deception,* ed. Donald Daniel and Katherine Herbig. New York: Pergamon.

Dayan, Moshe. 1976. *Story of My Life.* Tel-Aviv: Steimatzky.

De Rivera, Joseph. 1968. *The Psychological Dimension of Foreign Policy.* Columbus, Ohio: Merrill.

Deutsch, Karl, and Richard Merritt. 1965. "Effects of Events on National and International Images." In *International Behavior,* ed. Herbert Kelman. New York: Holt, Rinehart, and Winston.

Deutsch, Morton, and Harold Gerard. 1960. "A Study of Normative and Informational Social Influences upon Individual Judgment." In *Group Dynamics,* ed. Dorwin Cartwright and Alvin Zander, 2nd ed. Evanston, Ill.: Row, Peterson.

DeWeerd, H. A. 1962. "Strategic Surprise in the Korean War." *Orbis,* 6 (Fall):435–452.

Di Vesta, Francis, Donald Meyer, and Judson Mills. 1964. "Confidence in an Expert as a Function of His Judgments." *Human Relations,* 17 (August):235–242.

Dixon, Norman. 1976. *On the Psychology of Military Incompetence.* London: J. Cape.

Downs, Anthony. 1967. *Inside Bureaucracy.* Boston: Little, Brown.

Dror, Yehezkel. 1971. *Crazy States.* Lexington, Mass.: D. C. Heath.

—— 1978. "How to Spring Surprises on History." Synopsis of a paper presented at international conference, When Patterns Change: Turning Points in International Politics, Jerusalem.

—— 1980. "Comprehensive Strategic Intelligence for Rulers." Discussion paper for Organization for Economic Cooperation and Development (OECD) Development Center Conference on Social Intelligence, Paris, June 9–12.

Dulles, Allen. 1963. *The Craft of Intelligence.* New York: Signet.

Eban, Abba. 1977. *An Autobiography.* Tel-Aviv: Steimatzky.

Ellsworth, Robert, and Kenneth Adelman. 1979. "Foolish Intelligence." *Foreign Policy,* no. 36 (Fall):147–159.

Enthoven, Alain, and Wayne Smith. 1971. *How Much Is Enough?* New York: Harper and Row.

Epstein, Edward. 1980. "Deception and Estimates." In *Intelligence Requirements for the 1980s: Analysis and Estimates,* ed. Roy Godson. New Brunswick, N.J.: Transaction Books.

Erickson, John. 1972. "The Soviet Response to Surprise Attack: Three Directives, 22 June 1941." *Soviet Studies,* 23 (April):519–559.

———— 1975. *The Road to Stalingrad.* Vol. 1. London: Weidenfeld and Nicolson.

———— 1984. "Threat Identification and Strategic Appraisal by the Soviet Union, 1930–1941." In *Knowing One's Enemies: Intelligence Assessment before the Two World Wars,* ed. Ernest May. Princeton: Princeton University Press.

Feer, Fredric. 1980. "Coping with Deception." In *Intelligence Requirements for the 1980s: Analysis and Estimates,* ed. Roy Godson. New Brunswick, N.J.: Transaction Books.

Festinger, Leon, Stanley Schachter, and Kurt Back. 1960. "The Operation of Group Standards." In *Group Dynamics,* ed. Dorwin Cartwright and Alvin Zander, 2nd ed. Evanston, Ill.: Row, Peterson.

Finlay, David, Ole Holsti, and Richard Fagen. 1967. *Enemies in Politics.* Chicago: Rand McNally.

Fischer, David. 1970. *Historians' Fallacies.* New York: Harper and Row.

Fischhoff, Baruch. 1976. "Attribution Theory and Judgment under Uncertainty." In *New Directions in Attribution Research,* ed. J. H. Harvey, W. J. Ickes, and R. F. Kidd. Hillsdale, N.J.: Lawrence Erlbaum Associates.

Fischhoff, Baruch, and Ruth Beyth-Marom. 1976. "Failure Has Many Fathers." *Policy Sciences,* 7:388–393.

Fischhoff, Baruch, Paul Slovic, and Sarah Lichtenstein. 1977. "Knowing with Certainty: The Appropriateness of Extreme Confidence." *Journal of Experimental Psychology: Human Perception and Performance,* 3 (4):552–564.

———— 1980. "Lay Foibles and Expert Fables in Judgments about Risk." June. Eugene, Oregon. Also in *Progress in Resource Management and Environmental Planning,* ed. T. O'Riordan and R. K. Turner, vol. 3. Chichester: Wiley, 1981.

Freedman, Lawrence. 1977. *U.S. Intelligence and the Soviet Strategic Threat.* London: Macmillan.

Freeman, John, and Brian Job. 1979. "Scientific Forecasts in International Relations." *International Studies Quarterly,* 23 (March):113–143.

Garthoff, Raymond. 1978. "On Estimating and Imputing Intentions." *International Security,* 2 (Winter):22–32.

Gazit, Shlomo. 1980. "Estimates and Fortune-Telling in Intelligence Work." *International Security*, 4 (Spring):36–56.

——— 1981. *Modi'in, Ha'arakhah, Ve'azharah* (Intelligence, estimate, and warning). Jerusalem: The Leonard Davis Institute for International Relations. Hebrew.

Geller, E. Scott, and Gordon Pitz. 1968. "Confidence and Decision Speed in the Revision of Opinion." *Organizational Behavior and Human Performance*, 3:190–201.

George, Alexander. 1969. "The 'Operational Code': A Neglected Approach to the Study of Political Leaders and Decision Making." *International Studies Quarterly*, 13 (June):190–222.

——— 1974. "Adaptation to Stress in Political Decision Making: The Individual, Small Group, and Organizational Contexts." In *Coping and Adaptation*, ed. George Coelho, David Hamburg, and John Adams. New York: Basic Books.

——— 1979. "Warning and Response: Theory and Practice." In *International Violence: Terrorism, Surprise, and Control*, ed. Yair Evron. Jerusalem: The Hebrew University of Jerusalem.

——— 1980. *Presidential Decisionmaking in Foreign Policy: The Effective Use of Information and Advice.* Boulder, Colo.: Westview.

George, Alexander, and Richard Smoke. 1974. *Deterrence in American Foreign Policy: Theory and Practice.* New York: Columbia University Press.

Giza, Richard. 1980. "The Problems of the Intelligence Consumer." In *Intelligence Requirements for the 1980s: Analysis and Estimates*, ed. Roy Godson. New Brunswick, N.J.: Transaction Books.

Goodman, Allan. 1984. "Dateline Langley: Fixing the Intelligence Mess." *Foreign Policy*, no. 57 (Winter):160–179.

Goutard, Colonel A. 1959. *The Battle of France, 1940.* New York: Washburn.

Graham, Major-General Daniel. 1973. "Estimating the Threat: A Soldier's Job." *Army*, 23 (April):14–18.

——— 1979. "Analysis and Estimates." In *Intelligence Requirements for the 1980s: Elements of Intelligence*, ed. Roy Godson. Washington, D.C.: National Strategy Information Center.

Greene, Fred. 1965. "The Intelligence Arm: The Cuban Missile Crisis." In *Foreign Policy in the Sixties*, ed. Roger Hilsman and Robert Good. Baltimore: Johns Hopkins Press.

Hadidi, Salah al-. 1972. "A Witness to the 1967 War." Cited in *Al-Khawadith* (Beirut), August 25, 1972. Arabic.

Handel, Michael. 1977. "The Yom Kippur War and the Inevitability of Surprise." *International Studies Quarterly*, 21 (September):461–501.

——— 1980. "Avoiding Political and Technological Surprises in the 1980s." In *Intelligence Requirements for the 1980s: Analysis and Estimates*, ed. Roy Godson. New Brunswick, N.J.: Transaction Books.

———— 1981. *The Diplomacy of Surprise: Hitler, Nixon, Sadat.* Cambridge, Mass.: Center for International Affairs, Harvard University.

———— 1982. "Intelligence and Deception." *The Journal of Strategic Studies,* 5 (March):122–154.

———— 1984. "Intelligence and the Problem of Strategic Surprise." *The Journal of Strategic Studies,* 7 (September):229–281.

Hareven, Alouph. 1978. "Disturbed Hierarchy: Israeli Intelligence in 1954 and 1973." *The Jerusalem Quarterly,* no. 9 (Fall):3–19.

Harkabi, Yehoshafat. 1966. *Nuclear War and Nuclear Peace.* Jerusalem: Israel Program for Scientific Translations.

———— 1975. "Khavat Da'at Linsibot Hahafta'ah Bemilkhemet Yom Hakipurim" (Evaluation of the circumstances of the surprise in the Yom Kippur War). In *Aravim, Falastinim, Ve'Israel* (Arabs, Palestinians, and Israel). Jerusalem: Van Leer. Hebrew.

Heikal, Mohamed Hassanein. 1973. *The Cairo Documents.* New York: Doubleday.

Herzog, Chaim. 1975. *The War of Atonement.* Tel-Aviv: Steimatzky.

Heuer, Richards. 1978a. "Do You Think You Need More Information?" Paper prepared for internal dissemination within the U.S. intelligence community, October.

———— ed. 1978b. *Quantitative Approaches to Political Intelligence: The CIA Experience.* Boulder, Colo.: Westview.

———— 1979. "Improving Intelligence Analysis: Some Insights on Data, Concepts, and Management in the Intelligence Community." *The Bureaucrat,* 8 (Winter):2–11.

————1980a. "Memory: How Do We Remember What We Know?" *Analytical Methods Review,* July.

———— 1980b. "Strategies for Analytical Judgment." *Analytical Methods Review,* November.

————1980c. "Perception: Why Can't We See What Is There to Be Seen?" *Analytical Methods Review,* March.

———— 1981a. "Strategic Deception and Counterdeception: A Cognitive Process Approach." *International Studies Quarterly,* 25 (June):294–327.

———— 1981b. "Biases in Evaluation of Evidence." Manuscript.

———— 1982. "Cognitive Factors in Deception and Counterdeception." In *Strategic Military Deception,* ed. Donald Daniel and Katherine Herbig. New York: Pergamon.

Hilsman, Roger. 1956. *Strategic Intelligence and National Decisions.* Glencoe, Ill.: Free Press.

———— 1964. *To Move a Nation.* New York: Delta.

Hinsley, F. H., et al. 1979. *British Intelligence in the Second World War: Its Influence on Strategy and Operations.* Vol. 1. London: Her Majesty's Stationery Office.

Hoffman, Steven. 1972. "Anticipation, Disaster, and Victory: India 1962–71." *Asian Survey*, 12 (November):960–979.

Holst, Johan. 1966. "Surprise, Signals, and Reaction: The Attack on Norway." *Cooperation and Conflict* (Stockholm), 1 (2):31–45.

Holsti, Ole. 1962. "The Belief System and National Images: A Case Study." *Journal of Conflict Resolution*, 6 (September):244–252.

—— 1972. *Crisis, Escalation, War.* Montreal: McGill-Queen's University Press.

—— 1977. "Foreign Policy Decision Makers Viewed Psychologically: Cognitive Processes Approaches." In *Thought and Action in Foreign Policy*, ed. Matthew Bonham and Michael Shapiro. Basel: Birkhauser Verlag.

Hopple, Gerald, 1984. "Intelligence and Warning: Implications and Lessons of the Falkland Islands War." *World Politics*, 36:339–361.

Hovland, Carl, Irving Janis, and Harold Kelley. 1953. *Communication and Persuasion.* New Haven: Yale University Press.

Hovland, Carl, and Walter Weiss. 1951. "The Influence of Source Credibility on Communication Effectiveness." *The Public Opinion Quarterly*, 15 (Winter):635–650.

Hughes, Thomas. 1976. *The Fate of Facts in a World of Men—Foreign Policy and Intelligence Making.* Headline Series, no. 233. New York: Foreign Policy Association.

Huntington, Samuel. 1957. *The Soldier and the State.* New York: Vintage.

Janis, Irving. 1962. "Psychological Effects of Warnings." In *Man and Society in Disaster*, ed. George Baker and Dwight Chapman. New York: Basic Books.

—— 1971. "Groupthink among Policy Makers." In *Sanctions for Evil*, ed. Nevitt Sanford and Craig Comstock. San Francisco: Jossey-Bass.

—— 1972. *Victims of Groupthink.* Boston: Houghton Mifflin.

Janis, Irving, and Leon Mann. 1977. *Decision Making.* New York: Free Press.

Janowitz, Morris. 1960. *The Professional Soldier.* New York: Free Press.

Jervis, Robert. 1969. "Hypotheses on Misperception." In *International Politics and Foreign Policy*, ed. James Rosenau, rev. ed. New York: Free Press.

—— 1970. *The Logic of Images in International Relations.* Princeton: Princeton University Press.

—— 1976. *Perception and Misperception in International Politics.* Princeton: Princeton University Press.

—— 1977. "Minimizing Misperception." In *Thought and Action in Foreign Policy*, ed. Matthew Bonham and Michael Shapiro. Basel: Birkhauser Verlag.

—— 1986. "What's Wrong with the Intelligence Process?" *The International Journal of Intelligence and Counterintelligence*, 1 (Spring):28–41.

Johnson, Homer, and John Scileppi. 1969. "Effects of Ego-Involvement Conditions on Attitude Change to High and Low Credibility Communications." *Journal of Personality and Social Psychology*, 13 (1):31–36.

Jones, Edward, and Richard Nisbett. 1971. "The Actor and the Observer: Divergent Perceptions and the Causes of Behavior." In Edward Jones et al., *Attribution: Perceiving the Causes of Behavior.* Morristown, N.J.: General Learning Press.

Jouvenel, Bertrand de. 1967. *The Art of Conjecture.* New York: Basic Books.

Kahn, David. 1978. *Hitler's Spies.* New York: Macmillan.

Kahneman, Daniel. 1974. "Cognitive Limitations and Public Decision Making." Manuscript, London.

Kahneman, Daniel, Paul Slovic, and Amos Tversky, eds. 1982. *Judgment under Uncertainty: Heuristics and Biases.* New York: Cambridge University Press.

Kahneman, Daniel, and Amos Tversky. 1972. "Subjective Probability: A Judgment of Representativeness." *Cognitive Psychology,* 3:430–451.

—— 1973. "On the Psychology of Prediction." *Psychological Review,* 80 (4):237–251.

—— 1979. "Intuitive Prediction: Biases and Corrective Procedures." *Management Science,* 12:313–327.

Kam, Ephraim, ed. 1974. *Hussein Pote'akh Bemilkhamah* (Hussein wages war). Tel-Aviv: Ma'arakhot. Hebrew.

Kaul, Lieutenant-General B. M. 1971. *Confrontation with Pakistan.* New Delhi: Vikas Publications.

Kelley, Harold, and John Thibaut. 1969. "Group Problem Solving." In *The Handbook of Social Psychology,* ed. Gardner Lindzey and Elliot Aronson, 2nd ed., vol. 4. Reading, Mass.: Addison-Wesley.

Kelly, C. W., and C. R. Peterson. 1971. "Probability Estimates and Probabilistic Procedures in Current-Intelligence Analyses." International Business Machines Corporation, Federal Systems Division, Gaithersburg, Maryland.

Kennan, George. 1958. *Russia, the Atom, and the West.* New York: Harper and Row.

—— 1967. *Memoirs: 1925–1950.* Boston: Little, Brown.

Kent, Sherman. 1949. *Strategic Intelligence for American World Policy.* Princeton: Princeton University Press.

Kimche, Jon, and David Kimche. 1973. *Mishnei Evrey Hagiv'ah* (Both sides of the hill). Tel-Aviv: Ma'arakhot. Hebrew.

Kimmel, Husband. 1955. *Admiral Kimmel's Story.* Chicago: Regnery.

Kirby, Major-General S. Woodburn. 1957. *The War against Japan.* Vol. 1, *The Loss of Singapore.* London: Her Majesty's Stationery Office.

Kirkpatrick, Lyman. 1969. *Captains without Eyes.* New York: Macmillan.

—— 1973. *The U.S. Intelligence Community.* New York: Hill and Wang.

Kissinger, Henry. 1979. *White House Years.* Boston: Little, Brown.

Klineberg, Otto. 1965. *The Human Dimension in International Relations.* New York: Holt, Rinehart, and Winston.

Knorr, Klaus. 1956. *The War Potential of Nations*, Princeton: Princeton University Press.

———— 1964a. "Failures in National Intelligence Estimates: The Case of the Cuban Missiles." *World Politics*, 16 (April):455–467.

———— 1964b. "Foreign Intelligence and the Social Sciences." Research monograph no. 17. Center of International Studies, Princeton University.

———— 1970. *Military Power and Potential*. Lexington, Mass.: D.C. Heath.

———— 1976. "Threat Perception." In *Historical Dimensions of National Security Problems*, ed. Klaus Knorr. Lawrence, Kans.: University Press of Kansas.

———— 1979. "Strategic Intelligence: Problems and Remedies." In *Strategic Thought in the Nuclear Age*, ed. Laurence Martin. London: Heinemann.

———— 1983. "Strategic Surprise in Four European Wars." In *Military Strategic Surprise*, ed. Klaus Knorr and Patrick Morgan. New Brunswick, N.J.: Transaction Books.

Knorr, Klaus, and Patrick Morgan, eds. 1983. *Military Strategic Surprise*. New Brunswick, N.J.: Transaction Books.

Knorr, Klaus, and Oskar Morgenstern. 1968. "Political Conjecture in Military Planning." Policy memo no. 35. Center of International Studies, Princeton University.

Koht, Halvdan. 1941. *Norway: Neutral and Invaded*. London: Hutchinson.

Koriat, Asher, Sarah Lichtenstein, and Baruch Fischhoff. 1980. "Reasons for Confidence." *Journal of Experimental Psychology: Human Learning and Memory*, 6 (March):107–118.

Kuhn, Thomas. 1970. *The Structure of Scientific Revolutions*. 2nd enlarged ed. Chicago: University of Chicago Press.

Lanir, Zvi. 1983. *Hahafta'a Habsisit: Modi'in Bemashber* (Fundamental surprise: The national intelligence crisis). Tel-Aviv: Hakibutz Hame'ukhad. Hebrew.

Laqueur, Walter. 1985. *A World of Secrets: The Uses and Limits of Intelligence*. New York: Basic Books.

Latimer, Thomas. 1979. "U.S. Intelligence and the Congress." *Strategic Review*, 7 (Summer):47–56.

Leasor, James. 1968. *Singapore: The Battle That Changed the World*. London: Hodder and Stoughton.

Leckie, Robert. 1962. *Conflict: The History of the Korean War, 1950–53*. New York: Avon.

Levran, Brigadier-General Aharon. 1980. "Hafta'ah Vehatra'ah: Eyunim Beshe'elot Yesod" (Surprise and warning: On fundamental problems). *Ma'arkhot*, 276–277 (October-November):17–21. Hebrew.

Lewin, Ronald. 1978. *Ultra Goes to War*. London: Hutchinson.

Manchester, William. 1978. *American Caesar*. Boston: Little, Brown.

Mansur, Abul Kasim [pseud.]. 1979. "The Crisis in Iran: Why the U.S.

Ignored a Quarter Century of Warning." *Armed Forces Journal International*, 116 (January):26–33.

Marshall, Andrew. 1966. *Problems of Estimating Military Power.* RAND paper P-3417.

Martino, Joseph. 1972. *Technological Forecasting for Decisionmaking.* New York: American Elsevier Publishing Company.

Mason, Henry. 1963. "War Comes to the Netherlands: September 1939-May 1940." *Political Science Quarterly*, 78 (4):548–580.

Maxwell, Neville. 1970. *India's China War.* London: J. Cape.

May, Ernest. 1973. *"Lessons" of the Past.* New York: Oxford University Press.

McGarvey, Patrick. 1973. "DIA: Intelligence to Please." In *Readings in American Foreign Policy*, ed. Morton Halperin and Arnold Kanter. Boston: Little, Brown.

———— 1974. *CIA: The Myth and the Madness.* Baltimore: Penguin Books.

McGregor, Douglas. 1938. "The Major Determinants of the Prediction of Social Events." *The Journal of Abnormal and Social Psychology*, 33:179–204.

Meir, Golda. 1975. *My Life.* Tel-Aviv: Steimatzky.

Morgan, Patrick. 1983. "Examples of Strategic Surprise in the Far East." In *Military Strategic Surprise*, ed. Klaus Knorr and Patrick Morgan. New Brunswick, N.J.: Transaction Books.

Moritz, Frank. 1978. "Cross-Impact Analysis: Forecasting the Future of Rhodesia." In *Quantitative Approaches to Political Intelligence: The CIA Experience*, ed. Richards Heuer. Boulder, Colo.: Westview.

Mullik, B. N. 1971. *The Chinese Betrayal.* New Delhi: Allied Publishers.

Nakdimon, Shlomo. 1982. *Svirut Nemukhah* (Low probability). Tel-Aviv: Revivim. Hebrew.

Nisbett, Richard, and Lee Ross. 1980. *Human Inference: Strategies and Shortcomings of Social Judgment.* Englewood Cliffs, N.J.: Prentice-Hall.

Oberdorfer, Don. 1971. *Tet.* New York: Doubleday.

Oskamp, Stuart. 1965. "Overconfidence in Case-Study Judgments." *Journal of Consulting Psychology*, 29 (3):261–265.

Paige, Glenn. 1968. *The Korean Decision.* New York: Free Press.

Pao-min Chang. 1982. "The Sino-Vietnamese Dispute over the Ethnic Chinese." *The China Quarterly*, no. 90 (June):195–230.

Pearson, Frederic, and R. E. Doerga. 1978. "The Netherlands and the 1940 Nazi Invasion." *The Jerusalem Journal of International Relations*, 3 (Winter-Spring):25–50.

Perlmutter, Amos. 1975. "Israel's Fourth War, October 1973: Political and Military Misperceptions." *Orbis*, 19 (Summer):434–460.

Pettee, George. 1946. *The Future of American Secret Intelligence.* Washington, D.C.: Infantry Journal Press.

Phelps, Ruth, Stanley Halpin, Edgar Johnson, and Franklin Moses. 1979. *The Use of Subjective Probability in Army Intelligence Estimation and Data Evaluation.* Alexandria, Va.: U.S. Army Research Institute.

Pike Papers, The. 1976. U.S. Congress. House. Select Committee on Intelligence. CIA report, January 29, 1976. Published in a special supplement of *The Village Voice* (February).

Platt, Washington. 1957a. *Strategic Intelligence Production.* New York: Praeger.

——— 1957b. "Forecasting in Strategic Intelligence." *Military Review,* 37 (May):42–49.

Poteat, George. 1976. "The Intelligence Gap: Hypotheses on the Process of Surprise." *International Studies Notes,* 3 (Fall):14–18.

Prange, Gordon. 1981. *At Dawn We Slept.* New York: McGraw-Hill.

Pruitt, Dean. 1965. "Definition of the Situation as a Determinant of International Action." In *International Behavior,* ed. Herbert Kelman. New York: Holt, Rinehart, and Winston.

Quandt, William. 1977. *Decade of Decisions.* Berkeley: University of California Press.

Ransom, Harry. 1958. *Central Intelligence and National Security.* Cambridge, Mass.: Harvard University Press.

——— 1974. "Strategic Intelligence and Foreign Policy." *World Politics,* 27 (October):131–146.

Rees, David. 1970. *Korea: The Limited War.* Baltimore: Penguin.

Rich, William. 1981. "Pearl Harbor: History and Implications." *Military Intelligence,* 7 (January-March):47–51.

Ridgway, Matthew. 1967. *The Korean War.* New York: Doubleday.

Rokeach, Milton. 1960. *The Open and Closed Mind.* New York: Basic Books.

Rosenbaum, Milton, and Irwin Lewin. 1968. "Impression Formation as a Function of Source Credibility and Order of Presentation of Contradictory Information." *Journal of Personality and Social Psychology,* 10 (2):167–174.

Ross, Lee. 1977. "The Intuitive Psychologist and His Shortcomings: Distortions in the Attribution Process." In *Advances in Experimental Social Psychology,* ed. L. Berkowitz, vol. 10. New York: Academic Press.

Ross, Lee, and Craig Anderson. 1982. "Shortcomings in the Attribution Process: On the Origins and Maintenance of Erroneous Social Assessments." In *Judgment under Uncertainty: Heuristics and Biases,* ed. Daniel Kahneman, Paul Slovic, and Amos Tversky. New York: Cambridge University Press.

Rothstein, Robert. 1972. *Planning, Prediction, and Policymaking in Foreign Affairs.* Boston: Little, Brown.

Sarbin, Theodore. 1982. "Prolegomenon to a Theory of Counterdeception." In *Strategic Military Deception,* ed. Donald Daniel and Katherine Herbig. New York: Pergamon.

Schlesinger, Arthur. 1965. *A Thousand Days.* Boston: Houghton Mifflin.

Schweitzer, Nicholas. 1977. "Delphi as a Technique in Intelligence." Paper presented at the eighteenth annual convention of the International Studies Association, St. Louis, Missouri, March 18.

—— 1978. "Bayesian Analysis: Estimating the Probability of Middle East Conflict." In *Quantitative Approaches to Political Intelligence: The CIA Experience,* ed. Richards Heuer. Boulder, Colo.: Westview.

Scott, William. 1958. "Rationality and the Non-Rationality of International Attitudes." *Journal of Conflict Resolution,* 2, no. 1:8–16.

Sella, Amnon. 1978. " 'Barbarossa': Surprise Attack and Communication." *Journal of Contemporary History,* 13 (July):555–583.

Shapiro, Michael, and G. Matthew Bonham. 1973. "Cognitive Process and Foreign Policy Decision Making." *International Studies Quarterly,* 17 (June):147–174.

Sherwin, Ronald. 1982. "The Organizational Approach to Strategic Deception: Implications for Theory and Policy." In *Strategic Military Deception,* ed. Donald Daniel and Katherine Herbig. New York: Pergamon.

Sherwood, Robert. 1950. *Roosevelt and Hopkins.* Rev. ed. New York: Grosset and Dunlap.

Shirer, William. 1971. *The Collapse of the Third Republic.* New York: Pocket Books.

Shlaim, Avi. 1976. "Failures in National Intelligence Estimates: The Case of the Yom Kippur War." *World Politics,* 28 (April):348–380.

Shreckengost, R.C. 1977. "How to Produce Better Intelligence." Manuscript.

Singer, J. David. 1958. "Threat-Perception and the Armament-Tension Dilemma." *The Journal of Conflict Resolution,* 2 (1):90–105.

Slovic, Paul. 1972. *From Shakespeare to Simon: Speculations—and Some Evidence—about Man's Ability to Process Information.* Research Bulletin 12, no. 12. Oregon Research Institute.

—— 1978. "Judgment, Choice, and Societal Risk Taking." In *Judgment and Decision in Public Policy Formation,* ed. K. R. Hammond. AAAS Selected Symposium Series. Boulder, Colo.: Westview.

—— 1982. "Toward Understanding and Improving Decisions." In *Human Performance and Productivity,* ed. E. A. Fleishman. Hillsdale, N.J.: Erlbaum.

Slovic, Paul, Baruch Fischhoff, and Sarah Lichtenstein. 1976a. "The Certainty Illusion." Research Bulletin 16, no. 4. Oregon Research Institute.

—— 1976b. "Cognitive Processes and Societal Risk Taking." In *Cognitive and Social Behavior,* ed. J. S. Carroll and J. W. Payne. Potomac, Md.: Lawrence Erlbaum.

—— 1977. "Behavioral Decision Theory." *Annual Review of Psychology,* 28:1–39.

—— 1979. "Rating the Risks." *Environment,* 21 (April):14–39.

—— 1980. "Facts and Fears: Understanding Perceived Risk." In *Societal*

Risk Assessment: How Safe Is Safe Enough?, ed. Richard Schwing and Walter Albers. New York: Plenum.

——— 1981. "Perceived Risk: Psychological Factors and Social Implications." *Proceedings of the Royal Society*, 376:17–34.

Slovic, Paul, Howard Kunreuther, and Gilbert White. 1974. "Decision Processes, Rationality, and Adjustment to Natural Hazards." In *Natural Hazards, Local, National, and Global*, ed. Gilbert White. New York: Oxford University Press.

Slovic, Paul, and Sarah Lichtenstein. 1971. "Comparison of Bayesian and Regression Approaches to the Study of Information Processing in Judgment." *Organizational Behavior and Human Performance*, 6:649–744.

Smoke, Richard. 1977. *War: Controlling Escalation.* Cambridge, Mass.: Harvard University Press.

Snyder, Glen, and Paul Diesing. 1977. *Conflict among Nations.* Princeton: Princeton University Press.

Spanier, John. 1965. *The Truman-MacArthur Controversy and the Korean War.* New York: Norton.

Spector, Ronald. 1985. *Eagle against the Sun.* New York: The Free Press.

Stech, Frank. 1979. *Political and Military Intention Estimation: A Taxonometric Analysis.* Bethesda, Md.: Mathtech.

——— 1980a. "Self-Deception: The Other Side of the Coin." *The Washington Quarterly*, 3 (Summer):130–140.

——— 1980b. "Intelligence, Operations, and Intentions." *Military Intelligence*, 6 (July-September):37–43.

Stein, Janice Gross. 1977. "Freud and Descartes: The Paradoxes of Psychological Logic." *International Journal*, 32 (Summer):429–451.

——— 1980. " 'Intelligence' and 'Stupidity' Reconsidered: Estimation and Decision in Israel, 1973." *The Journal of Strategic Studies*, 3 (September):147–177.

——— 1982a. "The 1973 Intelligence Failure: A Reconsideration." *The Jerusalem Quarterly*, no. 24 (Summer):41–54.

——— 1982b. "Military Deception, Strategic Surprise, and Conventional Deterrence: A Political Analysis of Egypt and Israel, 1971–73." *The Journal of Strategic Studies*, 5 (March):94–121.

Steinbruner, John. 1974. *The Cybernetic Theory of Decision.* Princeton: Princeton University Press.

Strong, Major-General Kenneth. 1968. *Intelligence at the Top.* London: Cassell.

——— 1970. *Men of Intelligence.* London: Giniger.

Sullivan, David. 1980. "Evaluating U.S. Intelligence Estimates." In *Intelligence Requirements for the 1980s: Analysis and Estimates*, ed. Roy Godson. New Brunswick, N.J.: Transaction Books.

Szanton, Peter, and Graham Allison. 1976. "Intelligence: Seizing the Opportunity." *Foreign Policy*, no. 22 (Spring):183–205.

Talmon, Yaakov. 1973. "Heshbon Nefesh" (Introspection). *Haaretz*, Tel-Aviv, November 30. Hebrew.

Tanter, Raymond. 1977. "The Use of Modern Methods of Intelligence Estimation." Lecture delivered to the Ministry of Foreign Affairs, Government of Israel, Jerusalem, February 14.

Tanter, Raymond, and Janice Stein. 1976. "Surprise Attacks and Intelligence Estimation." Manuscript.

Taylor, Shelley. 1982. "The Availability Bias in Social Perception and Interaction." In *Judgment under Uncertainty: Heuristics and Biases*, ed. Daniel Kahneman, Paul Slovic, and Amos Tversky. New York: Cambridge University Press.

Toch, Hans. 1958. "The Perception of Future Events: Case Studies in Social Prediction." *Public Opinion Quarterly*, 22 (Spring):57–66.

Toland, John. 1982. *Infamy: Pearl Harbor and Its Aftermath*. New York: Doubleday.

Trepper, Leopold. 1975. *Hatizmoret Ha'adumah Shely* (My red orchestra). Jerusalem: Eydanim. Hebrew.

Truman, Harry. 1956. *Memoirs*. Vol. 2, *Years of Trial and Hope*. New York: Doubleday.

Turner, Barry. 1976. "The Organizational and Interorganizational Development of Disasters." *Administrative Science Quarterly*, 21 (September):378–396.

Tversky, Amos, and Daniel Kahneman. 1973. "Availability: A Heuristic for Judging Frequency and Probability." *Cognitive Psychology*, 5:207–232.

—— 1974. "Judgment under Uncertainty: Heuristics and Biases." *Science*, 185:1124–1131.

—— 1975. "Intuitive Judgment Biases and Corrective Procedures." Report prepared for Stanford Research Institute.

—— 1976. "Causal Thinking in Judgment under Uncertainty." Manuscript. Hebrew University, Jerusalem.

—— 1980. "Causal Schemas in Judgments under Uncertainty." In *Progress in Social Psychology*, ed. M. Fishbein. Hillsdale, N.J.: Erlbaum.

U.S. Congress. Senate. 1946a. *Report of the Joint Committee on the Investigation of the Pearl Harbor Attack*. 79th Cong., 2nd sess. Washington, D.C.

—— Senate. 1946b. *Minority Views of the Joint Committee on the Investigation of the Pearl Harbor Attack*. 79th Cong., 2nd sess.

—— Senate. 1951. Committees on Armed Services and Foreign Relations. *The Military Situation in the Far East*. 82nd Cong., 1st sess.

—— House. 1975. Hearings before the Select Committee on Intelligence. *U.S. Intelligence Agencies and Activities: The Performance of the Intelligence Community*. 94th Cong., 1st sess. (September-October).

—— Senate. 1976. *Foreign and Military Intelligence*. Final report of the Select Committee to Study Government Operations (The Church Committee). Book I. 94th Cong., 2nd sess., April 26.

——— House. 1979. Subcommittee on Evaluation, Permanent Select Committee on Intelligence. *Iran: Evaluation of U.S. Intelligence Performance Prior to November 1978.* January.

Verba, Sidney. 1961. *Small Groups and Political Behavior.* Princeton: Princeton University Press.

Vertzberger, Ya'akov. 1978a. "India's Border Crisis with China, 1962." *The Jerusalem Journal of International Relations,* 3 (Winter-Spring):117–142.

——— 1978b. "Hdinamika Shel Eevutey Tfisah Umdinuit Khutz: Nehro Vehasikhsukh Hasino-Hodi, 1959–1962" (The dynamics of misperception and foreign policy: Nehru and the Sino-Indian conflict, 1959–1962). Ph.D. diss., Hebrew University, Jerusalem. Hebrew.

——— 1982. "India's Strategic Posture and the Border War Defeat of 1962: A Case Study in Miscalculation." *The Journal of Strategic Studies,* 5 (September):370–392.

Wallach, Michael, and Nathan Kogan. 1965. "The Roles of Information, Discussion, and Consensus in Group Risk Taking." *Journal of Experimental Social Psychology,* 1:1–19.

Washburn, A. Michael, and Thomas Jones. 1978. "Anchoring Futures in Preferences." In *Forecasting in International Relations,* ed. Nazli Choucri and Thomas Robinson. San Francisco: D. H. Freeman.

Wasserman, Benno. 1960. "The Failure of Intelligence Predictions." *Political Studies,* 8 (June):156–169.

Whaley, Barton. 1969. *Stratagem: Deception and Surprise in War.* Cambridge, Mass.: M.I.T. Center for International Studies.

——— 1973. *Codeword BARBAROSSA.* Cambridge, Mass.: M.I.T. Press.

——— 1975. "The Causes of Surprise in War." Paper delivered at the Conference on Strategic Issues, the Leonard Davis Institute for International Relations, Jerusalem, April 8.

Whiting, Allen. 1960. *China Crosses the Yalu.* Stanford: Stanford University Press.

Wilensky, Harold. 1967. *Organizational Intelligence.* New York: Basic Books.

——— 1972. "Intelligence, Crises, and Foreign Policy: Reflections on the Limits of Rationality." In *Surveillance and Espionage in a Free Society,* ed. Richard Blum. New York: Praeger.

Williams, Phil. 1973. "Intelligence Failures in National Security Policy." *The Royal Air Forces Quarterly,* 13 (Autumn):223–227.

Williams, Brigadier-General Robert. 1974. "Surprise: The Danger Signals." *Army,* 24 (April):10–16.

Willoughby, Major-General Charles. 1956. *MacArthur: 1941–1951.* New York: McGraw-Hill.

Withey, Stephen. 1962. "Reaction to Uncertain Threat." In *Man and Society in Disaster,* ed. George Baker and Dwight Chapman. New York: Basic Books.

Wohlstetter, Roberta. 1962. *Pearl Harbor: Warning and Decision*. Stanford: Stanford University Press.

—— 1965. "Cuba and Pearl Harbor: Hindsight and Foresight." *Foreign Affairs*, 43 (July):691–707.

—— 1966. "Sunday, December 7, 1941, and the Monday Morning Quarterbacks." *Air Force and Space Digest*, December:82–86.

Wolfenstein, Martha. 1957. *Disaster: A Psychological Essay*. London: Routledge and Kegan Paul.

Woods, Donald. 1966. "Improving Estimates That Involve Uncertainty." *Harvard Business Review*, 44 (July–August):91–98.

Yasri, Brigadier-General Adel. 1974. *Rikhlat al-Sak al-Muallaka* (The travels of the hanged leg). Cairo. Arabic.

Index

Acheson, Dean, 14, 70, 71, 123, 162

Advance warning: of disaster, 10–11; of attack, 9, 22, 64, 186–189. *See also* Early warning indicators; Language of warnings; Strategic warnings

Aerial reconnaissance, 37, 39, 50, 95, 136, 156

Agranat Commission of Inquiry, 32, 74, 78, 92, 225–226

Alert (preparedness), 31, 32, 33

Allison, Graham, 176

Ambiguity, 116, 214

American decision makers, 207–208; and World War II, 14, 17, 38, 50, 81, 118, 183–184, 204; and Korean War, 65, 68–69, 123, 187

American intelligence, 1, 53–54, 150, 209–210, 218–219, 232, 237n3. *See also* Central Intelligence Agency; Defense Intelligence Agency

American intelligence and Korean War, 50, 120, 227; analysis of China's intentions and capabilities, 15, 16, 37–38, 59, 65, 69–70, 80, 95, 134, 151–153, 162, 166; analysis of North Korea's intentions and capabilities, 48, 58, 103, 123, 128, 187, 197–198, 203

American intelligence and Vietnam War, 41–42, 171, 206, 210

American intelligence and World War II, 38, 139, 183–186, 189, 192–194, 231, 237n4; analysis of Japan's intentions and capabilities, 16, 19, 72, 75, 136, 142, 210–211

American intelligence and Yom Kippur War, 15, 53, 123, 151, 173, 194, 198, 207–208, 227–228

Analysts. *See* Intelligence analysts

Arab counties, 35, 119, 145, 232; intentions of, 14, 15, 41, 60, 69, 71, 73, 105, 123, 230, 231; capabilities of, 59, 61, 74, 77, 80, 82, 105, 124. *See also* Egypt; Iraq; Israeli-Arab wars; Jordan; Syria

Arab-Israeli Handbook, 124

Assumptions, 214, 218, 220; erroneous, 8, 12–22, 66–67, 107, 117, 181–182, 194–195. *See also* Judgment

Badran, Shams, 77

Barak, Ehud, 236n5

"Barbarossa." *See* Soviet Union, German invasion of

Bar-Lev, Haim, 14, 63, 172

Basic measures (preparedness), 31, 32, 33–34, 228

Beaufre, André, 63, 81

Behavior, and expectations, 72, 88, 98, 127, 165, 177

Behavior of enemy, 48, 88–89, 93, 104, 118; information on, 41, 43, 181–182, 224; analysis of, 56, 64–69, 98–99, 123, 138, 174, 181–182, 200, 211. *See also* Capabilities of enemy; Deception; Intentions of enemy

Behavior of victims, 2, 4, 11, 13, 163, 190–192

Belgium, German invasion of, 3, 16